D0924879

THE DOLPHIN BOOK OF SPEECHES

George W. Hibbitt, Professor Emeritus of English at Columbia University, specialized in the study of speech. He received the Ph.D. degree from Columbia. Dr. Hibbitt is a member of the editorial board of Funk and Wagnalls' Standard Dictionary and has made a series of broadcasts on English usage for the National Broadcasting Company. He has contributed a number of articles to magazines and is the author of *How to Speak Effectively on All Occasions* (Dolphin Books C-310) and *Fundamentals of Speech* (Doubleday College Course Guide, U8).

The Dolphin Book of
SPEECHES

Edited by
GEORGE W. HIBBITT

Dolphin Books
Doubleday & Company, Inc.
Garden City, New York

The Dolphin Books edition is the first publication
of *The Dolphin Book of Speeches*

Dolphin Books edition: 1965

"I Have a Dream," by Martin Luther King, Jr. Copyright ©
1963 by Martin Luther King, Jr. Reprinted by permission of
Joan Daves.

Library of Congress Catalog Card Number 65–20060
Copyright © 1965 by George W. Hibbitt
All Rights Reserved
Printed in the United States of America

Contents

PART SEVEN.   HAIL AND FAREWELL

PART EIGHT.   MODERN PROBLEMS

Foreword

The speeches in this volume are examples of rhetoric—the art of speaking—chosen to represent the varying conceptions of the good speech from ancient to modern times and to illustrate the various components of which a memorable or effective speech is composed.

Greek orators spent years perfecting their techniques of speechmaking. Isocrates, a famous Greek teacher of rhetoric, is said to have earned about a hundred thousand dollars for his work; for the writing of a speech to be delivered by someone else on a special occasion he would be paid fifty thousand dollars. Today it would be difficult to name a man who is widely known primarily for his skill as an orator; indeed, even the word *oratory* has an old-fashioned implication. Instead, public figures are said to *communicate* their ideas, and are praised for straightforward, "natural" style (which they have been painstakingly taught by modern-day Isocrateses). Yet, whatever the terms we use, when, for example, we think of the speeches of Winston Churchill or John F. Kennedy, the glory of oratory—and our respect and admiration of fine examples of this art—still remain.

The selections here will give the reader an opportunity to study the problems every speaker faced and how he coped with them: problems such as organization of his material; choice of style; approach to a specific audience; choice of figures of speech and vocabulary; the use of wit; the projection of conviction and intelligence.

Consider how the situation and audience as well as the perception of the speaker influenced the speech in these situations: Socrates speaking to a jury that had just condemned him to death by poison; Savonarola addressing a people he believed to be enslaved by rich rulers; Cotton Mather preaching to a solemn, conservative Puritan congregation; William Jennings Bryan exhorting his party in the silver-minded West; Winston Churchill in the early days of World War II galvanizing an uneasy Parliament; President Kennedy appealing to an entire nation to change its ways of thinking and acting.

The end of oratory is to persuade the listener of the rightness and justice of the speaker's cause. So one further element must be added to the qualities of a speech: that the speaker himself believe in the honesty and propriety of his position. Aristotle said that the best speaker was a moral man, and this holds true today. A clear conscience contributes to a speech its essential clarity of ideas and directness.

With these factors in mind, look at the examples that follow and you will see how qualities of mind and emotions are woven into the orator's composition.

Bear in mind, too, that the criteria for formal speeches have changed through history as cultures and technology have changed. In ancient Greece, speeches were declaimed in the open and the first requirement of a speaker was the sheer ability to make himself heard. The Greek style required among other things long and involved sentences, as did the Latin style. Nowadays radio and television have vastly increased the size of the audience but the microphone takes care of the inadequacies of the voice. However, *time* has become crucial because of the monetary and technical requirements of these media. Even more important, the speaker faces an audience that is impatient, one that will not sit quietly for hours listening to an elaborate presentation. The public of today is attuned to speed and efficiency and the speaker must contend with this mood or go unheard. His sentences must be short; he must choose the most precise words; he must get right down immediately to what he has to say.

Orators today may chaff at the restrictions their audience imposes, yet these very limitations are new and exciting challenges to the further development of the art of speaking.

PART ONE

THRESHOLDS OF MYSTERY

Socrates

470?–399 B.C.

Socrates is the very "head and source" of philosophy. He was the first to introduce scientific inductive argumentation, to present universal conceptions for argument, to insist upon precise definition of terms, and also to present a study of ethics. With him formal logic begins. He questioned tenets of morality and insisted that there be an intellectual basis for moral principles. Knowledge was an integral part of right action. Socrates was about seventy years old when he fell from favor. His accuser, Meletus, in his indictment says, "Socrates is guilty of not believing in the gods believed in by the state and of introducing other new divinities. Moreover, he is guilty of corrupting the youth. The penalty proposed is death." The indictment was for an offense against the state and it became a public suit; and further it was a public suit on the basis of impiety. Plato wrote the "Apology" soon after the death of Socrates and predicted that those who voted for his condemnation did so by paying more attention to wealth and power than to virtue and their own consciences. Plato tells the reader that he was present at the trial of Socrates, and we may assume that nothing escaped his careful scrutiny and everything rested in his memory.

Socrates met the charge with calmness. His inward spirit checked him from preparing a formal speech in his defense. This is no "apology" in the popular English sense of the term but rather an exposition of his reasons to believe that he was a wise man and the reasons for the prejudice against him. He refused to speak as the judges wanted; he declared he had been, instead, a benefactor of the city. He claimed no special favor. They brought in the judgment of guilty and the penalty of death by poison.

On His Condemnation to Death

There are many reasons why I am not grieved, O men of Athens, at the vote of condemnation. I expected this, and am only surprised that the votes are so nearly equal; for I had thought that the majority against me would have been much larger; but now, had thirty votes gone over to the other side, I should have been acquitted. And I may say, I think, that I have escaped Meletus. And I may say something more; for without the assistance of Amytus and Lycon, he would not have had one fifth of the votes, as the law requires, in which case he would have incurred a fine of a thousand drachmae.

And so he proposes death to be the penalty. And what shall I propose on my part, O men of Athens? Clearly that which is my due. And what then is my due? What shall be done to the man who has never had the wit to be idle in his whole life—but has been careless of what concerns many—wealth, family interests, and military offices, and speaking in the assembly, and magistracies, and plots, and parties. Reflecting that I was really too honest a man to follow in this way and live, I did not go where I could do no good to you or to myself; but where I could do the greatest good privately to everyone of you, thither I went, and sought to persuade every man among you that he must look to himself, and seek virtue and wisdom before he looks to his private interests, and that this should be the order which he observes in all his actions. What shall be done to such a man? Doubtless some good things, O men of Athens, if he has his reward. What would be a reward suitable to a poor man who is your benefactor, who desires leisure that he may instruct you? There can be no reward so fitting as maintenance in the Prytaneum, O men of Athens, a reward which he deserves far more than the citizen who has won the prize at Olympia in the horse or chariot race, whether the chariots were drawn by two horses or by many. For I am in want, and he has enough; and he only gives you the appearance of happiness, and I give you the reality. And if I am to estimate the penalty justly, I say that maintenance in the Prytaneum is the just return.

Someone will say: Yes, Socrates, but cannot you hold your tongue, and then you may go into a foreign city to live on in exile, and no one will interfere with you. Now I have great difficulty in making you understand my answer to this. For if I tell you that to do as you say would be disobedient to the God, and therefore I cannot hold my tongue, you will not believe that I am serious; and if I say again that daily to talk about virtue, and of those other things about which you hear me examining myself and others, is the greatest good of man, and that the unexamined life is not worth living, you are still less likely to believe me. But as it is, I might have estimated the offence at what I could pay, for money I have none; and therefore I must ask you to proportion the fine according to my means. Well, perhaps I could afford a mina [approximately fifty dollars] and therefore I propose that penalty: Plato, Crito, Critobulus, and Apollodorus, my friends here, bid me say thirty minae, and they will be ample security to you.

Not much time will be gained, O men of Athens, in return for the evil name which you will get from the detractors of the city, who will say that you killed Socrates, a wise man; for when they want to reproach you, they will call me wise, even though I am not wise. If you had waited a little longer, your desire would have been fulfilled in the course of nature. For I am very advanced in years, as you may percieve, and near death. But I say this not to you all, but to those only who have condemned me to die. And I say this too to the same persons. Perhaps you think, O men of Athens, that I have been convicted through the want of arguments, by which I might have escaped punishment. Far otherwise: I have been convicted through want indeed, yet not of arguments, but of audacity and impudence, and of the inclination to say such things to you as would have been most agreeable to hear, had I lamented and bewailed and done and said many things unworthy of me, as I affirm, but such as you are accustomed to hear from others.

Neither did I then think that I ought, for the sake of avoiding danger, to do anything unworthy of a freeman, nor do I now repent of having so defended myself; but I should rather choose to die having so defended myself than to live in that way. For neither in a trial nor in battle is it right that I or anyone else should employ every possible means whereby he may avoid death; for in battle it is frequently evident that a man might escape death by laying down his arms and throwing himself on the mercy of his pursuers. And there are many other devices in every danger, by which to avoid death, if a man dares to do and say everything.

But this is not difficult, O men of Athens, to escape death, but it is much more difficult to avoid depravity, for it flies faster than death. And now I, being slow and aged, am overtaken by the slower of the two; but my accusers, being strong and active, have been overtaken by the swifter, wickedness. And now I depart, condemned by you to death; but they are condemned by truth, as guilty of iniquity and injustice: and I abide my sentence and so do they. These things, perhaps, ought so to be, and I think that they are for the best.

In the next place, I wish to predict to you who have condemned me, what your fate will be: for I am now in that condition in which men most frequently prophesy, namely, when they are about to die. I say then to you, O Athenians, who have condemned me to death, that immediately after my death a punishment will overtake you, far more severe, by Zeus, than that which you have inflicted on me. For you have done this thinking that you should be freed from the necessity of giving account of your life. The very contrary, however, as I declare, will happen to you. Your accusers will be greater in number whom I have restrained, though you did not perceive it; and they will be more severe, inasmuch as they are younger and you will be more indignant. For, if you think that by putting men to death you will restrain anyone from upbraiding you because you do not live well, you are much mistaken; for this method of escape is neither possible nor honorable, but that other is most honorable and most easy, not to put a check upon others, but for a man to take heed to himself, how he may be most perfect. Having predicted thus much to those of you who have condemned me, I take my leave of you.

But with you who have voted for my acquittal, I would gladly hold converse about what has taken place, while the officials are busy [preparing the formal record] and I am not yet taken to the place where I must die. Stay with me then, so long, O Athenians, for nothing hinders our conversing with each other, while we are permitted to do so; because I wish to make known to you, as being my friends, the meaning of that which has just now befallen me. To me then, O my judges—and in calling you judges I call you rightly—a strange thing has happened. For the accustomed prophetic voice of my guardian deity, on every former occasion, even in the most trifling affairs, opposed me, if I was about to do anything wrong; but now, that has befallen me which you yourselves behold, and which anyone would think, and which is supposed to be, the extremity of evil; yet neither when I departed from home in the morning did the warning of the god oppose me, nor when I came up here to the place of trial, nor in my address when I was about to say anything; yet on other occasions it has frequently restrained me in the midst of speaking. But now it has never throughout this proceeding opposed me, either in what I did or said. What then do I suppose to be the cause of this? I will tell you: what has happened to me appears to be a blessing; and it is impossible that we think rightly who suppose that death is an evil. A great proof of this to me is the fact that it is impossible but that the accustomed signal from the god should have opposed me, unless I had been about to meet with some good.

Moreover, we may hence conclude that there is great hope that death is a blessing. For to die is one of two things: to be dead is as to be nothing and have no sensation of anything whatever; or, as it is said, there is a certain change and passage of the soul from one place to another. And if it is a privation of all sensation, as it were, a sleep in which the sleeper has no dream, death would be a wonderful gain. For I think that if anyone, having selected a night in which he slept so soundly as not to have had a dream, and having compared this night with all the other nights and days of his life, should be required on consideration to say how many days and nights he had passed better and more pleasantly than this night throughout his life, I think that not only a private person, but even a great king himself would find them easy to number in comparison with other days and nights. If, therefore, death is a thing of this kind, I say it is a gain; for thus all futurity appears to be nothing more than one night.

But if, on the other hand, death is a removal from hence to another place, and what is said to be true, that all the dead are there, what greater blessing can there be than this, my judges? For if, on arriving at Hades, released from these who pretend to be judges, one shall find those who are true judges, and who are said to judge there, Minos, and Rhadamanthus, Aeacus, and Triptolemus, and such others of the demigods as were just during their own life, would this be a sad removal? At what price would you estimate a conference with Orpheus and Musaeus, Hesiod and Homer? I indeed should be willing to die often, if this be true. For to me, the sojourn there would be admirable when I should meet with Palamedes, and Ajax, son of Telamon, and any other of the ancients who has died by an unjust sentence. The comparing of my sufferings with theirs would, I think, be no unpleasing occupation. But the greatest pleasure would be to spend my time in questioning and examining the people there as I have done those here, and discovering who among them is wise, and who fancies himself to be so but is not. At what price, my judges, would not anyone estimate the opportunity of questioning him who led that mighty army against Troy, or Ulysses, or Sisyphus, or ten thousand others, whom one might mention, both men and women? With whom to converse and associate, and to question them, would be an inconceivable happiness! In any event I am sure that they put no man to death there; in other respects those who live there are more happy than those that are here, and are henceforth immortal, if at least what is said be true.

You, therefore, O my judges, ought to enjoy good hopes as to death, and to think upon this one truth that to a good man nothing is evil, neither while he lives nor when he is dead, nor are that man's concerns neglected by the gods. And what has befallen me is not the effect of chance; but this is clear to me that now must die, and, thus freed from my cares, that this is better for me. On this account the warning in no way turned me aside; and I bear no resentment toward those who condemned me, or against my accusers, although they did not condemn and accuse me with this intention, but thinking to injure me: in this they deserved to be blamed.

Thus much, however, I beg of them. Punish my sons, when they grow up, O judges, paining them as I have pained you, if they appear to you to care for riches or anything else before virtue, and if they think themselves to be something when they are nothing, reproach them as I have done you, for not attending to what they ought, and for conceiving themselves something when they are worth nothing. If you do this both I and my sons shall have met with just treatment from your hands.

It is now time to depart—for me to die, for you to live. But which of us is going to a better state is unknown to everyone but God.

Marc Antony
83?–30 B.C.

Marcus Antonius, or Marc Antony was a friend and lieutenant of Julius Caesar. He had been Caesar's protégé and was a dashing young soldier from a good family. As tribune he had vetoed a bill to strip Caesar of his army. At the time of Caesar's assassination, he was an elected Consul in Rome.

The funeral oration here forever set in magnificent English by Shakespeare was delivered over the body of Caesar and is reported by Don Cassius in his history of Rome and also by Plutarch in his life of Marc Antony. It was from Plutarch that Shakespeare drew his suggestions for the speech.

Though the speech belongs to Shakespeare, it nevertheless seems to flow from the bereaved Marc Antony himself and is, of itself, a masterpiece of oratory in the best tradition. Shakespeare adds the effects of the speech on the listeners, and the auditors thus become almost as important as the speech itself. Such is the purpose of oratory that the listeners be moved, and thus still does Antony every time this speech is repeated on stage.

In the action of the play, Brutus has just spoken. He was one of the assassins of Caesar and has just persuaded the crowd by his oratory that assassination was a work of justice, not envy, politics, or cold murder.

MARC ANTONY'S FUNERAL ORATION

ANTONY. Friends, Romans, countrymen, lend me your
       ears;
  I come to bury Caesar, not to praise him.
  The evil that men do lives after them;
  The good is oft interred with their bones;

So let it be with Caesar. The noble Brutus
Hath told you Caesar was ambitious:
If it were so, it was a grievous fault,
And grievously hath Caesar answer'd it.
Here, under leave of Brutus and the rest,—
For Brutus is an honorable man;
So are they all, all honorable men,—
Come I to speak in Caesar's funeral.
He was my friend, faithful and just to me:
But Brutus says he was ambitious;
And Brutus is an honorable man.
He hath brought many captives home to Rome,
Whose ransoms did the general coffers fill;
Did this in Caesar seem ambitious?
When that the poor have cried, Caesar hath wept:
Ambition should be made of sterner stuff:
Yet Brutus says he was ambitious;
And Brutus is an honorable man.
You all did see that on the Lupercal
I thrice presented him a kingly crown,
Which he did thrice refuse: was this ambition?
Yet Brutus says he was ambitious;
And, sure, he is an honorable man.
I speak not to disprove what Brutus spoke.
But here I am to speak what I do know.
You all did love him once, not without cause:
What cause withholds you then to mourn for him?
O judgment! thou art fled to brutish beasts,
And men have lost their reason. Bear with me;
My heart is in the coffin there with Caesar,
And I must pause till it come back to me.

FIRST CITIZEN.   Methinks there is much reason in his
    sayings.
SECOND CITIZEN.   If thou consider rightly of the matter,
    Caesar has had great wrong.
THIRD CITIZEN.   Has he, masters?
    I fear there will a worse come in his place.
FOURTH CITIZEN.   Mark'd ye his words? He would not the
    crown;
    Therefore 'tis certain he was not ambitious.

FIRST CITIZEN.   If it be found so, some will dear abide it.

SECOND CITIZEN.   Poor soul! his eyes are red as fire with
weeping.

THIRD CITIZEN.   There's not a nobler man in Rome than
Antony.

FOURTH CITIZEN.   Now mark him, he begins again to
speak.

ANTONY.   But yesterday the word of Caesar might
Have stood against the world: now lies he there,
And none so poor to do him reverence.
O masters, if I were disposed to stir
Your hearts and minds to mutiny and rage,
I should do Brutus wrong, and Cassius wrong,
Who, you all know, are honorable men:
But here's a parchment with the seal of Caesar;
I found it in his closet; 'tis his will:
Let but the commons hear this testament—
Which, pardon me, I do not mean to read—
And they would go and kiss dead Caesar's wounds
And dip their napkins in his sacred blood,
Yea, beg a hair of him for memory,
And, dying, mention it within their wills,
Bequeathing it as a rich legacy
Unto their issue.

FOURTH CITIZEN.   We'll hear the will: read it, Marc Antony.

ALL.   The will, the will! we will hear Caesar's will.

ANTONY.   Have patience, gentle friends, I must not
read it;
It is not meet you know how Caesar loved you.
You are not wood, you are not stones, but men;
And, being men, hearing the will of Caesar,
It will inflame you, it will make you mad:
'Tis good you know not that you are his heirs;
For if you should, O, what would come of it!

FOURTH CITIZEN.   Read the will; we'll hear it, Antony;
You shall read us the will, Caesar's will.

ANTONY.   Will you be patient? will you stay a while?
I have o'ershot myself to tell you of it:
I fear I wrong the honorable men

Whose daggers have stabb'd Caesar; I do fear it.

FOURTH CITIZEN. They were traitors: honorable men!

ALL. The will! The testament!

SECOND CITIZEN. They were villains, murderers: the will! read the will.

ANTONY. You will compel me, then, to read the will?
Then make a ring about the corpse of Caesar,
And let me show you him that made the will.
Shall I descend? and will you give me leave?

ALL. Descend.

SECOND CITIZEN. Descend.

THIRD CITIZEN. You shall have leave.

Antony comes down from the pulpit.

FOURTH CITIZEN. A ring; stand round.

FIRST CITIZEN. Stand from the hearse, stand from the body.

SECOND CITIZEN. Room for Antony, most noble Antony.

ANTONY. Nay, press not so upon me; stand far off.

ALL. Stand back. Room! Bear back.

ANTONY. If you have tears, prepare to shed them now.
You all do know this mantle: I remember
The first time ever Caesar put it on:
'Twas on a summer's evening, in his tent,
That day he overcame the Nervii:
Look, in this place ran Cassius' dagger through:
See what a rent the envious Casca made:
Through this the well-beloved Brutus stabb'd;
And as he pluck'd his cursed steel away,
Mark how the blood of Caesar follow'd it,
As rushing out of doors, to be resolved
If Brutus so unkindly knock'd, or no:
For Brutus, as you know, was Caesar's angel:
Judge, O you gods, how dearly Caesar loved him!
This was the most unkindest cut of all;
For when the noble Caesar saw him stab
Ingratitude, more strong than traitors' arms,
Quite vanquished him: then burst his mighty heart;
And, in his mantle muffling up his face
Even at the base of Pompey's statue,
Which all the while ran blood, great Caesar fell.

O, what a fall was there, my countrymen!
Then I, and you, and all of us fell down,
Whilst bloody treason flourish'd over us.
O, now you weep, and I perceive you feel
The dint of pity: these are gracious drops.
Kind souls, what, weep you when you but behold
Our Caesar's vesture wounded? Look you here:
Here is himself, marr'd, as you see, with traitors.

FIRST CITIZEN. O piteous spectacle!

SECOND CITIZEN. O noble Caesar!

THIRD CITIZEN. O woeful day!

FOURTH CITIZEN. O traitors, villains!

FIRST CITIZEN. O most bloody sight!

SECOND CITIZEN. We will be reveng'd!

ALL.   Revenge! About!
Seek! Burn! Fire! Kill! Slay!
Let not a traitor live!

ANTONY. Stay, countrymen.

FIRST CITIZEN. Peace there! hear the noble Antony.

SECOND CITIZEN. We'll hear him, we'll follow him, we'll
die with him.

ANTONY. Good friends, sweet friends, let me not stir
you up
To such a sudden flood of mutiny.
They that have done this deed are honorable;
What private griefs they have, alas, I know not,
That made them do it: they are wise and honorable,
And will, no doubt, with reasons answer you.
I come not, friends, to steal away your hearts:
I am no orator, as Brutus is;
But, as you know me all, a plain blunt man,
That love my friend; and that they know full well
That gave me public leave to speak of him:
For I have neither wit, nor words, nor worth,
Action, nor utterance, nor the power of speech,
To stir men's blood: I only speak right on;
I tell you that which you yourselves do know;
Show you sweet Caesar's wounds, poor dumb mouths,
And bid them speak for me: but were I Brutus,
And Brutus Antony, there were an Antony

Would ruffle up your spirits, and put a tongue
In every wound of Caesar, that should move
The stones of Rome to rise and mutiny.

ALL. We'll mutiny.

FIRST CITIZEN. We'll burn the house of Brutus.

THIRD CITIZEN. Away, then! come, seek the conspirators.

ANTONY. Yet hear me, countrymen; yet hear me speak.

ALL. Peace, ho! Hear Antony. Most noble Antony!

ANTONY. Why, friends, you go to do you know not what;
Wherein hath Caesar thus deserv'd your loves?
Alas, you know not; I must tell you, then:
You have forgot the will I told you of.

ALL. Most true. The will! Let's stay and hear the will.

ANTONY. Here is the will! and under Caesar's seal
To every Roman citizen he gives,
To every several man, seventy-five drachmas.

SECOND CITIZEN. Most noble Caesar! we'll revenge his
death.

THIRD CITIZEN. O royal Caesar!

ANTONY. Hear me with patience.

ALL. Peace, ho!

ANTONY. Moreover, he hath left you all his walks,
His private arbors and new-planted orchards,
On this side Tiber; he hath left them you,
And to your heirs for ever; common pleasures,
To walk abroad and recreate yourselves.
Here was a Caesar! when comes such another?

FIRST CITIZEN. Never, never. Come, away, away!
We'll burn his body in a holy place,
And with the brands fire the traitors' houses.
Take up the body.

SECOND CITIZEN. Go fetch fire.

THIRD CITIZEN. Pluck down benches.

FOURTH CITIZEN. Pluck down forms, windows, anything.
                Exeunt Citizens with the body.

ANTONY. Now let it work. Mischief, thou art afoot,
Take thou what course thou wilt.

                                Julius Caesar, III, ii, 79–266

Abraham Lincoln
1809–1865

This great speech of President Lincoln was, according to one story, written on his railroad trip from Washington to Gettysburg. According to Andrew Carnegie, who worked on the road as a young man, he supplied Lincoln with the pencil which he used to compose the speech on the back of an envelope.

By whatever means, in whatever restricted space, President Lincoln created a lasting literary monument. It was written with the whole of his reading in the Bible and Shakespeare in his mind. It is condensed with a sense of great style. He gave the speech November 19, 1863.

The audience at Gettysburg had been greatly impressed by the speaker who preceded the President; he was Senator Edward Everett from Massachusetts, whose roaring voice was heard at the very edge of the crowd. Everett's speech is now forgotten. Lincoln spoke with a small voice and was heard by few in the great gathering. His speech passed almost unnoticed in the newspapers the next day, but it is a speech that Americans have long remembered.

ADDRESS AT GETTYSBURG

Fourscore and seven years ago our fathers brought forth upon this continent a new nation, conceived in liberty, and dedicated to the proposition that all men are created equal.

Now we are engaged in a great civil war, testing whether that nation, or any nation so conceived and so dedicated, can long endure. We are met on a great battlefield of that war. We have come to dedicate a portion of that field as a final resting place for those who here gave their lives that that nation might live. It is altogether fitting and proper that we should do this.

But in a larger sense, we cannot dedicate, we cannot consecrate, we cannot hallow this ground. The brave men, living and dead, who struggled here, have consecrated it far above our poor power to add or detract. The world will little note nor long remember what we say here; but it can never forget what they did here. It is for us, the living, rather to be dedicated here to the unfinished work which they who fought here have thus far so nobly advanced. It is rather for us to be here dedicated to the great task remaining before us: that from these honored dead we take increased devotion to that cause for which they gave the last full measure of devotion; that we here highly resolve that these dead shall not have died in vain; that this nation, under God, shall have a new birth of freedom; and that government of the people, by the people, for the people, shall not perish from the earth.

Lyndon B. Johnson, PRESIDENT OF THE UNITED STATES
John W. McCormack, SPEAKER OF THE HOUSE OF
  REPRESENTATIVES
Michael J. Mansfield, SENIOR SENATOR FROM MON-
  TANA
Earl Warren, CHIEF JUSTICE OF THE SUPREME COURT

The men in this group all faced the same problem, to speak a eulogy for their departed Chief of State, John Fitzgerald Kennedy, assassinated at Dallas, Texas, November 22, 1963. President Johnson's brief message was delivered at the airfield when he returned from Dallas; the others at the ceremony in the Rotunda of the Capitol in Washington. It is of interest to see how each speaker approached this problem, each under a great emotional strain and confronting an audience that was both the government officials in the Rotunda and the distant national television audience.

EULOGIES ON JOHN FITZGERALD KENNEDY

Lyndon B. Johnson, President of the United States.
Delivered at Dulles International Air Force Base, November 23, 1963.

This is a sad time for all people.
We have suffered a loss that cannot be weighed.
For me it is a deep personal tragedy.
I know the world shares the sorrow that Mrs. Kennedy
    and her family bear.
I will do my best.
That is all I can do.
I ask for your help—and God's.

John W. McCormack, Speaker of the House of Representatives.

Delivered in the Rotunda of the Capitol, Washington, D.C., November 24, 1963.

As we gather here today bowed in grief, the heartfelt sympathy of members of the Congress and of our people are extended to Mrs. Jacqueline Kennedy and to Ambassador and Mrs. Joseph P. Kennedy and their loved ones. Their deep grief is also self-shared by countless millions of persons throughout the world, considered a personal tragedy, as if one had lost a loved member of his own immediate family.

Any citizen of our beloved country who looks back over its history cannot fail to see that we have been blessed with God's favor beyond most other peoples. At each great crisis in our history we have found a leader able to grasp the helm of state and guide the country through the troubles which beset it. In our earliest days, when our strength and wealth were so limited and our problems so great, Washington and Jefferson appeared to lead our people. Two generations later, when our country was torn in two by a fratricidal war, Abraham Lincoln appeared from the mass of the people as a leader able to reunite the nation.

In more recent times, in the critical days of the Depression and the great war forced upon us by Fascist aggression, Franklin Delano Roosevelt, later Harry S Truman appeared on the scene to reorganize the country and lead its revived citizens to victory. Finally, only recently, when the cold war was building up the supreme crisis of a threatened nuclear war capable of destroying everything —and everybody—that our predecessors had so carefully built, and which a liberty-loving world wanted, once again a strong and courageous man appeared to lead us.

No country need despair so long as God, in His infinite goodness, continues to provide the nation with leaders able to guide it through the successive crises which seem to be the inevitable fate of any great nation.

Surely no country ever faced more gigantic problems

than ours in the last few years, and surely no country could have obtained a more able leader in a time of such crisis. President John Fitzgerald Kennedy possessed all the qualities of greatness. He had deep faith, complete confidence, human sympathy and broad vision which recognize the true values of freedom, equality and the brotherhood which have always been the marks of the American political dreams.

He had the bravery and a sense of personal duty which made him willing to face up to the great task of being President in these trying times. He had the warmth and the sense of humanity which made the burden of the task bearable for himself and for his associates, and which made all kinds of diverse peoples and races eager to be associated with him in his task. He had the tenacity and determination to carry each stage of his great work through to its successful conclusion.

Now that our great leader has been taken from us in a cruel death, we are bound to feel shattered and helpless in the face of our loss. This is but natural, but as the first bitter pangs of our incredulous grief begin to pass we must thank God that we were privileged, however briefly, to have had this great man for our President. For he has now taken his place among the great figures of world history.

While this is an occasion of deep sorrow it should be also one of dedication. We must have the determination to unite and carry on the spirit of John Fitzgerald Kennedy for a strengthened America and a future world of peace.

Senator Michael J. Mansfield.
Delivered in the Rotunda of the Capitol, Washington, D.C., November 24, 1963.

There was a sound of laughter; in a moment, it was no more. And so she took a ring from her finger and placed it in his hands.

There was a wit in a man neither young nor old, but a wit full of an old man's wisdom and of a child's wisdom, and then, in a moment it was no more. And so she took a ring from her finger and placed it in his hands.

There was a man marked with the scars of his love of country, a body active with the surge of a life far, far from spent and, in a moment, it was no more. And so she took a ring from her finger and placed it in his hands.

There was a father with a little boy, a little girl and a joy of each in the other. In a moment it was no more, and so she took a ring from her finger and placed it in his hands.

There was a husband who asked much and gave much, and out of the giving and the asking wove with a woman what could not be broken in life, and in a moment it was no more. And so she took a ring from her finger and placed it in his hands, and kissed him and closed the lid of a coffin.

A piece of each of us died that moment. Yet, in death he gave of himself to us. He gave us of a good heart from which the laughter came. He gave us of a profound wit, from which a great leadership emerged. He gave us of a kindness and a strength fused into a human courage to seek peace without fear.

He gave us of his love that we, too, in turn, might give. He gave that we might give of ourselves, what we might give to one another until there would be no room, no room at all, for the bigotry, the hatred, prejudice and the arrogance which converged in that moment of horror to strike him down.

In leaving us—these gifts, John Fitzgerald Kennedy, President of the United States, leaves with us. Will we take them, Mr. President? Will we have, now, the sense and the responsibility and the courage to take them?

Chief Justice Earl Warren.
Delivered in the Rotunda of the Capitol, Washington, D.C., November 24, 1963.

There are few events in our national life that unite Americans and so touch the heart of all of us as the passing of a President of the United States.

There is nothing that adds shock to our sadness as the assassination of our leader, chosen as he is to embody the ideals of our people, the faith we have in our institutions and our belief in the fatherhood of God and the brotherhood of man.

Such misfortunes have befallen the nation on other occasions, but never more shockingly than two days ago.

We are saddened; we are stunned; we are perplexed.

John Fitzgerald Kennedy, a great and good President, the friend of all men of goodwill, a believer in the dignity and equality of all human beings, a fighter for justice and apostle of peace, has been snatched from our midst by the bullet of an assassin.

What moved some misguided wretch to do this horrible deed may never be known to us, but we do know that such acts are commonly stimulated by forces of hatred and malevolence, such as today are eating their way into the bloodstream of American life.

What a price we pay for this fanaticism!

It has been said that the only thing we learn from history is that we do not learn. But surely we can learn if we have the will to do so. Surely there is a lesson to be learned from this tragic event.

If we really love this country, if we truly love justice and mercy, if we fervently want to make this nation better for those who are to follow us, we can at least abjure the hatred that consumes people, the false accusations that divide us and the bitterness that begets violence.

Is it too much to hope that the martyrdom of our beloved President might even soften the hearts of those who would themselves recoil from assassination, but who do not shrink from spreading the venom which kindles thoughts of it in others?

Our nation is bereaved. The whole world is poorer because of his loss. But we can all be better Americans because John Fitzgerald Kennedy has passed our way, because he has been our chosen leader at a time in history when his character, his vision and his quiet courage have enabled him to chart for us a safe course through the shoals of treacherous seas that encompass the world.

And now that he is relieved of the almost superhuman burdens we imposed on him, may he rest in peace.

EXHORTATION AND ENLIGHTENMENT

PART TWO

EXPERIMENTAL AND EXPERIMENT

Isocrates

436–338 B.C.

Isocrates was one of the great orators of Greece. Son of of a prosperous flute manufacturer, Isocrates received his education from great teachers including the renowned Georgias who appears in the Dialogues of Plato. Isocrates was bashful and had a weak voice, but he must have been a really great teacher of rhetoric since he had a school of a hundred students each of whom paid a thousand drachmae, or approximately one thousand dollars, for instruction.

Although Isocrates was not a politician he continuously thought of the public good and the betterment of his city, Athens. The speeches of Isocrates were written for others to speak and were read by the thoughtful people of Athens, and he became for the Athenians an influential and creative thinker.

On the Panegyricus, *Isocrates spent from ten to fifteen years. It was published in 380 B.C. This speech can be studied as an example of the best Greek oratorical style of its time, with polish, proper figures of speech, opposing clauses, and the necessary words of transition so important in the Greek sentences. However great the length of the sentence, the primary thought is always kept clear.*

The title Panegyricus *means a speech at an open public meeting usually on the occasion of some festival such as the great Olympic games. Isocrates takes that occasion to state his theme that Greeks should all forgive each other their differences and the states should cease marauding each other, combine their forces, attack Asia, and thereby enrich themselves.*

He failed in his plea. When he was ninety-eight years old, he wrote his last discourse, the Panathenaicus, *wherein his rhetoric still holds its fire, zeal, style, and enthusiasm for his beloved Athens. He died a few years*

*after the Battle of Chaeronea of "voluntary starvation," as
the legend goes, because of the downfall of Greek liberty.
Milton has continued this legend in his Fifth English
Sonnet:*

> *. . . that Parliament
> Broke him, as that dishonest victory
> At Chaeronea, fatal to liberty
> Kil'd with report that Old man eloquent. . . .*

PANEGYRICUS

Many times have I wondered at those who first con-
voked the national assemblies and established the athletic
games, amazed that they should have thought the prowess
of men's bodies to be deserving of so great bounties, while
to those who had toiled in private for the public good and
trained their own minds so as to be able to help also their
fellow-men they apportioned no reward whatsoever when,
in all reason, they ought rather to have made provision for
the latter; for if all the athletes should acquire twice the
strength which they now possess, the rest of the world
would be no better off; but let a single man attain to wisdom, and all men will reap the benefit who are willing to
share his insight.

Yet I have not on this account lost heart nor chosen to
abate my labors; on the contrary, believing that I shall
have a sufficient reward in the approbation which my discourse will itself command, I have come before you to
give my counsels on the war against the barbarians and on
concord among ourselves. I am, in truth, not unaware that
many of those who have claimed to be sophists have
rushed upon this theme, but I hope to rise so far superior
to them that it will seem as if no word had ever been
spoken by my rivals upon this subject; and, at the same
time, I have singled out the highest kind of oratory that
which deals with the greatest affairs and, while best displaying the ability of those who speak, brings most profit
to those who hear; and this oration is of that character.

In the next place, the moment for action has not yet gone by, and so made it now futile to bring up this question; for then, and only then, should we cease to speak, when the conditions have come to an end and there is no longer any need to deliberate about them, or when we see that the discussion of them is so complete that there is left no room to improve upon what has been said. But so long as conditions go on as before, and what has been said about them is inadequate, is it not our duty to scan and study this question, the right decision of which will deliver us from our mutual warfares, our present confusion, and our greatest ills?

Furthermore, if it were possible to present the same subject matter in one form and in no other, one might have reason to think it gratuitous to weary one's hearers by speaking again in the same manner as his predecessors; but since oratory is of such a nature that it is possible to discourse on the same subject matter in many different ways—to represent the great as lowly or invest the things of old in a new manner or set forth events of recent date in an old fashion—it follows that one must not try to speak better than they . . . and it is my opinion that the study of oratory as well as the other arts would make the greatest advance if we should admire and honor, not those who make the first beginnings in their crafts, but those who are the most finished craftsmen in each, and not those who seek to speak on subjects on which no one has spoken before, but those who know how to speak as no one else could.

I, for my part, am concerned . . . with those who will not tolerate, but will resent, any carelessness of phrase, and will seek to find in my speeches a quality which they will not discover in others. Addressing myself to these, I shall proceed with my theme, after first vaunting a little further my own powers. For I observe that the other orators in their introductions seek to conciliate their hearers and make excuses for the speeches which they are about to deliver, sometimes alleging that their preparation has been on the spur of the moment, sometimes urging that it is difficult to find words to match the greatness of their theme. But as for myself, if I do not speak in a manner worthy of my subject and of my reputation and of the time which I have spent—not merely the hours which have been devoted to my speech but also the years which I have lived—I bid you show me no indulgence but hold me up to ridicule and scorn; for there is nothing of the sort which I do not deserve to suffer, if indeed, being no better than others, I make promises so great . . .

I am not at the present moment of the same mind as I was at the beginning of my speech. For then I thought that I should be able to speak in a manner worthy of my theme; now, however, I have not risen to its grandeur, and many of the thoughts which I had in mind to utter have escaped me. Therefore you must come to my aid and try to picture to yourselves what vast prosperity we should attain if we should turn the war which now involves ourselves against the peoples of the continent, and bring the prosperity of Asia across Europe. And you must not depart to your homes as men who have merely listened to an oration; nay, those among you who are men of action must exhort one another to try to reconcile our city with Lacedaemon; and those among you who make claim to eloquence must stop composing orations on "deposits" or on other trivial themes . . . and center your rivalry on this subject and study how you may surpass me in speaking on the same question, bearing ever in mind that it does not become men who promise great things to waste their time on little things, nor yet to make the kind of speeches which will improve no whit the lives of those whom they convince, but rather the kind which, if carried out in action, will both deliver the authors themselves from their present distress and win for them the credit of bringing to pass great blessings for the rest of the world.

Hannibal
247–183 B.C.

Livy (59 B.C.–A.D. 17) in his History of Rome *recounts the following speech as delivered by Hannibal to his soldiers. Obviously Livy, who lived much later than Hannibal, reconstructed this speech in the form and style that Livy imagined Hannibal would have spoken to his soldiers under the circumstances. Livy is recognized as a writer of accurate and extraordinary devotion to style, as the Latins knew it.*

Hannibal, a Carthaginian general, was one of the great military geniuses of all time. His strategy in crossing the Alps with his soldiers from the hot countries and his train of elephants remains one of the mysteries and great accomplishments in history. How Hannibal performed this feat has been the subject of much research. We know that his troops suffered hardships not only from the winter climate of the Alps and the difficult terrain, but from lack of food and all supplies. What then had Hannibal to offer them as a reward? He declares this in his speech.

He led his troops from a conquest in Spain through the Alps to the very gates of Rome. There he maintained himself and his army against the Roman legions until he was recalled to govern Carthage. But Carthage was destroyed, in time, by the Romans and Hannibal was ordered to Rome as a prisoner, but he poisoned himself rather than submit.

ADDRESS TO HIS SOLDIERS

If, soldiers, you shall by and by, in judging of your own fortune, preserve the same feelings which you experienced a little before in the example of the fate of others, we have already conquered; for neither was that merely a spectacle, but, as it were, a certain representation of your condition. And I know not whether fortune has not thrown around you still stronger chains and more urgent necessities than around your captives. On the right and left two seas enclose you, without your possessing even a single ship for escape. The river Po around you, the Po larger and more impetuous than the Rhone; the Alps behind, scarcely passed by you when fresh and vigorous, hem you in.

Here, soldiers, where you have first met the enemy, you must conquer or die; and the same fortune which has imposed the necessity of fighting holds out to you, if victorious, rewards than which men are not wont to desire greater, even from the immortal gods. If we were only about to recover by our valor Sicily and Sardinia, wrested from our fathers, the recompense would be sufficiently ample; but whatever, acquired and amassed by so many triumphs, the Romans possess, all, with its masters themselves, will become yours. To gain this rich reward, hasten, then, and seize your arms, with the favor of the gods.

Long enough, in pursuing cattle among the desert mountains of Lusitania and Celtiberia, you have seen no emolument from so may toils and dangers; it is time to make rich and profitable campaigns, and to gain the great reward of your labors, after having accomplished such a length of journey over so many mountains and rivers, and so many nations in arms. Here fortune has granted you the termination of your labors; here she will bestow a reward worthy of the service you have undergone. Nor, in proportion as the war is great in name, ought you to consider that the victory will be difficult. A despised enemy has often maintained a sanguinary contest, and renowned States and kings have been conquered by a very slight effort.

For, setting aside only the splendor of the Roman name, what remains in which they can be compared to you? To pass over in silence your service for twenty years, distinguished by such valor and success, you have made your way to this place from the pillars of Hercules, from the ocean and the remotest limits of the world, advancing victorious through so many of the fiercest nations of Gaul and Spain; you will fight with a raw army, which this very summer was beaten, conquered, and surrounded by the Gauls, as yet unknown to its general, and ignorant of him. Shall I compare myself—almost born, and certainly bred, in the tent of my father, that most illustrious commander, myself the subjugator of Spain and Gaul, the conqueror too not only of the Alpine nations, but, what is much more, of the Alps themselves—with this six-months' general, the deserter of his army?—to whom, if anyone, having taken away their standards, should today show the Carthaginians and Romans, I am sure that he would not know of which army he was consul.

I do not regard it, soldiers, as of small account that there is not a man among you before whose eyes I have not often achieved some military exploit; and to whom, in like manner, I, the spectator and witness of his valor, could not recount his own gallant deeds, particularized by time and place. With soldiers who have a thousand times received my praises and gifts, I, who was the pupil of you all before I became your commander, will march out in battle-array against those who are unknown to and ignorant of each other.

On whatever side I turn my eyes I see nothing but what is full of courage and energy: a veteran infantry; cavalry, both those with and those without the bridle, composed of the most gallant nations,—you, our most faithful and valiant allies, you Carthaginians, who are about to fight as well for the sake of your country as from the justest resentment. We are the assailants in the war, and descend into Italy with hostile standards, about to engage so much more boldly and bravely than the foe, as the confidence and courage of the assailants are greater than those of him who is defensive. Besides, suffering, injury, and indignity inflame and excite our minds: they first demanded me, your leader, for punishment, and then all of you who had laid siege to Saguntum; and had we been given up they would have visited us with the severest tortures.

That most cruel and haughty nation considers everything its own, and at its own disposal; it thinks it right that it should regulate with whom we are to have war, with whom peace; it circumscribes and shuts us up by the boundaries of mountains and rivers which we must not pass, and then does not adhere to those boundaries which it appointed. Pass not the Iberius; have nothing to do with the Saguntines. Saguntum is on the Iberius; you must not move a step in any direction. Is it a small thing that you take away my most ancient provinces—Sicily and Sardinia? Will you take Spain also? And should I withdraw thence, will you cross over into Africa?

Will cross, did I say? They have sent the two consuls of this year, one to Africa, the other to Spain: there is nothing left to us in any quarter, except what we can assert to ourselves by arms. Those may be cowards and dastards who have something to look back upon; whom, flying through safe and unmolested roads, their own lands and their own country will receive: there is a necessity for you to be brave, and, since all between victory and death is broken off from you by inevitable despair, either to conquer, or if fortune should waver, to meet death rather in battle than in flight. If this be well fixed and determined in the minds of you all, I will repeat, you have already conquered; no stronger incentive to victory has been given to man by the immortal gods.

Julius Caesar

100–44 B.C.

Julius Caesar's contemporaries thought of him as not only a soldier and politician but the orator next in greatness to Cicero. Unfortunately only fragments of his speeches have come down to us. This speech is recorded by Sallust, who was present at the trial of the Catiline conspirators. He was an excellent reporter, so that the speech is close to the pronouncement by Caesar himself.

In this speech, Caesar stated the position that the conspirators did not deserve death but life imprisonment and the confiscation of their property. No such law existed for life imprisonment and confiscation of property, and the Senate to whom he spoke was not ready on so short a notice to enact such a law. If the argument of Caesar had prevailed, the guards for the prisoners would have to be increased so long as the prisoners lived because there would always be the chance of escape; and if the prisoners did escape, there was the possibility that the conspirators might start anew. The words of Caesar carried weight, and he spoke so persuasively that Cicero and others felt there might be an adjournment. Cato rose and spoke immediately after Caesar and under his power adjournment was forgotten. The conspirators were sentenced to death and were then executed.

ON THE TREATMENT OF THE CONSPIRATORS

It becomes all men, conscript fathers, who deliberate on dubious matters, to be influenced neither by hatred, affection, anger, nor pity. The mind, when such feelings obstruct its view, cannot easily see what is right; nor has any human being consulted, at the same moment, his passions and his interest. When the mind is freely exerted, its reasoning is sound; but passion, if it gain possession of it, becomes its tyrant, and reason is powerless.

I could easily mention, conscript fathers, numerous examples of kings and nations, who, swayed by resentment or compassion, have adopted injudicious courses of conduct; but I had rather speak of those instances in which our ancestors, in opposition to the impulse of passion, acted with wisdom and sound policy.

In the Macedonian war, which we carried on against King Perses, the great and powerful state of Rhodes, which had risen by the aid of the Roman people, was faithless and hostile to us; yet, when the war was ended, and the conduct of the Rhodians was taken into consideration, our forefathers left them unmolested, lest any should say that war was made upon them for the sake of seizing their wealth, rather than of punishing their faithlessness. Throughout the Punic wars, too, though the Carthaginians, both during peace and in suspensions of arms, were guilty of many acts of injustice, yet our ancestors never took occasion to retaliate, but considered rather what was worthy of themselves than what might justly be inflicted on their enemies.

Similar caution, conscript fathers, is to be observed by yourselves, that the guilt of Lentulus, and the other conspirators, may not have greater weight with you than your own dignity, and that you may not regard your indignation more than your character. If, indeed, a punishment adequate to their crimes be discovered, I consent to extraordinary measures; but if the enormity of their crime exceeds whatever can be devised, I think that we should inflict only such penalties as the laws have provided.

Most of those who have given their opinions before me have deplored, in studied and impressive language, the sad fate that threatens the republic; they have recounted the barbarities of war, and the afflictions that would fall on the vanquished; they have told us that maidens would be dishonored, and youths abused; that children would be torn from the embraces of their parents; that matrons would be subjected to the pleasure of the conquerors; that temples and dwelling-houses would be plundered; that massacres and fires would follow; and that every place would be filled with arms, corpses, blood and lamentation. But to what end, in the name of the eternal gods! was such eloquence directed? Was it intended to render you indignant at the conspiracy? A speech, no doubt, will inflame him whom so frightful and monstrous a reality has not provoked! Far from it: for to no man does evil, directed against himself, appear a light matter; many, on the contrary, have felt it more seriously than was right.

But to different persons, conscript fathers, different degrees of license are allowed. If those who pass a life sunk in obscurity commit any error, through excessive anger, few become aware of it, for their fame is as limited as their fortune; but of those who live invested with extensive power, and in an exalted station, the whole world knows the proceedings. Thus in the highest position there is the least liberty of action; and it becomes us to indulge neither partiality nor aversion, but least of all animosity; for what in others is called resentment is in the powerful termed violence and cruelty.

I am, indeed, of opinion, conscript fathers, that the utmost degree of torture is inadequate to punish their crime; but the generality of mankind dwell on that which happens last, and, in the case of malefactors, forget their guilt, and talk only of their punishment, should that punishment have been inordinately severe. I feel assured, too, that Decimus Silanus, a man of spirit and resolution, made the suggestions which he offered, from zeal for the state, and that he had no view, in so important a matter, to favor or to enmity; such I know to be his character, and such his discretion. Yet his proposal appears to me, I will not say cruel (for what can be cruel that is directed against such characters?), but foreign to our policy. For, assuredly, Silanus, either your fears, or their treason, must have induced you, a consul-elect, to propose this new kind of punishment. Of fear it is unnecessary to speak, when, by the prompt activity of that distinguished man our consul, such numerous forces are under arms; and as to the punishment, we may say, what is, indeed, the truth, that in trouble and distress death is a relief from suffering, and not a torment; that it puts an end to all human woes; and that, beyond it, there is no place either for sorrow or joy.

But why, in the name of the immortal gods, did you not add to your proposal, Silanus, that, before they were put to death, they should be punished with the scourge? Was it because the Porcian law forbids it? But other laws forbid condemned citizens to be deprived of life, and allow them to go into exile. Or was it because scourging is a severer penalty than death? Yet what can be too severe, or too harsh, toward men convicted of such an offence? But if scourging be a milder punishment than death, how is it consistent to observe the law as to the smaller point, when you disregard it as to the greater?

But who, it may be asked, will blame any severity that shall be decreed against these parricides of their country? I answer that time, the course of events, and fortune, whose caprice governs nations, may blame it. Whatever shall fall on the traitors, will fall on them justly; but it is for you, conscript fathers, to consider well what you resolve to inflict on others. All precedents productive of evil effects have had their origin from what was good; but when a government passes into the hands of the ignorant or un-principled, any new example of severity, inflicted on deserving and suitable objects, is extended to those that are improper and undeserving of it. The Lacedaemonians, when they had conquered the Athenians, appointed thirty men to govern their state. These thirty began their administration by putting to death, even without a trial, all who were notoriously wicked, or publicly detestable; acts at which the people rejoiced, and extolled their justice. But afterward, when their lawless power gradually increased, they proceeded, at their pleasure, to kill the good and bad indiscriminately, and to strike terror into all; and thus the state, overpowered and enslaved, paid a heavy penalty for its imprudent exultation.

Within our own memory, too, when the victorious Sylla ordered Damasippus, and others of similar character, who had risen by distressing their country, to be put to death, who did not commend the proceeding? All exclaimed that wicked and factious men, who had troubled the state with their seditious practices, had justly forfeited their lives. Yet this proceeding was the commencement of great bloodshed. For whenever any one coveted the mansion or villa, or even the plate or apparel of another, he exerted his influence to have him numbered among the proscribed. Thus they, to whom the death of Damasippus had been a subject of joy, were soon after dragged to death themselves; nor was there any cessation of slaughter, until Sylla had glutted all his partisans with riches.

Such excesses, indeed, I do not fear from Marcus Tullius, or in these times. But in a large state there arise many men of various dispositions. At some other period, and under another consul, who, like the present, may have an army at his command, some false accusation may be credited as true; and when, with our example for a precedent, the consul shall have drawn the sword on the authority of the senate, who shall stay its progress, or moderate its fury?

Our ancestors, conscript fathers, were never deficient in conduct or courage; nor did pride prevent them from imitating the customs of other nations, if they appeared deserving of regard. Their armor, and weapons of war, they borrowed from the Samnites; their ensigns of authority, for the most part, from the Etrurians; and, in short, whatever appeared eligible to them, whether among allies or among enemies, they adopted at home with the greatest readiness, being more inclined to emulate merit than to be jealous of it. But at the same time, adopting a practice from Greece, they punished their citizens with the scourge, and inflicted capital punishment on such as were condemned. When the republic, however, became powerful, and faction grew strong from the vast number of citizens, men began to involve the innocent in condemnation, and other like abuses were practiced; and it was then that the Porcian and other laws were provided, by which condemned citizens were allowed to go into exile. This lenity of our ancestors, conscript fathers, I regard as a very strong reason why we should not adopt any new measures of severity. For assuredly there was greater merit and wisdom in those, who raised so mighty an empire from humble means, than in us, who can scarcely preserve what they so honorably acquired. Am I of opinion, then, you will ask, that the conspirators should be set free, and that the army of Catiline should thus be increased? Far from it; my recommendation is that their property be confiscated, and that they themselves be kept in custody in such of the municipal towns as are best able to bear the expense; that no one hereafter bring their case before the senate, or speak on it to the people; and that the senate now give their opinion that he who shall act contrary to this, will act against the republic and the general safety.

Georges Jacques Danton
1759–1794

Danton is known as a fiery French Revolutionist, but he won his early fame as a lawyer and had a popular following because of his oratory. He founded the order of Cordeliers, a society of radical revolutionists, and he championed the extreme left in the National Assembly. His first conspicuous use of his gift of oratory outside of the law was to urge the mob to storm the Bastille. He became the head of the provisional republican government and minister of justice; he set up the Revolutionary Tribunal and steered the first Committee of Public Safety.

The speech here given in part was delivered in the National Assembly in 1792. His speeches were not carefully prepared but they show nevertheless a power of phrase and style and their delivery must have been one of passionate fervor. He was described by his contemporaries as Jove the Thunderer. But Robespierre, who led extremists, was displeased with him and he was distrusted. He was seized, rushed through a trial and guillotined on April 5, 1794.

His audiences were eager for extreme statements, easily fired by suggestions of revolt and destruction, and what effect such a speaker had is frightening to estimate.

To Dare Again, Ever to Dare!

It seems a satisfaction for the ministers of a free people to announce to them that their country will be saved. All are stirred, all are enthused, all burn to enter the combat.

You know that Verdun is not yet in the power of our enemies, and that its garrison swears to immolate the first who breathes a proposition of surrender.

One portion of our people will guard our frontiers, another will dig and arm the entrenchments, the third with pikes will defend the interior of our cities. Paris will second these great efforts. The commissioners of the Commune will solemnly proclaim to the citizens the invitation to arm and march to the defense of the country. At such a moment you can proclaim that the capital deserves the esteem of all France. At such a moment this national assembly becomes a veritable committee of war. We ask that you concur with us in directing this sublime movement of the people, by naming commissioners to second and assist all these great measures. We ask that any one refusing to give personal service or to furnish arms shall meet the punishment of death. We ask that proper instructions be given to the citizens to direct their movements. We ask that carriers be sent to all the departments to notify them of the decrees that you proclaim here. The tocsin we shall sound is not the alarm signal of danger; it orders the charge on the enemies of France. [*Applause.*] To conquer we have need to dare, to dare again, ever to dare! And the safety of France is insured.

Napoleon Bonaparte
1769–1821

Napoleon Bonaparte, born at Ajaccio, Corsica, educated there in a military school, then further educated in military science in Paris, profited well enough to become the military master of Europe. His rise was the combination of good fortune and an indomitable will. He acquired a well-deserved reputation as an orator through his stirring proclamations and his persuasive effect in evoking from his men loyalty to him and his causes. His most famous speech was, perhaps, contained in a single sentence. Thiers relates that when the Army of Egypt came within sight of the pyramids shining as if gilded by the rays of the sun, the army "halted as if seized by curiosity and admiration." But Napoleon, seizing the moment in history, galloped before his men pointing to the pyramids, exclaiming: "Soldiers, from the summits of the pyramids, forty centuries look down upon you."

To His Soldiers on Entering Milan

Soldiers:—You have rushed like a torrent from the top of the Apennines; you have overthrown and scattered all that opposed your march. Piedmont, delivered from Austrian tyranny, indulges her natural sentiments of peace and friendship toward France. Milan is yours, and the republican flag waves throughout Lombardy. The dukes of Parma and Modena owe their political existence to your generosity alone.

The army which so proudly threatened you can find no barrier to protect it against your courage; neither the Po, the Ticino, nor the Adda could stop you for a single day. These vaunted bulwarks of Italy opposed you in vain; you passed them as rapidly as the Apennines.

These great successes have filled the heart of your country with joy. Your representatives have ordered a festival to commemorate your victories, which has been held in every district of the republic. There your fathers, your mothers, your wives, sisters, and mistresses rejoiced in your good fortune and proudly boasted of belonging to you.

Yes, soldiers, you have done much—but remains there nothing more to do? Shall it be said of us that we knew how to conquer, but not how to make use of victory? Shall posterity reproach us with having found Capua in Lombardy?

But I see you already hasten to arms. An effeminate repose is tedious to you; the days which are lost to glory are lost to your happiness. Well, then, let us set forth! We have still forced marches to make, enemies to subdue, laurels to gather, injuries to revenge. Let those who have sharpened the daggers of civil war in France, who have basely murdered our ministers and burnt our ships at Toulon, tremble!

The hour of vengeance has struck; but let the people of all countries be free from apprehension; we are the friends of the people everywhere, and those great men whom we have taken for our models. To restore the Capitol, to replace the statues of the heroes who rendered it illustrious, to rouse the Roman people, stupefied by several ages of slavery—such will be the fruit of our victories, they will form an era for posterity; you will have the immortal glory of changing the face of the finest part of Europe. The French people, free and respected by the whole world, will give to Europe, a glorious peace, which will indemnify them for the sacrifices of every kind which for the last six years they have been making. You will then return to your homes and your country. Men will say, as they point you out, "He belonged to the Army of Italy."

Albert Jeremiah Beveridge

1862–1927

Albert Beveridge in 1899 became the Republican Senator from Indiana and served until 1911. After a quiet period, he returned to the field of politics and ran again for the Senate in 1922, but he was defeated. He was an ardent follower of the policies of President Theodore Roosevelt and believed in "the big stick" and the magnificence of powerful armies. His speeches reflect this glowing fervor for his country and the policies he believed would bring enrichment of the United States.

The speech here was given at the opening of the Indiana Republican Campaign at Tomlinson Hall, Indianapolis, September 16, 1898.

The western states in their political conventions followed the lead of Beveridge and espoused the same cause and attitude. Included are passages from the beginning, the middle, and the end. It should be noted that this speech was delivered to a Republican Convention, so that Beveridge could count on certain sentiments and opinions of his listeners.

The March of the Flag

Fellow Citizens:—It is a noble land that God has given us; a land that can feed and clothe the world; a land whose coast lines would inclose half the countries of Europe; a land set like a sentinel between the two imperial oceans of the globe, a greater England with a nobler destiny.

It is a mighty people that He has planted on this soil; a people sprung from the most masterful blood of history; a people perpetually revitalized by the virile, man-producing working-folk of all the earth; a people imperial by virtue of their power, by right of their institutions, by authority of their Heaven-directed purposes—the propagandists and not the misers of liberty.

It is a glorious history our God has bestowed upon His chosen people; a history with faith in our mission and our future; a history whose keynote was struck by the Liberty Bell; a history of statesmen who flung the boundaries of the Republic out into unexplored lands and savage wildernesses; a history of soldiers who carried the flag across blazing deserts and through the ranks of hostile mountains, even to the gates of sunset; a history of a multiplying people who overran a continent in half a century; a history of prophets who saw the consequences of evils inherited from the past and of martyrs who died to save them; a history divinely logical, in the process of whose tremendous reasoning we find ourselves today.

Therefore, in this campaign, the question is larger than a party question. It is an American question. It is a world question. Shall the American people continue their march toward the commercial supremacy of the world? Shall free institutions broaden their blessed reign as the children of liberty wax in strength, until the empire of our principles is established over the hearts of all mankind?

Have we no mission to perform, no duty to discharge to our fellow-man? Has God endowed us with gifts beyond our deserts and marked us as the people of His peculiar favor, merely to rot in our own selfishness, as men and nations must, who take cowardice for their companions and self for their duty—as China has, as India has, as Egypt has?

Shall we be as the man who had one talent and hid it, or as he who had ten talents and used them until they grew to riches? And shall we reap the reward that waits on our discharge of our high duty as the sovereign power on earth; shall we occupy new markets for what our farmers raise, new markets for what our merchants sell—aye, and, please God, new markets for what our ships shall carry?

Shall we avail ourselves of new sources of supply of what we do not raise or make, so that what are luxuries today will be necessities tomorrow? Shall our commerce be encouraged until, with Oceanica, the Orient, and the world, American trade shall be the imperial trade of the entire globe?

Shall we conduct the mightiest commerce of history with the best money known to man, or shall we use the pauper money of Mexico, of China, and of the Chicago platform?

What are the great facts of this administration? Not a failure of revenue; not a perpetual battle between the executive and legislative departments of government; not a rescue from dishonor by European syndicates at the price of tens of millions in cash and national humiliation unspeakable. These have not marked the past two years—the past two years, which have blossomed into four splendid months of glory.

But a war has marked it, the most holy war ever waged by one nation against another—a war for civilization, a war for a permanent peace, a war, which, under God, although we knew it not, swung open to the republic the portals of the commerce of the world. And the first question you must answer with your vote is whether you indorse that war. We are told that all citizens and every platform indorse the war, and I admit, with the joy of patriotism, that this is true. But that is only among ourselves, and we are of and to ourselves no longer. This election takes place on the stage of the world, with all earth's nations for our auditors. . . .

And the burning question of this campaign is, whether the American people will accept the gifts of events; whether they will rise as lifts their soaring destiny; whether they will proceed upon the lines of our past; or whether, for the first time, the American people doubt their mission, question fate, prove apostate to the spirit of their race, and halt the careless march of free institutions.

Hawaii is ours; Porto Rico is to be ours; at the prayer of her people Cuba finally will be ours; in the islands of the East, even to the Gates of Asia, coaling stations are to be ours at the very least; the flag of a liberal government is to float over the Philippines and may it be the banner that Taylor unfurled in Texas and Fremont carried to the coast.

The opposition tells us that we are not to govern a people without their consent. I answer: The rule of liberty, that all just government derives its authority from the consent of the governed, applies only to those who are capable of self-government. I answer: We govern the Indians without their consent, we govern our children without their consent. I answer: How do you assume that our government would be without their consent? Would the people of the Philippines prefer the just, humane, civilizing government of this republic to the savage, bloody rule of pillage and extortion from which we have rescued them?

And, regardless of this formula of words, made only for enlightened, self-governing peoples, do we owe no duty to the world? Shall we turn these people back to the reeking hands? Shall we abandon them to their fate, with the wolves of conquest all about them—with Germany, Russia, France, even Japan, hungering for them? Shall we save them from those nations, to give them a self-rule of tragedy? It would be like giving a razor to a babe and telling it to shave itself. It would be like giving a typewriter to an Eskimo and telling him to publish one of the great dailies of the world. This proposition of the opposition makes the Declaration of Independence preposterous as the reading of Job's lamentations would be at a wedding. . . .

Will you say by your vote that American ability to govern has decayed; that a century's experience in self-rule has failed of a result? Will you affirm by your vote that you are an infidel to American vigor and power and practical sense? Or, that we are of the ruling race of the world; that ours is the blood of government; ours the heart of dominion; ours the brain and genius of administration? Will you remember that we do but what our fathers did —we but pitch the tents of liberty farther westward, farther southward—we only continue the march of the flag.

The march of the flag! In 1789 the flag of the Republic waved over 4,000,000 souls in thirteen states, and their savage territory which stretched to the Mississippi, to

Canada, to the Floridas. The timid minds of that day said that no new territories were needed, and, for the hour, they were right. But Jefferson, through whose intellect the centuries marched; Jefferson, who dreamed of Cuba as an American state; Jefferson, the first Imperialist of the Republic—Jefferson acquired that imperial territory which swept from the Mississippi to the mountains, from Texas to the British possessions, and the march of the flag began!

The infidels to the gospel of liberty raved, but the flag swept on! the title to that noble land out of which Oregon, Washington, Idaho, and Montana have been carved was uncertain; Jefferson, strict constructionist of constitutional power though he was, obeyed the Anglo-Saxon impulse within him, whose watchword then and whose watchword throughout the world today is, "Forward!": another empire was added to the Republic and the march of the flag went on! . . .

A screen of land from New Orleans to Florida shut us from the Gulf, and over this and the Everglade Peninsula waved the saffron flag of Spain; Andrew Jackson seized both, the American stood at his back, and under Monroe, the Floridas came under the dominion of the Republic, and the march of the flag went on! . . .

Then Texas responded to the bugle calls of liberty, and the march of the flag went on! And at last, we waged war with Mexico, and the flag swept over the southwest, over peerless California, past the Gate of Gold to Oregon on the North, and from ocean to ocean its folds of glory blazed.

And now, obeying the same voice that Jefferson heard and obeyed . . . our President today plants the flag over the islands of the seas, outposts of commerce, citadels of national security, and the march of the flag goes on! . . .

Fellow Americans, we are God's chosen people. Yonder at Bunker Hill and Yorktown His providence was above us. At New Orleans and on ensanguined seas His hand sustained us. Abraham Lincoln was His Minister, and His was the Altar of Freedom the boy in blue set on a hundred battlefields. His power directed Dewey in the East, and delivered the Spanish fleet into our hands on the eve of

Liberty's natal day, as he delivered the elder armada into the hands of our English sires two centuries ago. His great purposes are revealed in the progress of the flag, which surpasses the intentions of congresses and cabinets, and leads us like a holier pillar of cloud by day and pillar of fire by night into situations unforeseen by finite wisdom, and duties unexpected by the unprophetic heart of selfishness. The American people cannot use a dishonest medium of exchange; it is ours to set the world its example of right and honor. We cannot fly from our world duties; it is ours to execute the purpose of a fate that has driven us to be greater than our small intentions. We cannot retreat from any soil where Providence has unfurled our banner; it is ours to save that soil for liberty and civilization. For liberty and civilization are God's promise fulfilled, the flag must henceforth be the symbol and the sign to all mankind—the flag!—

> Flag of the free heart's hope and home,
>   By angel hands to valor given,
> Thy stars have lit the welkin dome,
>   And all their hues were born in heaven!
> Forever wave that standard sheet,
>   Where breathes the foe but falls before us,
> With freedom's soil beneath our feet
>   And freedom's banner streaming o'er us!

Nicholas Murray Butler
1862–1947

Nicholas Murray Butler was President of Columbia University in New York City from 1902 until 1945. Although an educator, he was active in politics and was once the candidate for the vice-presidency. As an internationally known American, Butler was recognized as one of the great after-dinner speakers of his day along with Theodore Roosevelt, Chauncey Depew, Mark Twain, and Brander Matthews. This address, delivered before the Phi Beta Kappa Society of Vassar College, June 10, 1901, reflects his vigor of mind and intellectual perception. His directives to students of that day are equally valid to students of the present. Parts of the speech follow.

THE EVIDENCES OF AN EDUCATION

"If you had had children, sir," said Boswell, "would you have taught them anything?" "I hope," replied Doctor Johnson, "that I should have willingly lived on bread and water to obtain instruction for them; but I would not have set their future to hazard, for the sake of thrusting into their heads knowledge of things for which they might not perhaps have either taste or necessity. You teach your daughters the diameters of the planets, and wonder when you have done that that they do not delight in your company." From which it appears that Doctor Johnson, by a sort of prolepsis, was moved to contribute to the discussion of one of the vexed questions of our time. Who is the educated man? By what signs shall we know him?

First among the evidences of an education I name correctness and precision in the use of the mother tongue. Important as this power is, and is admitted to be, it is a comparatively new thing in education. The modern European languages took on educational significance only when the decentralization of culture began at the close of the Middle Ages. So late as 1549 Jacques du Bellay supported the study of French with the mild assertion that it is "not so poor a tongue as many think it." Mulcaster, writing a little later, found it necessary to tell why his book on education was put into English rather than in Latin, and to defend the vernacular when he referred to its educational usefulness. Melanchthon put German in a class with Greek and Hebrew, and contrasted all three unfavorably with Latin. Indeed it was not until the present German Emperor plainly told the Berlin School Conference of 1890 that a national basis was lacking in German education; that the foundation of the gymnasium course of study must be German; that the duty of the schoolmasters was to train the young to become Germans, not Greeks and Romans; and that the German language must be made the center around which all other subjects revolved, that a revision of the official school program was brought about that made place for the really serious study of the German language and literature. And today, where the influence of the English universities and of not a few American colleges is potent, the study of English is slight and insignificant indeed. The superstition that the best gate to English is through the Latin is anything but dead.

One's hold upon the English tongue is measured by his choice of words and by his use of idiom. The composite character of modern English offers a wide field for apt and happy choice of expression. The educated man, at home with his mother tongue, moves easily about in its Saxon, Romanic, and Latin elements, and has gained by long experience and wide reading a knowledge of the mental incidence of words as well as of their artistic effect. He is hampered by no set formulas, but manifests in his speech, spoken and written, the characteristic powers and appreciation of his nature. The educated man is of necessity, therefore, a constant reader of the best written English. He reads not for conscious imitation, but for unconscious distinction between correct English on the one hand, and pedantic, or, as it is sometimes called, "elegant" English on the other. He is more likely to "go to bed" than to "retire," "to get up" than to "arise," to have "legs" rather than "limbs," to "dress" than to "clothe himself," and to "make a speech" rather than to "deliver an oration." He knows that "if you hear poor English and read poor English, you will pretty surely speak poor English and write poor English," and governs himself accordingly. He realizes the power and place of idiom and its relation to grammar, and shows his skill by preserving a balance between the two in his style.

As a second evidence of an education, I name those refined and gentle manners which are the expression of fixed habits of thought and action. "Manners are behavior and good breeding," as Addison said, but they are more. It is not without significance that the Latin language has but a single word (*mores*) both for usages, habits, manners, and for morals. Real manners, the manners of a truly educated man or woman, are an outward expression of intellectual and moral conviction. Sham manners are a veneer which falls away at the dampening touch of the first selfish suggestion. Manners have a moral significance, and find their basis in that true and deepest self-respect which is built upon respect for others. An infallible test of character is to be found in one's manners toward those whom, for one reason or another, the world may deem his inferiors. A man's manners toward his equals or his superiors are shaped by too many motives to render their interpretation either easy or certain. Manners do not make the man, but manners reveal the man.

As a third evidence of an education, I name the power and habit of reflection. It is a frequent charge against us moderns, particularly against Americans, that we are losing the habit of reflection, and the high qualities which depend upon it. We are told that the loss is a necessary result of our hurried and busy lives, of our diverse interests, and of the annihilation of space and time by steam and electricity.

If it be true—and there are some counts in the indictment which it is difficult to deny—then one of the most precious evidences of an education is slipping from us, and we must redouble our efforts to keep fast hold upon it. For an unexamined life, as Socrates unceasingly insisted, is not worth living. The life which asks no questions of itself, which traces events back to no cause and forward to no purposes, which raises no vital issues of principle, and which seeks no interpretation of what passes within and without, is not a human life at all; it is the life of an animal. The trained and the untrained mind are perhaps in sharpest contrast at this very point. An armory of insights and convictions always ready for applications to new conditions, is a mark of a trained and educated mind. The educated man has standards of truth, of human experience, and wisdom by which new proposals are judged. These standards can be gained only through reflection. The undisciplined mind is a prey to every passing fancy and the victim of every plausible doctrinaire. He has no permanent forms of judgment which give him character.

As a fourth evidence of an education, I name the power of growth. There is a type of mind which, when trained to a certain point, crystallizes, as it were, and refuses to move forward thereafter. This type of mind fails to give one of the essential evidences of an education. It has perhaps acquired much and promised much; but somehow or other the promise is not fulfilled. It is not dead, but in a trance.

A human mind continuing to grow and to develop throughout a long life is a splendid and impressive sight. Broadened views, widened sympathies, deepened insights are the accompaniments of growth.

As a fifth evidence of an education, I name efficiency —the power to do. The time has long since gone by, if it ever was, when contemplation pure and simple, withdrawal from the world and its activities, or intelligent incompetence was a defensible ideal of education. Today the truly educated man must be, in some sense, efficient. With brain, tongue, or hand he must be able to express his knowledge, and so leave the world other than he found it. Do something and be able to do it well; express what you know in some helpful and substantial form; produce, and do not everlastingly feel only and revel in feelings—these are counsels which make for a real education and against that sham form of it which is easily recognized as well-informed incapacity.

These five characteristics, then, I offer as evidences of an education—correctness and precision in the use of the mother tongue; refined and gentle manners, which are the expression of fixed habits of thought and action; the power and habit of reflection; the power of growth; and efficiency, or the power to do. On this plane the physicist, may meet with the philologian, and the naturalist with the philosopher, and each recognize the fact his fellow is an educated man, though the range of their information is widely different, and the centers of their highest interests are far apart. They are knit together in a brotherhood by the close tie of those traits which have sprung out of the reaction of their minds and wills upon that which has fed them and brought them strength. Without these traits men are not truly educated and their erudition, however vast, is of no avail; it furnishes a museum, not a developed human being.

It is these habits, of necessity made by ourselves alone, begun in the days of school and college, and strengthened with maturer years and broader experience, that serve to show to ourselves and to others that we have discovered the secret of gaining an education.

Dwight David Eisenhower
1890–

General of the Army Dwight D. Eisenhower, Supreme Commander of the Allied Expeditionary Force personally broadcast his message about the invasion of the Continent on June 6, 1944, and to his men sent this Order of the Day. The "Order" was distributed to the commanders of the vessels carrying the men across the channel and each commander read the message to his men. This message, succinct, direct, straightforward, told them of the kind of spirit their leader possessed.

The second speech, given in part, was delivered at a dinner in his honor by the City of New York on June 19, 1945. The difference in tone, in quality, in phrases can be detected. The first speech was written under great emotional tension; the second is a reflection on past events.

ORDER OF THE DAY, JUNE 6, 1944

Soldiers, sailors and airmen of the Allied Expeditionary Force: You are about to embark upon a great crusade, toward which we have striven these many months. The eyes of the world are upon you. The hopes and prayers of liberty-loving people everywhere march with you.

In company with our brave Allies and brothers in arms on other fronts, you will bring about the destruction of the German war machine, the elimination of the Nazi tyranny over the oppressed peoples of Europe, and the security for ourselves in a free world.

Your task will not be an easy one. Your enemy is well trained, well equipped and battle-hardened. He will fight savagely.

But this is the year 1944. Much has happened since the

Nazi triumphs of 1940–41. The United Nations have inflicted upon the Germans great defeats in open battle, man to man. Our air offensive has seriously reduced their strength in the air and their capacity to wage war on the ground.

Our home fronts have given us an overwhelming superiority in weapons and munitions of war, and placed at our disposal great reserves of trained fighting men.

The tide has turned. The free men of the world are marching together to victory. I have full confidence in your courage, devotion to duty and skill in battle. We will accept nothing less than full victory. Good luck.

Let us all beseech the blessing of Almighty God upon this great and noble undertaking.

PEACE AN ABSOLUTE NECESSITY, JUNE 19, 1945

I want to say one thing in defense of the regular officer of the Army brought to mind by the wonderful commendation given to me personally between the introductory remarks.

There is no greater pacifist than the regular officer.

Any man who is forced to turn his attention to the horrors of the battlefield, to the grotesque shapes that are left there for the burying squads—he doesn't want war. He never wants it. He is an agent of his Government to do a necessary and very desperate task. And it is to the welfare of the United States always to see that they have people studying those things and ready in emergency to do what the regular officer has done in this war, namely, furnish the technical leadership for the tactical, applied power of a whole nation.

America's record in production and on the battle line is one that will fill our histories forever, and today you should turn your thoughts to what you have done, and I mean, America. And remember that you can do it because self-confidence is one of the great things that brings greater achievements still in the future.

We are still at war. I hope that the rejoicing in which we indulge because of the crushing of the Nazi will never blind us to the task we still have in the Pacific. The reason I bring this up is this—it is to your interest always to remember it. . . .

We cannot be isolated from the world.

From New York to my headquarters in Frankfort it is exactly sixteen hours by air. You are that close to trouble all the time if trouble starts in Europe. It is to our interest to see that we are strong. To repeat a remark I made this noon: Weakness cannot cooperate with anything. Only strength can cooperate.

As I see it, peace is an absolute necessity to this world. Civilization itself, in the face of another catastrophe such as we have faced in the last three years—and for other nations more—would tremble, possibly decay and be destroyed. We must face those problems of peace and with the same resolution that America showed in 1941 and '42 when not the greatest optimist would believe that within eleven months after landing in Normandy the American arms and Allied arms would stand triumphant on the Elbe.

I believe that we should let no specious argument of any kind deter us from exploring every direction in which peace can be maintained. I believe we should be strong, but we should be tolerant. We should be ready to defend our right but we should be considerate and recognize the rights of the other man.

The business of preserving peace is a practical thing but practicality and idealism are not necessarily mutually antagonistic. We can be idealistic and we can be practical along with it.

You have great hospitals in your city that are filled with wounded men. I call them "my wounded men;" they came back from my theatre. I don't want to see any more of them there, ever.

I feel that if the brains and the intelligence, the genius of America are placed on this problem, if we can forget self, if we can forget politics, if we can forget personal ambition, we can solve this problem, and we must solve the problem or we will all be lost.

No man can tell me that America with its glorious mixture of races, of creeds, its Jews, its Catholics, its Protestants—it cannot lose, and we can't lose this one.

Douglas MacArthur
1880–1964

General of the Army Douglas MacArthur had an illustrious yet stormy career in the Army and as director of the occupation of Japan after the surrender of the Japanese. He was an outspoken man of great integrity, and a brilliant conversationalist, but he was particularly fluent as an orator. His speech to Congress after his dismissal from command in Korea by President Truman was a masterpiece of eloquence almost out of the nineteenth century, yet no one will forget who reads that speech that "Old Soldiers Never Die."

General MacArthur believed, however, that his best speech was that of "Duty, Honor and Country" which he delivered at the United States Military Academy, West Point, N.Y. on the award to the General of the Sylvanus Medal, May 12, 1962.

DUTY, HONOR AND COUNTRY

No human being could fail to be deeply moved by such a tribute as this, coming from a profession I have served so long and a people I have loved so well. It fills me with an emotion I cannot express. But this award is not intended primarily for a personality, but to symbolize a great moral code—the code of conduct and chivalry of those who guard this beloved land of culture and ancient descent.

"Duty," "honor," "country"—those three hallowed words reverently dictate what you want to be, what you can be, what you will be. They are your rallying point to build courage when courage seems to fail, to regain faith when there seems to be little cause for faith, to create hope when hope becomes forlorn.

Unhappily, I possess neither that eloquence of diction, that poetry of imagination, nor that brilliance of metaphor to tell you all that they mean.

The unbeliever will say they are but words, but a slogan, but a flamboyant phrase. Every pedant, every demagogue, every cynic, every hypocrite, every troublemaker, and, I am sorry to say, some others of an entirely different character, will try to downgrade them even to the extent of mockery and ridicule.

But these are some of the things they build. They build your basic character. They mold you for your future roles as the custodians of the Nation's defense. They make you strong enough to know when you are weak, and brave enough to face yourself when you are afraid.

They teach you to be proud and unbending in honest failure, but humble and gentle in success; not to substitute words for actions; not to seek the path of comfort, but to face the stress and spur of difficulty and challenge; to learn to stand up in the storm, but to have compassion on those who fall; to master yourself before you seek to master others; to have a heart that is clean, a goal that is high; to learn to laugh, yet never forget how to weep; to reach into the future, yet never neglect the past; to be serious, yet never take yourself too seriously; to be modest so that you will remember the simplicity of true greatness; the open mind of true wisdom, the meekness of true strength.

They give you a temperate will, a quality of imagination, a vigor of the emotions, a freshness of the deep springs of life, a temperamental predominance of courage over timidity, an appetite for adventure over love of ease.

They create in your heart the sense of wonder, the unfailing hope of what next, and the joy and inspiration of life. They teach you in this way to be an officer and a gentleman.

And what sort of soldiers are those you are to lead? Are they reliable? Are they brave? Are they capable of victory?

Their story is known to all of you. It is the story of the American man at arms. My estimate of him was formed on the battlefields many, many years ago, and has never changed. I regarded him then, as I regard him now, as one of the world's noblest figures; not only as one of the finest military characters, but also as one of the most stainless . . .

In twenty campaigns, on a hundred battlefields, around a thousand campfires, I have witnessed that enduring fortitude, that patriotic self-abnegation, and that invincible determination which have carved his statue in the hearts of his people.

From one end of the world to the other, he has drained deep the chalice of courage. As I listened to these songs in memory's eye I could see those staggering columns of the First World War, bending under soggy packs on many a weary march, from dripping dusk to drizzly dawn, slogging ankle deep through mire of shell-pocked roads; to form grimly for the attack, blue-lipped, covered with sludge and mud, chilled by the wind and rain, driving home their objectives, and for many, to the judgment seat of God.

Always for them: Duty, honor, country. Always their blood, and sweat and tears, as they saw the way and the light. And twenty years after, on the other side of the globe, again the filth of dirty fox-holes, and the stench of ghostly trenches, the slime of dripping dugouts, those boiling suns of relentless heat, those torrential rains of devastating storms, the loneliness and utter desolation of jungle trails, the bitterness of long separation of those they loved and cherished, the deadly pestilence of tropical disease, the horror of stricken areas of war.

Their resolute and determined defense, their swift and sure attack, their indomitable purpose, their complete and decisive victory, always, through the bloody haze or their last reverberating shot, the vision of gaunt, ghastly men, reverently following your password of duty, honor, country . . .

You face a world of change . . . We deal not with things of this world alone, but with the illimitable distances and yet unfathomed mysteries of the universe. We are reaching out for a new and boundless frontier. We speak in terms of harnessing the cosmic energy, of making the winds and tides work for us. . . .

And through all this welter of change and development your mission remains fixed, determined, inviolable. It is to win our wars. Everything else in your professional career is but corollary to this vital dedication. All other public purpose, all other public projects, all other public needs, great or small, will find others for their accomplishments: but you are the ones who are trained to fight.

This does not mean that you are warmongers. On the contrary, the soldier above all other people prays for peace, for he must suffer and bear the deepest wounds, and scars of war. But always in our ears ring the ominous words of Plato, that wisest of philosophers: "Only the dead have seen the end of war."

The shadows are lengthening for me. The twilight is here. My days of old have vanished—tone and tints . . . Their memory is one of wondrous beauty, watered by years and coaxed and caressed by the smiles of yesterday . . . I listen then but with thirsty ear, for the witching melody of faint bugles blowing reveille, of far drums beating the long roll.

In my dream I hear again the crash of guns, the rattle of musketry, the strange, mournful murmur of the battle-field. But in the evening of my memory I come back to West Point. Always there echoes and re-echoes: Duty, honor, country.

Today marks my final roll call with you. But I want you to know that when I cross the river, my last conscious thoughts will be of the corps, and the corps, and the corps.

I bid you farewell.

PART THREE

CRIME, PUNISHMENT, AND REWARDS

Marcus Tullius Cicero
106–43 B.C.

*Marcus Tullius Cicero was born in an ancient, honored
family that had never taken part in the political affairs of
Rome, and the young man upset the family tradition by
entering the political arena as a lawyer. He had received
an excellent liberal education and shown such promise in
his early years that his schoolfellows told their parents
what a bright young boy he was. He studied philosophy
under Philo the Academic and oratory under Molo, the
ablest rhetorician of the day. He received special instruction from Diodotus the Stoic in the subtleties of argumentation. He daily declaimed with young noblemen in both
Greek and Latin.*

*He reached the highest position in Roman life and repu-
tation through his eloquence and his integrity as a civil
magistrate. His outstanding honesty set him apart from
many Romans who sought power and wealth. In the end,
his friends turned against him even when he had defended
them in court. One of these men, Pompilius, killed Cicero
as he was being carried to a ship to sail from his native
land.*

*Of some 107 orations only seventy-seven of Cicero's
speeches remain in whole or part. He wrote many letters,
philosophical essays, and works on the method of oratory.
His four orations against Catiline are of special mention.
Here the first is given.*

*This speech was delivered to the Roman Senate in the
Temple of Concord. The chronological events leading to
it are as follows: Cicero had been elected Consul and
Catiline had been defeated for that office; Catiline had
behind him a small army of disgruntled toughs who were
seeking power and spoils, and with these men Catiline
planned an assassination of Cicero for November 6, 63 B.C.;
Cicero learned of this plot from a woman who had been*

*told the secret; Cicero had his house guarded and the
assassination was prevented; On November 7 Cicero went
to the Senate and delivered the "First Oration Against
Catiline." The conspirator himself was present as a member of the Senate and heard the speech. He was angered
by it and left the Senate and went to his young, threatening army to foment further plans against Cicero and Rome.
The three other orations followed as Cicero gathered his
information on Catiline's plans and declared them to the
Senate.*

First Oration Against Catiline

When, O Catiline, do you mean to cease abusing our
patience? How long is that madness of yours still to mock
us? When is there to be an end of that unbridled audacity
of yours, swaggering about as it does now? Do not the
mighty guards placed on the Palatine Hill—do not the
watches posted throughout the city—does not the alarm of
the people, and the union of all good men—does not the
precaution taken of assembling the senate in this most
defensible place—do not the looks and countenances of
this venerable body here present, have any effect upon
you? Do you not feel that your plans are detected? Do
you not see that your conspiracy is already arrested and
rendered powerless by the knowledge which every one
here possesses of it? What is there that you did last night,
what the night before—where is it that you were—who
was there that you summoned to meet you—what design
was there which was adopted by you, with which you
think that any one of us is unacquainted?

Shame on the age and on its principles! The senate is
aware of these things; the consul sees them; and yet this
man lives. Lives! aye, he comes even into the senate. He
takes a part in the public deliberations; he is watching
and marking down and checking off for slaughter every
individual among us. And we, gallant men that we are,
think that we are doing our duty to the republic if we
keep out of the way of his frenzied attacks.

You ought, O Catiline, long ago to have been led to execution by command of the counsel. That destruction which you have been long plotting against us ought to have already fallen on your own head.

What? Did not that most illustrious man, Publius Scipio, the Pontifex Maximus, in his capacity of a private citizen, put to death Tiberius Gracchus, though but slightly undermining the constitution? And shall we, who are the consuls, tolerate Catiline, openly desirous to destroy the whole world with fire and slaughter? For I pass over older instances, such as how Caius Servilius Ahala with his own hand slew Spurius Maelius when plotting a revolution in the state. There was—there was once such virtue in this republic that brave men would repress mischievous citizens with severer chastisement than the most bitter enemy. For we have a resolution of the senate, a formidable and authoritative decree against you, O Catiline; the wisdom of the republic is not at fault, nor the dignity of this senatorial body. We, we alone—I say it openly—we, the consuls, are wanting in our duty.

The senate once passed a decree that Lucius Opimius, the consul, should take care that the republic suffered no injury. Not one night elapsed. There was put to death, on some mere suspicion of disaffection, Caius Gracchus, a man whose family had borne the most unblemished reputation for many generations. There was slain Marcus Fulvius, a man of consular rank, and all of his children. By a like decree of the senate the safety of the republic was intrusted to Caius Marius and Lucius Valerius, the consuls. Did not the vengeance of the republic, did not execution overtake Lucius Saturninus, a tribune of the people, and Caius Servilius, the praetor, without the delay of one single day? But we, for these twenty days, have been allowing the edge of the senate's authority to grow blunt, as it were. For we are in possession of a similar decree of the senate, but we keep it locked up in its parchment— buried, I may say, in the sheath; and according to this decree you ought, O Catiline, to be put to death this instant. You live—and you live, not to lay aside, but to persist in your audacity. I wish, O conscript fathers, to be merciful; I wish not to appear negligent amid such danger to the state; but I do not accuse myself of remissness and culpable inactivity. A camp is pitched in Italy, at the entrance of Etruria, in hostility to the republic; the number of the enemy increases every day; and yet the general of that camp, the leader of those enemies, we see within the walls—aye, and even in the senate—planning every day some internal injury to the republic. If, O Catiline, I should not order you to be arrested, to be put to death, I should I suppose, have to fear lest all good men should say that I had acted tardily, rather than that any one should affirm that I acted cruelly. But yet this, which ought to have been done long since, I have good reason for not doing as yet; I will put you to death, then, when there shall be not one person possible to be found so wicked, so abandoned, so like yourself, as not to allow that it has been rightly done. As long as one person exists who can dare to defend you, you shall live; but you shall live as you do now, surrounded by my many and trusted guards, so that you shall not be able to stir one finger against the republic: many eyes and ears shall still observe and watch you as they have hitherto done, though you shall not perceive them.

For what is there, O Catiline, that you can still expect, if night is not able to veil your nefarious meetings in darkness, and if private houses cannot conceal the voice of your conspiracy within their walls—if everything is seen and displayed? Change your mind: trust me: forget the slaughter and conflagration you are meditating. You are hemmed in on all sides: all your plans are clearer than the day to us; let me remind you of them. Do you recollect that on the 21st of October I said in the senate, that on a certain day, which was to be the 27th of October, C. Manlius, the satellite and servant of your audacity, would be in arms? Was I mistaken, Catiline, not only in so important, so atrocious, so incredible a fact, but, what is much more remarkable, in the very day? I said also in the senate that you had fixed the massacre of the nobles for the 28th of October, when many chief men of the senate had left Rome, not so much for the sake of saving themselves as of checking your designs. Can you deny that on that very day you were so hemmed in by my guards and my vigilance, that you were unable to stir one finger against the republic; when you said that you would be content with the flight of the rest, and the slaughter of us who remained? What? when you made sure that you would be able to seize Praeneste on the 1st of November by a nocturnal attack, did you not find that that colony was fortified by my order, by my garrison, by my watchfulness and care? You do nothing, you plan nothing, think of nothing which I not only do not hear but which I do not see and know every particular of.

Listen while I speak of the night before. You shall now see that I watch far more actively for the safety than you do for the destruction of the republic. I say that you came the night before (I will say nothing obscurely) into the Scythe-dealers' street, to the house of Marcus Lecca; that many of your accomplices in the same insanity and wickedness came there, too. Do you dare to deny it? Why are you silent? I will prove it if you do deny it; for I see here in the senate some men who were there with you.

O ye immortal gods, where on earth are we? in what city are we living? what constitution is ours? There are here—here in our body, O conscript fathers, in this the most holy and dignified assembly of the whole world, men who meditate my death, and the death of all of us, and the destruction of this city, and of the whole world. I, the consul, see them; I ask them their opinion about the republic, and I do not yet attack, even by words, those who ought to be put to death by the sword. You were, then, O Catiline, at Lecca's that night; you divided Italy into sections; you settled where every one was to go; you fixed whom you were to leave at Rome, whom you were to take with you; you portioned out the divisions of the city for conflagration; you undertook that you yourself would at once leave the city, and said that there was then only this to delay you, that I was still alive. Two Roman knights were found to deliver you from this anxiety, and to promise that very night, before daybreak, to slay me in my bed. All this I knew almost before your meeting had broken up. I strengthened and fortified my house with a stronger guard; I refused admittance, when they came, to those whom you sent in the morning to salute me, and of whom I had foretold to many eminent men that they would come to me at that time.

As, then, this is the case, O Catiline, continue as you have begun. Leave the city at last: the gates are open; depart. That Manlian camp of yours has been waiting too long for you as its general. And lead forth with you all your friends, or at least as many as you can; purge the city of your presence; you will deliver me from a great fear, when there is a wall between me and you. Among us you can dwell no longer—I will not bear it, I will not permit it, I will not tolerate it. Great thanks are due to the immortal gods, and to this very Jupiter Stator, in whose temple we are, the most ancient protector of this city, that we have already so often escaped so foul, so horrible, and so deadly an enemy to the republic. But the safety of the commonwealth must not be too often allowed to be risked on one man. As long as you, O Catiline, plotted against me while I was the consul elect, I defended myself not with a public guard, but by my own private diligence. When, in the next consular comitia, you wished to slay me when I was actually consul, and your competitors also, in the Campus Martius, I checked your nefarious attempt by the assistance and resources of my own friends, without exciting any disturbance publicly. In short, as often as you attacked me, I by myself opposed you, and that, too, though I saw that my ruin was connected with great disaster to the republic. But now you are openly attacking the entire republic.

You are summoning to destruction and devastation the temples of the immortal gods, the houses of the city, the lives of all the citizens; in short, all Italy. Wherefore, since I do not yet venture to do that which is the best thing, and which belongs to my office and to the discipline of our ancestors, I will do that which is more merciful if we regard its rigor, and more expedient for the state. For if I order you to be put to death, the rest of the conspirators will still remain in the republic; if, as I have long been exhorting you, you depart, your companions, these worthless dregs of the republic, will be drawn off from the city too. What is the matter, Catiline? Do you hesitate to do that when I order you which you were already doing of your own accord? The consul orders an enemy to depart from the city. Do you ask me, Are you to go into banishment? I do not order it; but if you consult me, I advise it.

For what is there, O Catiline, that can now afford you any pleasure in this city? for there is no one in it, except that band of profligate conspirators of yours, who does not fear you—no one who does not hate you. What brand of domestic baseness is not stamped upon your life? What disgraceful circumstance is wanting to your infamy in your private affairs? From what licentiousness have your eyes, from what atrocity have your hands, from what iniquity has your whole body ever abstained? Is there one youth, when you have once entangled him in the temptations of your corruption, to whom you have not held out a sword for audacious crime, or a torch for licentious wickedness?

What? when lately by the death of your former wife you had made your house empty and ready for a new bridal, did you not even add another incredible wickedness to this wickedness? But I pass that over, and willingly allow it to be buried in silence, that so horrible a crime may not be seen to have existed in this city, and not to have been chastised. I pass over the ruin of your fortune, which you know is hanging over you against the Ides of the very next month; I come to those things which relate not to the infamy of your private vices, not to your domestic difficulties and baseness, but to the welfare of the republic and to the lives and safety of us all.

Can the light of this life, O Catiline, can the breath of this atmosphere be pleasant to you, when you know that there is not one man of those here present who is ignorant that you, on the last day of the year, when Lepidus and Tullus were consuls, stood in the assembly armed; that you had prepared your hand for the slaughter of the consuls and chief men of the state, and that no reason or fear of yours hindered your crime and madness, but the fortune of the republic? And I say no more of these things, for they

are not unknown to every one. How often have you en-
deavored to slay me, both as consul-elect and as actual
consul? how many shots of yours, so aimed that they
seemed impossible to be escaped, have I avoided by some
slight stooping aside, and some dodging, as it were, of my
body? You attempt nothing, you execute nothing, you de-
vise nothing that can be kept hid from me at the proper
time; and yet you do not cease to attempt and to contrive.
How often already has that dagger of yours been wrested
from your hands? how often has it slipped through them
by some chance, and dropped down? and yet you cannot
any longer do without it; and to what sacred mysteries it
is consecrated and devoted by you I know not, that you
think it necessary to plunge it in the body of the consul.

But now, what is that life of yours that you are leading?
For I will speak to you not so as to seem influenced by the
hatred I ought to feel, but by pity, nothing of which is
due to you. You came a little while ago into the senate:
in so numerous an assembly, who of so many friends and
connections of yours saluted you? If this in the memory of
man never happened to any one else, are you waiting for
insults by word of mouth, when you are overwhelmed by
the most irresistible condemnation of silence? Is it nothing
that at your arrival all those seats were vacated? that all
the men of consular rank, who had often been marked out
by you for slaughter, the very moment you sat down, left
that part of the benches spare and vacant? With what
feelings do you think you ought to bear this? On my honor,
if my slaves feared me as all your fellow-citizens fear you,
I should think I must leave my house. Do not you think
you should leave the city? If I saw that I was even un-
deservedly so suspected and hated by my fellow-citizens,
I would rather flee from their sight than be gazed at by
the hostile eyes of every one. And do you, who, from the
consciousness of your wickedness, know that the hatred of
all men is just and has long been due to you, hesitate to
avoid the sight and presence of those men whose minds
and senses you offend? If your parents feared and hated
you, and if you could by no means pacify them, you
would, I think, depart somewhere out of their sight. Now

your country, which is the common parent of all of us, hates and fears you, and has no other opinion of you than that you are meditating parricide in her case; and will you neither feel awe of her authority, nor deference for her judgment, nor fear of her power?

And she, O Catiline, thus pleads with you, and after a manner silently speaks to you: There has now for many years been no crime committed but by you; no atrocity has taken place without you; you alone unpunished and unquestioned have murdered the citizens, have harassed and plundered the allies; you alone have had power not only to neglect all laws and investigations, but to overthrow and break through them. Your former actions, though they ought not to have been borne, yet I did bear as well as I could; but now that I should be wholly occupied with fear of you alone, that at every sound I should dread Catiline, that no design should seem possible to be entertained against me which does not proceed from your wickedness, this is no longer endurable. Depart then, and deliver me from this fear; that, if it be a just one, I may not be destroyed; if an imaginary one, that at least I may at last cease to fear.

If, as I have said, your country were thus to address you, ought she not to obtain her request, even if she were not able to enforce it? What shall I say of your having given yourself into custody? what of your having said, for the sake of avoiding suspicion, that you were willing to dwell in the house of Marcus Lepidus? And when you were not received by him, you dared even to come to me, and begged me to keep you in my house; and when you had received answer from me that I could not possibly be safe in the same house with you, when I considered myself in great danger as long as we were in the same city, you came to Quintus Metellus, the praetor, and being rejected by him, you passed on to your associate, that most excellent man, Marcus Marcellus, who would be, I suppose you thought, most diligent in guarding you, most sagacious in suspecting you, and most bold in punishing you; but how far can we think that man ought to be from bonds and imprisonment who has already judged himself deserving of being given into custody?

Since, then, this is the case, do you hesitate, O Catiline, if you cannot remain here with tranquillity, to depart to some distant land, and to trust your life, saved from just and deserved punishment, to flight and solitude? Make a motion, say you, to the senate (for that is what you demand), and if this body votes that you ought to go into banishment, you say that you will obey. I will not make such a motion, it is contrary to my principles, and yet I will let you see what these men think of you. Begone from the city, O Catiline, deliver the republic from fear; depart into banishment, if that is the word you are waiting for. What now, O Catiline? Do you not perceive, do you not see the silence of these men? they permit it, they say nothing; why wait you for the authority of their words, when you see their wishes in their silence?

But had I said the same to this worthy young man, Publius Sextius, or to that brave man, Marcus Marcellus, before this time the senate would deservedly have laid violent hands on me, consul though I be, in this very temple. But as to you, Catiline, while they are quiet they approve, while they permit me to speak they vote, while they are silent they are loud and eloquent. And not they alone, whose authority forsooth is dear to you, though their lives are unimportant, but the Roman knights, too, those most honorable and excellent men, and the other virtuous citizens who are now surrounding the senate, whose numbers you could see, whose desires you could know, and whose voices you a few minutes ago could hear —aye, whose very hands and weapons I have for some time been scarcely able to keep off from you; but those, too, I will easily bring to attend you to the gates if you leave these places you have been long desiring to lay waste.

And yet, why am I speaking? that anything may change your purpose? that you may ever amend your life? that you may meditate flight or think of voluntary banishment? I wish the gods may give you such a mind; though I see, if alarmed at my words you bring your mind to go into banishment, what a storm of unpopularity hangs over me, if not at present, while the memory of your wickedness is fresh, at all events hereafter. But it is worth while to incur that, as long as that is but a private misfortune of my own, and is unconnected with the dangers of the republic. But we cannot expect that you should be concerned at your own vices, that you should fear the penalties of the laws, or that you should yield to the necessities of the republic, for you are not, O Catiline, one whom either shame can recall from infamy, or fear from danger, or reason from madness.

Wherefore, as I have said before, go forth, and if you wish to make me, your enemy as you call me, unpopular, go straight into banishment. I shall scarcely be able to endure all that will be said if you do so; I shall scarcely be able to support my load of unpopularity if you do go into banishment at the command of the consul; but if you wish to serve my credit and reputation, go forth with your ill-omened band of profligates; betake yourself to Manlius, rouse up the abandoned citizens, separate yourself from the good ones, wage war against your country, exult in your impious banditti, so that you may not seem to have been driven out by me and gone to strangers, but to have gone invited to your friends.

Though why should I invite you, by whom I know men have been already sent on to wait in arms for you at the Forum Aurelium; who I know has fixed and agreed with Manlius upon a settled day; by whom I know that that silver eagle, which I trust will be ruinous and fatal to you and to all your friends, and to which there was set up in your house a shrine, as it were, of your crimes, has been already set forward. Need I fear that you can long do without that which you used to worship when going out to murder, and from whose altars you have often transferred your impious hand to the slaughter of citizens?

You will go at last where your unbridled and mad desire has been long hurrying you. And this causes you no grief, but an incredible pleasure. Nature has formed you, desire has trained you, fortune has preserved you for this insanity. Not only did you never desire quiet, but you never even desired any war but a criminal one; you have collected a band of profligates and worthless men, abandoned not only by all fortune but even by hope.

Then what happiness will you enjoy! with what delight will you exult! in what pleasure will you revel! when in so numerous a body of friends you neither hear nor see one good man. All the toils you have gone through have always pointed to this sort of life; your lying on the ground not merely to lie in wait to gratify your unclean desires, but even to accomplish crimes; your vigilance, not only when plotting against the sleep of husbands, but also against the goods of your murdered victims, have all been preparations for this. Now you have an opportunity of displaying your splendid endurance of hunger, of cold, of want of everything; by which in a short time you will find yourself worn out. All this I effected when I procured your rejection from the consulship, that you should be reduced to make attempts on your country as an exile, instead of being able to distress it as consul, and that that which had been wickedly undertaken by you should be called piracy rather than war.

Now that I may remove and avert, O conscript fathers, any in the last reasonable complaint from myself, listen, I beseech you, carefully to what I say, and lay it up in your inmost hearts and minds. In truth, if my country, which is far dearer to me than my life—if all Italy—if the whole republic were to address me, Marcus Tullius, what are you doing? will you permit that man to depart whom you have ascertained to be an enemy? whom you see ready to become the general of the war? whom you know to be expected in the camp of the enemy as their chief, the author of all this wickedness, the head of the conspiracy, the instigator of the slaves and abandoned citizens, so that he shall seem not driven out of the city by you, but let loose by you against the city? will you not order him to be thrown into prison, to be hurried off to execution, to be put to death with the most prompt severity? What hinders you? is it the customs of our ancestors? But even private men have often in this republic slain mischievous citizens. Is it the laws which have been passed about the punishment of Roman citizens? But in this city those who have rebelled against the republic have never had the rights of citizens. Do you fear odium with posterity? You are showing fine gratitude to the Roman people which has raised you, a man known only by your own actions, of no ancestral renown, through all the degrees of honor at so early an age to the very highest office, if from fear of unpopularity or of any danger you neglect the safety of your fellow-citizens. But if you have a fear of unpopularity, is that arising from the imputation of vigor and boldness, or that arising from that of inactivity and indecision most to be feared? When Italy is laid waste by war, when cities are attacked and houses in flames, do you not think that you will be then consumed by a perfect conflagration of hatred?

To this holy address of the republic, and to the feelings of those men who entertain the same opinion, I will make this short answer: If, O conscript fathers, I thought it best that Catiline should be punished with death, I would not have given the space of one hour to this gladiator to live in. If, forsooth, those excellent men and most illustrious cities not only did not pollute themselves, but even glorified themselves by the blood of Saturninus, and the Gracchi, and Flaccus, and many others of old time, surely I had no cause to fear lest for slaying this parricidal murderer of the citizens any unpopularity should accrue to me with posterity. And if it did threaten me to ever so great a degree, yet I have always been of the disposition to think unpopularity earned by virtue and glory not unpopularity.

Though there are some men in this body who either do not see what threatens, or dissemble what they do see; who have fed the hope of Catiline by mild sentiments, and have strengthened the rising conspiracy by not believing it; influenced by whose authority many, and they not wicked, but only ignorant, if I punished him would say that I had acted cruelly and tyrannically. But I know that if he arrives at the camp of Manlius to which he is going, there will be no one so stupid as not to see that there has been a conspiracy, no one so hardened as not to confess it.

But if this man alone were put to death, I know that this disease of the republic would be only checked for a while, not eradicated forever. But if he banishes himself, and takes with him all his friends, and collects at one point all the ruined men from every quarter, then not only will this full-grown plague of the republic be extinguished and eradicated, but also the root and seed of all future evils.

We have now for a long time, O conscript fathers, lived among these dangers and machinations of conspiracy; but somehow or other, the ripeness of all wickedness, and of this long-standing madness and audacity, has come to a head at the time of my consulship. But if this man alone is removed from this piratical crew, we may appear, perhaps, for a short time relieved from fear and anxiety, but the danger will settle down and lie hid in the veins and bowels of the republic. As it often happens that men afflicted with a severe disease, when they are tortured with heat and fever, if they drink cold water seem at first to be relieved, but afterwards suffer more and more severely; so this disease which is in the republic, if relieved by the punishment of this man, will only get worse and worse, as the rest will be still alive.

Wherefore, O conscript fathers, let the worthless be-gone—let them separate themselves from the good—let them collect in one place—let them, as I have often said before, be separated from us by a wall; let them cease to plot against the consul in his own house—to surround the tribunal of the city praetor—to besiege the senate house with swords—to prepare brands and torches to burn the city; let it, in short, be written on the brow of every citizen what are his sentiments about the republic. I promise you this, O conscript fathers, that there shall be so much diligence in us the consuls, so much authority in you, so much virtue in the Roman knights, so much unanimity in all good men, that you shall see everything made plain and manifest by the departure of Catiline—everything checked and punished.

With these omens, O Catiline, begone to your impious and nefarious war, to the great safety of the republic, to your own misfortune and injury, and to the destruction of those who have joined themselves to you in every wickedness and atrocity. Then do you, O Jupiter, who were consecrated by Romulus with the same auspices as this city, whom we rightly call the stay of this city and empire, repel this man and his companions from your altars and from the other temples—from the lives and fortunes of all the citizens; and overwhelm all the enemies of good men, the foes of the republic, the robbers of Italy, men bound together by a treaty and infamous alliance of crimes, dead and alive, with eternal punishments.

Emile Zola
1840–1902

Zola, a novelist, a passionate observer of human life and sympathetic to those who he felt had been subjected to injustice. He was moved by the miscarriage of justice in the case of Captain Alfred Dreyfus, who had been accused of writing a letter indicating that he would supply information about the French army to the German military attaché in Paris. The basis of the evidence was the similarity of the handwriting in the letter with that of Captain Dreyfus. But Captain Dreyfus was both a Jew and an Alsatian and these facts counted against him. In 1894 he was sentenced to degradation and life imprisonment at Devil's Island, the French penal colony, off French Guiana.

Zola played a very important part in this Dreyfus Affair, and in the newspaper Aurore, on January 13, 1898, in a letter beginning with the words J'accuse, he wrote a denunciation of the government for the hounding of the unfortunate officer. Zola was indicted for libel. The result was that the whole Dreyfus case was reopened and Dreyfus vindicated. Zola was condemned for this. He delivered this address to the jury at his trial in Paris, February 21, 1898.

APPEAL FOR DREYFUS

In the chamber at the sitting of January 22, M. Meline, the Prime Minister, declared, amid the frantic applause of his complaisant majority, that he had confidence in the twelve citizens to whose hands he intrusted the defense of the army. It was of you, gentlemen, that he spoke. And just as General Billot dictated its decision to the court martial intrusted with the acquittal of Major Esterhazy, by appealing from the tribune for respect for the *chose jugée*, so likewise M. Meline wished to give you the order to condemn me out of respect for the army which he accuses me of having insulted!

I denounce to the conscience of honest men this pressure brought to bear by the constituted authorities upon the justice of the country. These are abominable political maneuvers, which dishonor a free nation. We shall see, gentlemen, whether you will obey.

But it is not true that I am here in your presence by the will of M. Meline. He yielded to the necessity of prosecuting me only in great trouble, in terror of the new step which the advancing truth was about to take. This everybody knew. If I am before you, it is because I wished it. I alone decided that this obscure, this abominable affair, should be brought before your jurisdiction, and it is I alone of my free will who chose you,—you, the loftiest, the most direct emanation of French justice,—in order that France might at last know all, and give her opinion. My act had no other object, and my person is of no account. I have sacrificed it, in order to place in your hands not only the honor of the army, but the imperiled honor of the nation.

It appears that I was cherishing a dream in wishing to offer you all the proofs: considering you to be the sole worthy, the sole competent judge. They have begun by depriving you with the left hand of what they seemed to give you with the right. They pretended, indeed, to accept your jurisdiction, but if they had confidence in you to avenge the members of the court martial, there were still other officers who remained superior even to your jurisdiction. Let who can, understand. It is absurdity doubled with hypocrisy, and it is abundantly clear that they dreaded your good sense,—that they dared not run the risk of letting us tell all and of letting you judge the whole matter. They pretend that they wished to limit the scandal. What do you think of this scandal? Of my act, which consisted in bringing the matter before you,—in wishing the people, incarnate in you, to be the judge? They pretend also that they could not accept a revision in disguise, thus confessing that in reality they have but one dread, that of your sovereign control. The law has in you its entire representation, and it is this law of the people elect that I have wished for,—this law which, as a good citizen, I hold in profound respect, and not the suspicious procedure whereby they hoped to make you a derision.

I am thus excused, gentlemen, for having brought you here from your private affairs without being able to inundate you with the full flood of light of which I dreamed. The light, the whole light,—this was my sole, my passionate desire! And this trial has just proved it. We have had to fight—step by step—against an extraordinarily obstinate desire for darkness. A battle has been necessary to obtain every atom of truth. Everything has been refused us. Our witnesses have been terrorized in the hope of preventing us from proving our point. And it is on your behalf alone that we have fought, that this proof might be put before you in its entirety, so that you might give your opinion without remorse in your consciences. I am certain, therefore, that you will give us credit for our efforts, and that, moreover, sufficient light has been thrown upon the affair.

You have heard the witnesses; you are about to hear my counsel, who will tell you the true story: the story that maddens everybody and which no one knows. I am, therefore, at my ease. You have the truth at last, and it will do its work. M. Meline thought to dictate your decision by intrusting to you the honor of the army. And it is in the name of the honor of the army that I too appeal to your justice.

I give M. Meline the most direct contradiction. Never have I insulted the army. I spoke, on the contrary, of my sympathy, my respect for the nation in arms, for our dear soldiers of France, who would rise at the first menace to defend the soil of France. And it is just as false that I attacked the chiefs, the generals who would lead them to victory. If certain persons at the War Office have compromised the army itself by their acts, is it to insult the whole army to say so? Is it not rather to act as a good citizen to separate it from all that compromises it, to give the alarm, so that the blunders which alone have been the cause of our defeat shall not occur again, and shall not lead us to fresh disaster?

I am not defending myself, moreover. I leave history to judge my act, which was a necessary one; but I affirm that the army is dishonored when gendarmes are allowed to embrace Major Esterhazy after the abominable letters written by him. I affirm that that valiant army is insulted daily by the bandits who, on the plea of defending it, sully it by their degrading championship,—who trail in the mud all that France still honors as good and great. I affirm that those who dishonor that great national army are those who mingle cries of *"Vive l'armée!"* with those of *"A bas les juifs!"* and *"Vive Esterhazy!" Grand Dieu!* the people of St. Louis, of Bayard, of Condé, and of Hoche: the people which counts a hundred great victories, the people of the great wars of the Republic and the Empire, the people whose power, grace, and generosity have dazzled the world, crying *"Vive Esterhazy!"* It is a shame the stain of which our efforts on behalf of truth and justice can alone wash off!

You know the legend which has grown up: Dreyfus was condemned justly and legally by seven infallible officers, whom it is impossible even to suspect of a blunder without insulting the whole army. Dreyfus expiates in merited torments his abominable crime. And as he is a Jew, a Jewish syndicate is formed, an international *sans patrie* syndicate, disposing of hundreds of millions, the object of which is to save the traitor at any price, even by the most shameless intrigues. And thereupon this syndicate began to heap crime on crime: buying consciences, casting France into a disastrous agitation, resolved on selling her to the enemy, willing even to drive all Europe into a general war rather than renounce its terrible plan.

It is very simple, nay childish, if not imbecile. But it is with this poisoned bread that the unclean Press has been nourishing our people now for some months. And it is not surprising if we are witnessing a dangerous crisis; for when folly and lies are thus sown broadcast you necessarily reap insanity.

Gentlemen, I would not insult you by supposing that

you have yourselves been duped by this nursery tale. I know you; I know who you are. You are the heart and the reason of Paris, of my great Paris; where I was born, which I love with an infinite tenderness, which I have been studying and writing of now for forty years. And I know likewise what is now passing in your brains; for, before coming to sit here as defendant, I sat here on the bench where you are now. You represent there the average opinion; you try to illustrate prudence and justice in the mass. Soon I shall be in thought with you in the room where you deliberate, and I am convinced that your effort will be to safeguard your interests as citizens, which are, of course, the interests of the whole nation. You may make a mistake, but you will do so in the thought that while securing your own weal you are securing the weal of all.

I see you at your homes at evening under the lamp; I hear you talk with your friends; I accompany you into your factories and shops. You are all workers—some tradesmen, others manufacturers, some exercising liberal professions. And your very legitimate anxiety is the deplorable state into which business has fallen. Everywhere the present crisis threatens to become a disaster. The receipts fall off; transactions become more and more difficult. So that the idea which you have brought here, the thought which I read in your countenances, is that there has been enough of this and that it must be ended. You have not gone the length of saying, like many: "What matters it that an innocent man is at the Ile du Diable? Is the interest of a single man worth this disturbing a great country?" But you say, nevertheless, that the agitation which we are raising, we who hunger for truth and justice, costs too dear! And if you condemn me, gentlemen, it is that thought which will be at the bottom of your verdict. You desire tranquillity for your homes, you wish for the revival of business, and you may think that by punishing me you will stop a campaign which is injurious to the interests of France.

Well, gentlemen, if that is your idea, you are entirely mistaken. Do me the honor of believing that I am not defending my liberty. By punishing me you would only

magnify me. Whoever suffers for truth and justice becomes august and sacred. Look at me. Have I the look of
a hireling of a liar, and a traitor? Why should I be playing
a part? I have behind me neither political ambition nor
sectarian passion. I am a free writer, who has given his
life to labor; who tomorrow will reenter the ranks and
resume his suspended task. And how stupid are those who
call me an Italian;—me, born of a French mother, brought
up by grandparents in the Beauce, peasants of that vigorous soil; me, who lost my father at seven years of age,
who did not go to Italy till I was fifty-four. And yet, I am
proud that my father was from Venice,—the resplendent
city whose ancient glory sings in all memories. And even if
I were not French, would not the forty volumes in the
French language, which I have sent by millions of copies
throughout the world, suffice to make me a Frenchman?

So I do not defend myself. But what a blunder would be
yours if you were convinced that by striking me you would
reestablish order in our unfortunate country. Do you not
understand now that what the nation is dying of is the
obscurity in which there is such an obstinate determination
to leave it? The blunders of those in authority are being
heaped upon those of others; one lie necessitates another,
so that the mass is becoming formidable. A judicial
blunder was committed, and then to hide it a fresh crime
against good sense and equity has had daily to be committed! The condemnation of an innocent man has involved the acquittal of a guilty man, and now today you
are asked in turn to condemn me because I gave utterance
to my pain beholding our country embarked on this terrible course. Condemn me, then! But it will be one more
fault added to the others—a fault the burden of which
you will bear in history. And my condemnation, instead
of restoring the peace for which you long, and which we
all of us desire, will be only a fresh seed of passion and
disorder. The cup, I tell you, is full; do not make it run
over!

Why do you not exactly estimate the terrible crisis
through which the country is passing? They say that we
are the authors of the scandal, that it is lovers of truth and

justice who are leading the nation astray, and urging it to riot. Really this is a mockery! To speak only of General Gillot—was he not warned eighteen months ago? Did not Colonel Picquart insist that he should take in hand the matter of revision, if he did not wish the storm to burst and overturn everything! Did not M. Scheurer-Kestner, with tears in his eyes, beg him to think of France and save her from such a catastrophe? No! our desire has been to facilitate everything, to allay everything; and if the country is now in trouble, the responsibility lies with the power which, to cover the guilty, and in the furtherance of political interests, has denied everything, hoping to be strong enough to prevent the truth from being shed. It has maneuvered in behalf of darkness, and it alone is responsible for the present distraction of conscience!

The Dreyfus case! ah, gentlemen, that has now become a very small affair. It is lost and far-away in view of the terrifying questions to which it has given rise. There is no longer any Dreyfus case. The question now is whether France is still the France of the rights of man, the France that gave freedom to the world, and that ought to give it justice. Are we still the most noble, the most fraternal, the most generous nation? Shall we preserve our reputation in Europe for equity and humanity? Are not all the victories that we have won called in question? Open your eyes, and understand that, to be in such confusion, the French soul must have been stirred to its depths in the face of a terrible danger. A nation cannot be thus upset without imperiling its moral existence. This is an exceptionally serious hour; the safety of the nation is at stake.

And when you shall have understood that, gentlemen, you will feel that but one remedy is possible,—to tell the truth, to do justice. Anything that keeps back the light, anything that adds darkness to darkness, will only prolong and aggravate the crisis. The role of good citizens, of those who feel it to be imperatively necessary to put an end to this matter, is to demand broad daylight. There are already many who think so. The men of literature, philosophy, and science are rising on every hand in the name of intelligence and reason. And I do not speak of the foreigner, of the shudder that has run through all Europe. Yet the foreigner is not necessarily the enemy. Let us not speak of the nations that may be our adversaries to-morrow. Great Russia, our ally, little and generous Holland; all the sympathetic peoples of the north; those lands of the French tongue, Switzerland and Belgium,—why are men's hearts so full, so overflowing with fraternal suffering? Do you dream then of a France isolated in the world? When you cross the frontier, do you wish them to forget your traditional renown for equity and humanity?

Dreyfus is innocent. I swear it! I stake my life on it—my honor! At this solemn moment, in the presence of this tribunal, which is the representative of human justice: before you, gentlemen, who are the very incarnation of the country, before the whole of France, before the whole world, I swear that Dreyfus is innocent. By my forty years of work, by the authority that this toil may have given me, I swear that Dreyfus is innocent. By the name I have made for myself by my works which have helped for the expansion of French literature, I swear that Dreyfus is innocent. May all that melt away, may my works perish, if Dreyfus be not innocent! He is innocent. All seems against me—the two Chambers, the civil authority, the most widely-circulated journals, the public opinion which they have poisoned. And I have for me only the ideal,—an ideal of truth and justice. But I am quite calm; I shall conquer. I was determined that my country should not remain the victim of lies and injustice. I may be condemned here. The day will come when France will thank me for having helped to save her honor.

Clarence S. Darrow

1857–1938

Clarence S. Darrow, the greatest criminal lawyer of his generation, had hoped to be an essayist and novelist, but the attraction of the law was too great. In 1894 he came to public notice by his brilliant defense of Eugene V. Debs, President of the American Railway Union, who had been arrested in the Chicago railroad riots. After this case, Darrow decided to withdraw from general practice and defend only the "underdog."

The Leopold-Loeb trial of 1924 became one of the great defenses in the legal history of the United States. Here were two young men one 18 and one 19 accused of murder; they were Jewish; their parents were reputed wealthy; there was a possibility of insanity. To the astonishment of everyone, Clarence Darrow's clients pleaded guilty to homicide and chose to present their case to the judge for sentencing and not to a jury. This speech given here, in part, is consequently a plea to the judge for mercy as opposed to the penalty of death.

Notice with what ease and subtlety Darrow brings in the name of one of the prosecuting attorneys and plays with it throughout his plea.

A Plea for Mercy for Leopold and Loeb

Your Honor, it has been almost three months since the great responsibility of this case was assumed by my associates and myself. I am willing to confess that it has been three months of great anxiety. A burden which I gladly would have been spared excepting for my feeling of affection toward some of the members of these unfortunate families. This responsibility is almost too great for any one to assume; but we lawyers can no more choose than the court can choose.

Our anxiety over this case has not been due to the facts that are connected with this most unfortunate affair, but to the almost unheard of publicity it has received; to the fact that the newspapers all over this country have been giving it space such as they have almost never before given to any case.

And when the public is interested and demands a punishment, no matter what the offense, great or small, it thinks of only one punishment, and that is death.

It may not be a question that involved the taking of human life; it may be a question of the mere prejudice alone; but when the public speaks as one man it thinks only of killing.

We have been in this stress and strain for three months. We did what we could and all we could to gain the confidence of the public, who in the end really control, whether wisely or unwisely.

It was anounced that there were millions of dollars to be spent on this case. Wild and extravagant stories were freely published as though they were facts. Here was to be an effort to save the lives of two boys by the use of money in fabulous amounts such as these families never had.

We announced to the public that no excessive use of money would be made in this case, neither for lawyers nor for psychiatrists, or any other way. We have faithfully kept that promise.

The psychiatrists, as has been shown by the evidence in this case, are receiving a per diem, and only a per diem, which is the same as is paid by the State.

The attorneys, at their own request, have agreed to take such amounts as the officers of the Chicago Bar Association may think is proper in this case.

If we fail in this defense it will not be for lack of money. It will be on account of money. Money has been the most serious handicap that we have met. There are times when poverty is fortunate.

I insist, your Honor, that had this been the case of two

boys of these defendants' age, unconnected with families supposed to have great wealth, there is not a State's Attorney in Illinois who would not have consented at once to a plea of guilty and a punishment in the penitentiary for life. Not one.

No lawyer could have justified any other attitude. No prosecutor could have justified it.

We are here with the lives of two boys imperiled, with the public aroused. For what?   RHETORICAL

Because, unfortunately, the parents have money. Nothing else.

I told your Honor in the beginning that never had there been a case in Chicago, where on a plea of guilty a boy under twenty-one had been sentenced to death. I will raise that age and say, never has there been a case where a human being under the age of twenty-three has been sentenced to death. And, I think I am safe in saying, although I have not examined all the records and could not—but I think I am safe in saying—that never has there been such a case in the State of Illinois.

And yet this court is urged, aye, threatened, that he must hang two boys contrary to precedents, contrary to the acts of every judge who ever held court in this State.

Why?

Tell me what public necessity there is for this?

I have heard in the last six weeks nothing but the cry for blood. I have heard from the office of the State's Attorney only ugly hate.

I have heard precedents quoted which would be a disgrace to a savage race.

I have seen a court urged to the point of threats to hang two boys, in the face of science, in the face of philosophy, in the face of humanity, in the face of experience, in the face of all the better and more humane thought of the ages.

Now, your Honor, I shall discuss that [case (cited by Prosecutor Marshall from Blackstone wherein a young man of sixteen was hanged for the murder of a young girl)] more in detail a little later, and I only say it now because my friend Mr. Savage—did you pick him for his name or

PRONOUN
GAME

his ability or his learning?—because my friend Mr. Savage, in as cruel a speech as he knew how to make, said to this court that we plead guilty because we were afraid to do anything else.

Your Honor that is true.

It was not correct that we would have defended these boys in court; we believe we have been fair to the public. Anyhow, we have tried, and we have tried under terribly hard conditions.

We did plead guilty before your Honor, because we were afraid to submit our cause to a jury. I would not for a minute deny to this court or to this community a realization of the serious danger we were in and how perplexed we were before we took this most unusual step.

I can tell your Honor why.

I have found that years and experience with life tempers one's emotions and makes him more understanding of his fellow man.

When my friend Savage is my age, or even yours, he will read his address to this court with horror. _EXTENSION_

I know perfectly well that where responsibility is divided by twelve, it is easy to say:

"Away with him."

But, your Honor, if these boys hang, you must do it. There can be no division of responsibility here. You can never explain that the rest overpowered you. It must be your deliberate, cool, premeditated act, without a chance to shift responsibility. _MURDER LANGUAGE (SEMANTICS)_

Your Honor will never thank me for unloading this responsibility upon you, but you know that I would have been untrue to my clients if I had not concluded to take this chance before a court, instead of submitting it to a poisoned jury in the city of Chicago. I did it knowing that it would be an unheard of thing for any court, no matter who, to sentence these boys to death.

Your Honor, I must for a moment criticize the arguments that have preceded me. I can read to you in a minute my friend Marshall's argument, barring Blackstone. But the rest of his arguments and the rest of Brother Savage's argument I can sum up in a minute: *Cruel; das-*

tardly; premeditated; fiendish; abandoned; and malignant heart; sounds like a cancer—*cowardly,* cold blooded!

Now that is what I have listened to for three days against two minors, two children, who have no right to sign a note or make a deed.

Cowardly?

Well, I don't know. Let me tell you something that I think is cowardly, whether their acts were or not. Here is Dick Loeb and Nathan Leopold, and the State objects to anybody calling one "Dickie" and the other "Babe" although everybody else does, but they think they can hang them easier if their names are Richard and Nathan, so we will call them Richard and Nathan.

Eighteen and nineteen years old at the time of the homicide.

Here are three officers watching them. They are led out and in this jail and across the bridge waiting to be hanged. Not a chance to get away. Handcuffed when they get out of this room. Not a chance. Penned like rats in a trap; and for a lawyer with physiological eloquence to wave his fist in front of their faces and shout "Cowardly," does not appear to me as a brave act . . .

Have they any rights? Is there any reason, your Honor, why their proud names and all the future generations that bear them shall have this bar sinister written across them? How many boys and girls, how many unborn children will feel it? It is bad enough as it is, God knows.

Now I must say a word more and then I will leave this with you where I should have left it long ago. None of us are unmindful of the public; courts are not, and juries are not. We place our fate in the hands of a trained court, thinking that he would be more mindful and considerate than a jury. I cannot say how people feel. I have stood here for three months as one might stand at the ocean trying to sweep back the tide. I hope the seas are subsiding and the wind falling, and I believe they are, but I wish to make no pretense to this court. The easy thing and the popular thing to do is to hang my clients. I know it. Men and women who do not think will applaud. The cruel and thoughtless will approve. It will be easy today;

but in Chicago, and reaching out over the length and breadth of the land, more and more fathers and mothers, who are gaining an understanding and asking questions not only about these poor boys, but about their own— those will join in no acclaim at the death of my clients.

I know that your Honor stands between the future and the past. For me the future means the hopes of the young. I plead for life, charity, kindness, sympathy and understanding. And the future is with me.

Your honor may hang these boys but if you do you will make it harder for every boy and girl in this land and for the babes as yet unborn.

I am pleading that all life is worth saving and that mercy is the highest attribute of man. My greatest reward, hope and compensation will be that I have done something for the tens of thousands of boys who must follow the path these two poor young Jews have trod.

> So I be written in the Book of Love
> I do not care about that book above;
> Erase my name, or write it as you will,
> So I be written in the Book of Love.

Samuel Langhorn Clemens

1835–1910

Samuel Langhorn Clemens is better recognized by his pseudonym "Mark Twain." Clemens is best known today as the creator of Tom Sawyer and Huck Finn. Nevertheless, in his lifetime, Clemens was in great demand as an after-dinner speaker of wit, irony, and even bitter sarcasm. This speech was delivered at the seventy-first dinner of the New England Society in the City of New York, December 22, 1876. His audience, therefore, was well acquainted with vagaries of weather throughout New England.

NEW ENGLAND WEATHER

Gentlemen:—I reverently believe that the Maker who made us all, makes everything in New England—but the weather. [*Laughter*] I don't know who makes that, but I think it must be raw apprentices in the Weather Clerk's factory, who experiment and learn how in New England for board and clothes, and then are promoted to make weather for countries that require a good article and will take their custom elsewhere if they don't get it. [*Laughter*] There is a sumptuous variety about New England weather that compels the stranger's admiration—and regret. [*Laughter*] The weather is always doing something there; always attending strictly to business; always getting up new designs and trying them on people to see how they will go. [*Laughter*] But it gets through more business in spring than any other season. In spring I have counted one hundred and thirty-six different kinds of weather inside of four and twenty hours. [*Laughter*] It was I that made the fame and fortune of that man that had that marvelous collection of weather on exhibition at the Centennial that so astounded foreigners. He was going to travel all over the world to get specimens from all the climes. I said: "Don't you do it; you come to New England on a favorable spring day." I told him what we could do, in the way of style, variety and quantity. [*Laughter*] Well, he came, and he made his collection in four days. [*Laughter*] As to variety, —why, he confessed that he got hundreds of kinds of weather that he had never heard of before. And as to quantity—well, after he had picked out and discarded all that was blemished in any way, he not only had weather enough, but weather to spare; weather to hire out; weather to sell; to deposit; weather to invest; weather to give to the poor. [*Laughter and applause*]

The people of New England are by nature patient and forbearing; but there are some things which they will not stand. Every year they kill a lot of poets for writing about "Beautiful Spring." [*Laughter*] These are generally casual visitors, who bring their notions of spring from somewhere else, and cannot, of course, know how the natives feel about spring. And so, the first thing they know, the opportunity to enquire how they feel has permanently gone by. [*Laughter*]

Yes, one of the brightest gems in the New England weather is the dazzling uncertainty of it. There is only one thing certain about it, you are certain there is going to be plenty of weather [*Laughter*]—a perfect grand review; but you never can tell which end of the procession is going to move first. You can fix up for drought; you leave your umbrella in the house and sally out with your sprinkling pot, and ten to one you get drowned. [*Applause*] You make up your mind that the earthquake is due; you stand from under and take hold of something to steady yourself, and the first thing you know you get struck by lightning. [*Laughter*] These are great disappointments. But they can't be helped. [*Laughter*] The lightning there is peculiar; it is so convincing. When it strikes a thing, it doesn't leave enough of that thing behind for you to tell whether—well, you'd think it was something valuable, and a Congressman had been there. [*Loud laughter and applause*]

And the thunder. When the thunder commences to merely tune up, and scrape, and saw, and key up the instrument for the performance, strangers say: "Why, what awful thunder you have here!" But when the baton is raised and the real concert begins you'll find that the stranger is down in the cellar with his head in the ash-barrel. [*Laughter*]

Now, as to the size of the weather in New England—lengthways, I mean. It is utterly disproportioned to the size of that little country. [*Laughter*] Half the time, when it is packed as full as it can stick you will see that New England weather sticking out beyond the edges and projecting around hundreds and hundreds of miles over the neighboring States. [*Laughter*] She can't hold a tenth part of her weather. You can see cracks all about, where she has strained herself trying to do it. [*Laughter*]

I could speak volumes about the inhuman perversity of the New England weather, but I will give you but a single specimen. I like to hear rain on a tin roof, so I covered part of my roof with tin, with an eye to that luxury. Well, sir, do you think it ever rains on the tin? No, sir; skips it every time. [*Laughter*]

Mind, in this speech I have been trying merely to do honor to the New England weather; no language could do it justice. [*Laughter*] But after all, there are at least one or two things about that weather (or, if you please, effects produced by it) which we residents would not like to part with. [*Applause*] If we had not our bewitching autumn foliage, we should still have to credit the weather with one feature which compensates for all its bullying vagaries —the ice-storm—when a leafless tree is clothed with ice from the bottom to the top—ice that is bright and clear as crystal; every bough and twig is strung with ice-beads, frozen dew-drops, and the whole tree sparkles, cold and white, like the Shah of Persia's diamond plume. [*Applause*] Then the wind waves the branches, and the sun comes out and turns all of those myriads of beads and drops to prisms, that glow and hum and flash with all manner of colored fires, which change and change again, with inconceivable rapidity, from blue to red, from red to green, and green to gold; the tree becomes a sparkling fountain, a very explosion of dazzling jewels; and it stands there the acme, the climax, the supremest possibility in art or nature of bewildering, intoxicating, intolerable magnificence! One cannot make the words too strong. [*Long-continued applause*]

Month after month I lay up hate and grudge against the New England weather; but when the ice-storm comes at last, I say: "There, I forgive you now; the books are square between us; you don't owe me a cent; go and sin some more; your little faults and foibles count for nothing; you are the most enchanting weather in the world!" [*Applause and laughter*]

John H. Glenn, Jr.

1921–

Lieutenant Colonel John H. Glenn, Jr., of the United States Marine Corps was the first astronaut of the United States to orbit the earth. His flight of February 20, 1962, was historic and every citizen was eager to hear the report of America's first man in space. After his return he spoke to a joint session of the Congress at Washington and over the air to the world. Whatever he said of his trip into space would be eagerly listened to and read.

Lieutenant Colonel Glenn did not disappoint his auditors. He spoke not as a trained rhetorician but as a simple citizen who had pursued the same kind of education that a hundred million others had followed. He spoke naturally, plainly, directly, and throughout humbly. He impressed every listener with his honesty of reporting and his honesty of heart. Other speeches which he made in the course of his trips around the United States bore out the promise of his first speech to Congress.

A New Era

Mr. Speaker, Mr. President, Members of the Congress, I am only too aware of the tremendous honor that is being shown us at this joint meeting of the Congress today. When I think of past meetings that involved heads of state and equally notable persons, I can only say I am most humble to know that you consider our efforts to be in the same class.

This has been a great experience for all of us present and for all Americans, of course, and I am certainly glad to see that pride in our country and its accomplishments is not a thing of the past.

I still get a hard-to-define feeling inside when the flag goes by—and I know that all of you do, too. Today as we rode up Pennsylvania Avenue from the White House and saw the tremendous outpouring of feeling on the part of so many thousands of our people I got this same feeling all over again. Let us hope that none of us ever loses it.

The flight of *Friendship 7* on February 20 involved more than one man in the spacecraft in orbit.

I can think of many people who were involved in this, but I think of none more than just a few sitting in the front row right up here. I'd like to have them stand up. If my parents would stand up, please. My dad and mother.

My son and daughter, Dave and Lynn.

And the real rock in our family, my wife, Anne. I'm real proud of her.

There are many more people, of course, involved in our flight in *Friendship 7;* many more things involved, as well as people. There was the vision of Congress that established this national program of space exploration. Beyond that, many thousands of people were involved, civilian contractors and many subcontractors in many different fields; many elements—civilian, civil service and military, all blending their efforts toward a common goal. . . .

From the original vision of the Congress to consummation of this orbital flight has been over 3 years. This, in itself, states eloquently the case for the hard work and devotion of the entire Mercury teams. This has not been another job. It has been a dedicated labor such as I have not seen before. . . .

Friendship 7 is just a beginning, a successful experiment. It is another plateau in our step-by-step program of increasingly ambitious flights.

With all the experience we have had so far, where does this leave us?

As was to be expected, not everything worked perfectly on my flight. We may well need to make changes—and these will be tried out on subsequent 3-orbit flights, later this year, to be followed by 18-orbit, 24-hour missions.

Beyond that we look forward to Project Gemini—a two man orbital vehicle with greatly increased capability for advanced experiments. There will be additional rendez-vous experiments in space, technical and scientific observations, then, Apollo orbital, circumlunar and finally, lunar landing flights.

What did we learn from the *Friendship 7* flight that will help us obtain these objectives?

Some specific items have already been covered briefly in the news reports. And I think it is more than passing interest to all of us that information attained from these flights is readily available to all nations of the world.

The launch itself was conducted openly and with the news media representatives from around the world in attendance. Complete information is released as it is evaluated and validated. This is certainly in sharp contrast with similar programs conducted elsewhere in the world and elevates the peaceful intent of our program. . . .

But these things we know. The Mercury spacecraft and systems design concepts are sound and have now been verified during manned flight in space. We also proved that man can operate intelligently in space and can adapt rapidly to this new environment.

Zero G or weightlessness—at least for this period of time —appears to be no problem. As a matter of fact, lack of gravity is rather a fascinating thing.

Objects within the cockpit can be parked in midair. For example, at one time during the flight, I was using a hand held camera. Another system needed attention; so it seemed quite natural to let go of the camera, take care of the other chore in the spacecraft, then reach out, grasp the camera and go back about my business.

There seemed little sensation or speed although the craft was traveling at about 5 miles per second—a speed that I, too, find difficult to comprehend.

In addition to closely monitoring on board systems, we were able to make numerous outside observations.

The view from that altitude defies description.

The horizon colors are brilliant and sunsets spectacular.

It is hard to beat a day in which you are permitted the luxury of seeing four sunsets. . . .

I feel we are on the brink of an area of expansion of

knowledge about ourselves and our surroundings that is beyond description or comprehension at this time.

Our efforts today and what we have done so far are but small building blocks in a huge pyramid to come. . . .

Experimenters with common green mold, little dreamed what effect their discovery of penicillin would have.

The story has been told of Disraeli, Prime Minister of England at the time, visiting the laboratory of Faraday, one of the early experimenters with basic electrical principles. After viewing various demonstrations of electrical phenomena, Disraeli asked, "But what possible use is it?" Faraday replied, "Mister Prime Minister, what good is a baby?"

That is the stage of development in our program today—in its infancy. And it indicates a much broader potential impact, of course, than even the discovery of electricity did. We are just probing the surface of the greatest advancements in man's knowledge of his surroundings that has ever been made, I feel . . .

Knowledge begets knowledge. The more I see, the more impressed I am—not with what we know—but with how tremendous the areas are that are as yet unexplored.

Exploration, knowledge, and achievement are good only in so far as we apply them to our future actions. Progress never stops. We are now on the verge of a new era, I feel.

DEFENSE, RIGHTS, AND LIBERTY

PART FOUR

DEFENSE, RIGHTS AND LIBERTY

Demosthenes
385?–322 B.C.

Demosthenes, son of a wealthy Athenian arms manu-
facturer, was a delicate youth made fatherless when he
was still quite young. The guardians appointed by his fa-
ther soon wasted away his inheritance. When Demosthe-
nes was sixteen he listened to a law case at Athens and
was impressed with the lawyer's speech and the response
he aroused in his auditors; he then determined to study
oratory. However, he did not wait long to try his hand at
the law, and when he was seventeen he prosecuted the
guardians of his estate and a debtor and won both cases.

He had been criticized because of his stuttering, his in-
terruptive speech and respiration, ungraceful gestures,
feeble voice, and lack of rhetorical style. He overcame
these defects by speaking to the roaring sea with his
mouth full of pebbles; he ran up difficult hillsides to im-
prove his breathing and practiced his speeches before a
mirror to improve his facial control.

Demosthenes was at his height of eloquence when the
city-state of Athens was at her lowest ebb: the laws lacked
their authority; Athenians gave themselves over to luxury,
indolence, and gluttony. Demosthenes hated what he saw.
Philip II of Macedon (382–336 B.C.) was threatening
Athens and for fourteen years Demosthenes opposed
Philip and all his works in the public assembly. Throughout
this period he never changed his position; and when Philip
finally took Athens, the citizens of the city rewarded De-
mosthenes for his honesty and courage.

This honored award took the form of a crown of gold.
Aeschines, a well-known orator, opposed the gift, saying
that it had been bestowed unlawfully by the President of
the Senate, Ctesiphon. The basis for this charge was that
the award had been decreed before Demosthenes had
made his required report of expenditures on the use of a

fund, and that such a gift should not be received in the theater but rather in the building set aside for public assemblies, the Pnyx. The antagonism of Aeschines and the calm reasoning of Demosthenes brought great throngs to Athens. In the end Demosthenes triumphed by a vote of the people. Since Aeschines received less than the fifth part of the votes as was necessary in law, he was required to leave Athens for exile.

Demosthenes had his enemies, however, and they found cause to accuse, try, and condemn him for bribery. He escaped to Aegina, an island from which he could still see his country. He was allowed later to return but became involved in a plot against the Macedonians and was accused of treason. He went to the island of Calauria and there in the Temple of Poseidon at the age of about sixty took poison.

Of Greek oratory before Demosthenes there were two schools: that of Lysias, wherein mild persuasion caught the attention; and that of Thucydides, where the speech was a bold, animated attack to influence the emotions of the listeners. Demosthenes developed the third style, which included parts of both. When Demosthenes was asked what was the first requirement in an orator, he replied simply, "Delivery." When he was asked for the second and third requisites he gave the same answer.

On the Crown

I begin, men of Athens, by praying to every God and Goddess, that the same goodwill, which I have ever cherished toward the commonwealth and all of you, may be requited to me on the present trial. I pray likewise—and this especially concerns yourselves, your religion, and your honor—that the Gods may put it in your minds, not to take counsel of my opponent touching the manner in which I am to be heard—that would indeed be cruel!—but of the laws and of your oath; wherein (besides other obligations) it is prescribed that you shall hear both sides alike. This means, not only that you must pass no pre-condemnation, not only that you must extend your goodwill equally to both, but also that you must allow the parties to adopt such order and course of defense as they severally choose to prefer.

Many advantages hath Aeschines over me in this trial; and two especially, men of Athens. First, my risk in the contest is not the same. It is assuredly not the same for me to forfeit your regard, or for my adversary not to succeed with his indictment. To me—but I will say nothing toward at the outset of my address. My second disadvantage is, the natural disposition of mankind to take pleasure in hearing invectives and accusations, and to be amazed by those who praise themselves. To Aeschines is assigned the part which gives pleasure; that which is (I may fairly say,) offensive to all, is left for me. And if, to escape from this, I shall appear to be without defense against the charges, without proof of my claims to honor; whereas, if I proceed to give an account of my conduct and measures, I shall be forced to speak frequently of myself—I will endeavor then to do with all becoming modesty. What I am driven to by the necessity of the case, will be fairly chargeable to my opponent who has instituted such a prosecution.

As I am, it appears, on this day to render an account both of my private life and my public measures, I would fain, at the outset, call the Gods to my aid; and in your presence I implore them, first, that the goodwill which I have ever cherished toward the commonwealth and all of you may be fully requited to me on the present trial; next that they may direct you to such a decision upon this indictment, as will conduce to your common honor, and to the good conscience of each individual.

To all his scandalous abuse of my private life, observe my plain and honest answer. If you know me to be such as alleged—for I have lived nowhere else but among you— let not my voice be heard, however transcendent my statesmanship! Rise up this instant and condemn me! But if, in your opinion and judgment, I am far better and of better descent than my adversary; if (to speak without offense) I am not inferior, I or mine, to any respectable citizen; then give no credit to him for his other statements —it is plain they were all equally fictions—but to let the same goodwill which you have uniformly exhibited upon many former trials, be manifest now. With all your malice, Aeschines, it was very simple to suppose that I should turn from the discussion of measures and policy to notice your scandal. I will do no such thing; I am not so crazed. Your lies and calumnies about my political life I will examine forthwith; for that loose ribaldry, I shall have a word hereafter if the jury desire to hear it.

The crimes whereof I am accused are many and grievous; for some of them the laws enact heavy,—most severe penalties. The scheme of this present proceeding includes a combination of spiteful insolence, insult, railing, aspersions, and everything of the kind; while for the said charges and accusations, if they are true, the state has not the means of inflicting an adequate punishment, or anything like it. For it is not the right to debar another of access to the people and privilege of speech; moreover, to do so by way of malice and insult—by heaven!—is neither honest, nor constitutional, nor just. . . . In short, whatever else he [Aeschines] saw me doing in your prejudice, whatever mentioned or not mentioned in his catalogue of slander, there are laws for such things, and punishments, and trials, and judgments, with sharp and severe penalties; all of which he might have enforced against me; and had he done so—had he thus pursued the proper method with me, his charges would have been consistent with his conduct. But now he has declined the straightforward and just course, avoided all proofs of guilt at the time, and after this long interval gets up, to play his part withal, a heap of accusation, ribaldry, and scandal. Then he arraigns me, but prosecutes the defendant. His hatred of me makes the prominent part of the whole contest; yet, without having ever met me upon that ground, he openly seeks to deprive a third party of his privileges. Now, men of Athens, besides all other arguments that may be urged in Ctesiphon's behalf, this, methinks, may very fairly be alleged—that we should try our own quarrel by ourselves; not leave our private dispute, and look at what third party we can damage. That surely were the height of injustice.

As to the arguments which he jumbles together about the counter-written laws [those laws alleged to have been violated were copied and hung on a board side by side with the impugned decree as Aeschines had described in his speech against Ctesiphon] I hardly suppose you comprehend them—I myself could not understand the greater part. However I shall argue a just case in a straightforward way. So far from saying that I am not accountable, as the prosecutor just now falsely asserted, I acknowledge that I am all my life accountable for what as your statesman I have undertaken or advised; but for what I have voluntarily given to the people out of my own private fortune, I deny that I am any day accountable—do you hear, Aeschines?—nor is any other man, let him even be one of the nine archons.

"Oh, but you were a Conservator of Walls!" says he. Yes; and for that reason was I justly praised, because I gave the sums expended and did not charge them. A charge requires auditing and examiners; a donation merits thanks and praise: therefore the defendant made this motion in my favor.

That this is a settled principle in your hearts as well as in the laws, I can show by many proofs easily. First, Nausicles has often been crowned by you for what he expended out of his funds whilst he was general. Secondly, Diotimus was crowned for his present of shields; and Charidemus too, again, Neoptolemus here, superintendent of divers works has been favored for his donations.

In private, if you do not all know that I have been liberal and humane and charitable to the distressed, I am silent; I will say not a word; I will offer no evidence on the subject, either of persons whom I have ransomed from the enemy, or of persons whose daughters I helped to portion, or anything of the kind. For this is my maxim. I hope that the party receiving an obligation should ever remember it, the party conferring should forget it immediately, if the one is to act with honesty, the other without meanness. To remind and speak of your bounties is next door to reproaching. I will not act so; nothing shall induce me.

Whatever my reputation is in these respects, I am content with it.

I will have done, then, with private topics, but say another word or two upon public. If you can mention, Aeschines, a single man under the sun, whether Greek or barbarian, who has not suffered by Philip's power formerly and Alexander's now, well and good; I concede to you that my fortune or misfortune (if you please), has been the cause of everything. But if many that never saw me or heard my voice have been grievously afflicted, not individuals only, but whole cities and nations, how much juster and fairer is it to consider that to the common fortune apparently of all men, to a tide of events overwhelming and lamentable, these disasters are to be attributed. You, disregarding all this, accuse me whose ministry has been among my countrymen, knowing all the while that a part (if not the whole) of your calumny falls upon the people, and yourself in particular. For if I assumed the sole and absolute direction of our consuls, it was upon you, the other speakers, to accuse me; but if you were constantly present in all the assemblies, if the state invited public discussion of what was expected expedient, and if these measures were then believed by all to be the best, and especially by you (for certainly from no good-will did you leave me in possession of hopes and admiration and honors, all of which attended on my policy, but doubtless because you were compelled by the truth and had nothing better to advise), is it not iniquitous and monstrous to complain now of measures, than which you could suggest none better at the time?

Among all other people I find these principles in a manner defined and settled—Does a man willfully offend? He is the object of wrath and punishment. Hath a man erred unintentionally? There is a pardon instead of punishment for him. Has a man devoted himself to what seemed for the general good, and without any fault or misconduct been in common with all disappointed of success? Such a one deserved not obliquy or reproach, but sympathy. These principles will not be found in our statutes only: Nature herself has defined them by her unwritten laws and the feelings of humanity. Aeschines, however, has so far surpassed all men in brutality and malignity, that even things which he cited himself as misfortune he imputes to me as crimes.

And besides—as if he himself had spoken everything with candor and good-will—he told you to watch me, and mind that I did not cajole and deceive you, calling me a great orator, a juggler, a sophist, and the like; as though, if a man say of another what applies to himself, it must be true, and the hearers are not to inquire who the person is that makes the charge. Certain I am that you are all acquainted with my opponent's character, and believe these charges to be more applicable to him than to me. And of this I am sure, that my oratory—let it be so: though, indeed, I find that the speaker's power depends for the most part on the hearers; for according to your reception and favor it is that the wisdom of a speaker is esteemed—if I, however, possess any ability of this sort, you will find it has been exhibited always in public business on your behalf, never against you or on personal matters; whereas that of Aeschines has been displayed not only in speaking for the enemy, but against all persons who ever offended or quarreled with him. It is not for justice or the good of the commonwealth that he employs it. A citizen of worth and honor should not call upon judges impaneled in the public service to gratify his anger or hatred or anything of that kind; nor should he come before you upon such grounds. The best thing is not to have these feelings; but, if it cannot be helped, they should be mitigated and restrained.

I should conclude, Aeschines, that you undertook this cause to exhibit your eloquence and strength of lungs, not to obtain satisfaction for any wrong. But it is not the language of an orator, Aeschines, that has any value, nor yet the tone of his voice, but his adopting the same views with the people, and his hating and loving the same persons that his country does. He that is thus minded will say everything with loyal intention; he that courts persons from whom the commonwealth apprehends danger to herself rides not on the same anchorage with the people, and, therefore, has not the same expectation of safety. But—do you see?—I have: for my objects are the same with those of my countrymen; I have no interest separate or distinct. Is that so with you? How can it be—when immediately after the battle you went as ambassador to Philip, who was at that period the author of your country's calamities, notwithstanding that you had before persisted in refusing that office, as all men know?

And who is it that deceives the state? Surely the man who speaks not what he thinks. On whom does the crier pronounce a curse? Surely on such a man. What greater crime can an orator be charged with than that his opinions and his language are not the same? Such is found to be your character. And yet you open your mouth, and dare to look these men in the face! Do you think they don't know you?—or are sunk in such slumber and oblivion as not to remember the speeches which you delivered in the assembly, cursing and swearing that you had nothing to do with Philip, and that I brought that charge against you out of personal enmity, without foundation? No sooner came the news of the battle than you forgot all that; you acknowledged and avowed that between Philip and yourself there subsisted a relation of hospitality and friendship —new names these for your contract of hire. For upon what plea of equality or justice could Aeschines, son of Glaucothea the timbrel player, be the friend or acquaintance of Philip, I cannot see. No you were hired to ruin the interests of your countrymen; and yet, though you yourself have been caught in open treason, and been informed against yourself after the fact, you revile and reproach me for things which you will find any man is chargeable with sooner than I.

Many great and glorious enterprises has the commonwealth, Aeschines, undertaken and succeeded in through me; and she did not forget them. Here is the proof. On the election of a person to speak the funeral oration immediately after the event, you were proposed, but the people would not have you, notwithstanding your fine voice, nor Demades, though he had just made the peace, nor Hegemon, nor any other of your party—but me. And when you and Pythocles came forward in a brutal and shameful manner (O merciful heaven!) and urged the same accusations against me which you do now, and abused me, they elected me all the more. The reason—you are not ignorant of it—yet I will tell you. The Athenians knew as well the loyalty and zeal with which I conducted their affairs, as the dishonesty of you and your party; for what you denied upon oath in our prosperity, you confessed in the misfortunes of the republic. They considered, therefore, that men who got security for their politics by the public disasters had been their enemies long before, and were then avowedly such. They thought it right, also, that the person who was to speak in honor of the fallen and celebrate their valor should not have sat under the same roof or at the same table with their antagonists; that he should not revel there and sing a paean over the calamities of Greece in company with their murderers, and then come here and receive distinction; that he should not with his voice act the mourner of their fate, but that he should lament over them with his heart. This they perceived in themselves and in me, but not in any of you; therefore they elected me, and not you. Nor, while the people felt thus, did the fathers and brothers of the deceased, who were chosen by the people to perform their obsequies, feel differently. For having to order the funeral banquet (according to custom) at the house of the nearest relative to the deceased, they ordered it at mine. And with reason: because, though each to his own was nearer of kin than I was, none was so near to them all collectively. He that had the deepest interest in their safety and success had upon their mournful disaster the largest share of sorrow for them all.

Many other accusations and falsehoods he urged against me, O Athenians, but one thing surprised me more than all, that, when he mentioned the late misfortunes of the country, he felt not as became a well-disposed and upright citizen; he shed no tear, experienced no such emotion; with a loud voice exulting, and straining his throat, he imagined apparently that he was accusing me, while he was giving proof against himself that our distresses touch him not in the same manner as the rest.

But why do I censure him for this when with calumny far more shocking has he assailed me? He that charges me with Philippizing—O heaven and earth!—what would he not say? By Hercules and the gods! if one had honestly to inquire, discarding all expression of spite and falsehood, who the persons really are on whom the blame of what has happened may by common consent fairly and justly be thrown, it would be found they are the persons in the various states like Aeschines not like me—persons who, while Philip's power was feeble and exceedingly small, and we were constantly warning and exhorting and giving salutary counsel, sacrificed the general interests for the sake of selfish lucre, deceiving and corrupting their respective countrymen, until they made them slaves . . . All these, O Athenians, are men of the same politics in their own countries as this party among you—profligates and parasites and miscreants, who have each of them crippled their fatherlands; toasted away their liberty, first to Philip and last to Alexander; who measure happiness by their belly and all that is base, while freedom and independence, which the Greeks of olden time regarded as the test and standard of well-being, they have annihilated.

Of this base and infamous conspiracy and profligacy—or rather O Athenians, if I am to speak in earnest, of this betrayal of Grecian liberty—Athens is by all mankind acquitted, owing to my counsels; and I am acquitted by you. Then do you ask me, Aeschines, for what merit I claim to be honored? I will tell you. Because, while all the statesmen of Greece, beginning with yourselves, have been corrupted formerly by Philip and now by Alexander, me neither opportunity nor fair speeches, nor large promises, nor hope, nor fear, nor anything else, could tempt or induce to betray aught that I considered just and beneficial to my country. Whatever I have advised my fellow citizens, I never advised like you men, leaning as in a balance to the side of profit; all my proceedings have been those of a soul upright, honest, and incorrupt; entrusted with affairs of greater magnitude than any of my contemporaries, I have administered them all honestly and faithfully. Therefore I do claim to be honored.

As to this fortification, for which you ridiculed me, of the walls and fosse, I regard them as deserving of thanks and praise, and so they are; but I place them nowhere near my acts of administration. Not with stones nor with bricks did I fortify Athens, nor is this the ministry on which I most pride myself. Would you view my fortifications aright, you will find arms and states and posts and harbors and galleys and horses and men for their defense. These are the bulwarks with which I protected Attica as far as was possible by human wisdom; with these I fortified our territory, not the circle of Piraeus or the city. Nay, more; I was not beaten by Philip in estimates or preparations; far from it; but the generals and forces of the allies were overcome by his fortune. Where are the proofs of this? They are plain and evident. Consider.

What was the course becoming a loyal citizen—a statesman serving his country with all possible forethought and zeal and fidelity? Should he not have covered Attica on the seaboard with Euboea, on the midland frontier with Boeotia, on the Peloponnesian with the people of that confine? Should he not have provided for the conveyance of corn along a friendly coast all the way to Piraeus? preserved certain places that belonged to us by sending off succors, and by advising and moving accordingly—brought others into alliance and confederacy with us—cut off the principal resources of the enemy, and supplied what the commonwealth was deficient in? All this has been accomplished by my decrees and measures; and whoever will examine them without prejudice, men of Athens, will find they were rightly planned and faithfully executed; that none of the proper seasons were lost or missed or thrown away by me; nothing which depended on one man's ability and prudence was neglected. But if the power of some deity or fortune, or the worthlessness of commanders, or the wickedness of you that betrayed your countries, or all these things together, injured and eventually ruined our cause, of what is Demosthenes guilty? Had there been in each of the Greek cities one such man as I was in my station among you, or rather, had Thessaly possessed one single man, and Arcadia one, of the same sentiments as myself, none of the Greeks either beyond or within Thermopylae would have suffered their present calamities; all would have been free and independent, living prosperously in their own countries with perfect safety and security, thankful to you and the rest of the Athenians for such manifold blessings through me.

You mention the good men of olden times; and you are right so to do. Yet it is hardly fair, O Athenians, that he should get the advantage of that respect which you have for the dead, to compare and contrast me with them—me who am living among you; for what mortal is ignorant that toward the living there exists always more or less of ill-will, whereas the dead are no longer hated by even an enemy? Such being human nature, am I to be tried and judged by the standard of my predecessors? Heaven forbid! It is not just or equitable, Aeschines. Let me be compared with you, or any person you like of your party who are still alive. And consider this—whether it is more honorable and better for the state, that because of the services of a former age, prodigious though they are beyond all power of expression, those of the present generation should be unrequited and spurned or that all who give proof of their good intentions should have their share of honor and regard from the people. Yet, indeed—if I must say so much—my politics and principles, if considered fairly, will be found to resemble those of the illustrious ancients, and to have had the same objects in view while yours resemble those of their calumniators; for it is certain there were persons in those times who ran down the living, and praised people dead and gone, with a malignant purpose like yourself.

Two things, men of Athens, are characteristic of a well-disposed citizen—so may I speak of myself and give the least offense: in authority his constant aim should be the dignity and preeminence of the commonwealth; in all times and circumstances his spirit should be loyal. This depends upon nature; power and might upon other things. Such a spirit, you will find, I have ever sincerely cherished.

Only see. When any person demanded—when they brought Amphictyonic suits against me—when they menaced—when they promised—when they set miscreants like wild beasts upon me—never in any way have I abandoned my affection for you. From the very beginning I chose an honest and straightforward course in politics, to support the honor, the power, the glory of my fatherland, these to exalt, in these to have my being. I do not walk the market place gay and cheerful because the stranger has prospered, holding out my right hand and congratulating those whom I think will report it yonder, and on any news of our success shudder and groan and stoop to the earth, like these impious men who rail at Athens, as if in so doing they did not rail at themselves; who look abroad, and if the foreigner thrive by the distresses of Greece, are thankful for it, and say we should keep him so thriving to all time.

Never, O ye gods, may those wishes be confirmed by you! If possible, inspire even in these men a better sense and feeling! But if they are, indeed, incurable, destroy them by themselves; exterminate them on land and sea; and for the rest of us, grant that we may speedily be released from our present fears, and enjoy a lasting deliverance!

William Pitt, Earl of Chatham
1708–1778

William Pitt came to full development of his parlia-
mentary power when his criticism of the War of Austrian
Succession brought about the downfall of Robert Walpole
in 1742. Through his shrewd management as head of a co-
alition government he brought about the defeat of the
French in Canada. He left the Whig party over questions
about the American Colonies and, with Burke, tried to lead
the government into a policy of reasonable co-operation
with America. Yet George III and his ministers were
deaf and blind to all reason in this area. Because of illness
Pitt had not been in the House for twelve months. He
suddenly appeared there when no one had expected him
and delivered this speech on January 14, 1766. The royal
speech to which he refers informed Parliament that mat-
ters of great importance had occurred in America, and or-
ders had been sent to insure the support of the lawful
authority. The Stamp Act of 1765 had already been
passed and as a result of this unwise action the disorders
began to arise. The debate concerning America followed
the King's speech and became one of the greatest occa-
sions in the history of the House of Commons. Grenville
with technical accuracy and logic had just spoken and Pitt
gave this speech as a reply. Though the manuscript does
not exist as a whole, the parts of it have been put together
from available sources.

Has Parliament the Right to Tax America?

Mr. Speaker,

I came to town but today. I was a stranger to the tenor
of his Majesty's Speech and the proposed address until I
heard them read in this House. Unconsulted and uncon-

nected I have not the means of information. I am fearful of offending through mistake, and therefore beg to be indulged with a second reading of the proposed address. [*The address is then read.*] I commend the King's Speech, and approve of the address in answer. As it decides nothing, every gentleman being left at perfect liberty to take such a part concerning America as he might afterwards see fit. I speak not with respect to parties. I stand in this place single and independent.

As to the late ministry [*turning to Grenville who sat near him*] every capital measure they have taken has been entirely wrong. As to the present gentlemen, to those at least whom I have in my eye [*looking at Conway*] I have no objection. Their characters are fair; and I am always glad when men of fair characters engage in his Majesty's service. Some of them have done me the honor to ask my opinion before they would engage. They will do me the justice to own, I advised them to engage; but, notwithstanding,—I love to be explicit,—I cannot give them my confidence: pardon me gentlemen [*bowing to the Ministry*], confidence is a plant of slow growth in an aged bosom; youth is the season of credulity. By comparing events with each other, reason from effects to causes, methinks I plainly discover the traces of an overruling influence . . . I have had the honor to serve the Crown, and if I could have submitted to influence, I might have still continued to serve; but I would not be responsible for others. I have no local attachments; it is indifferent to me whether a man was rocked in his cradle on this side or that of the Tweed.

When the resolution was taken in the House to tax America, I was ill in bed. If I could have endured to have been carried in my bed, so great was the agitation of my mind for the consequences, I would have solicited some kind hand to have laid me down on this floor, to have borne my testimony against it. It is now an Act that has passed. I would speak with decency of every Act of this House, but must beg indulgence to speak of it with freedom. The subject of debate is of greater importance than ever engaged the attention of this House, that subject only excepted when nearly a century ago, it was a question whether you yourselves were to be bond or free. The manner in which this affair will be terminated will decide the judgment of posterity on the glory of this Kingdom, and the wisdom of its government during the present reign.

As my health and life are so very infirm and precarious that I may not be able to attend on the day that may be fixed by the House for the consideration of America, I must now, though somewhat inseasonably, leaving the expediency of the Stamp Act to another time, speak to a point of infinite moment, I mean to the right. Some seem to have considered it as a point of honor, and leave all measures of right and wrong to follow a delusion that may lead us to destruction. On a question that may mortally wound the freedom of three million of virtuous and brave subjects beyond the Atlantic Ocean, I cannot be silent. America being neither really nor virtually represented in Westminster, cannot be held legally, constitutionally, or reasonably subject to obedience to any money bill of this Kingdom.

It is my opinion that this Kingdom has no right to lay a tax upon the colonies. At the same time I assert the authority of this Kingdom over the colonies to be sovereign and supreme, in every circumstance of government and legislation whatsoever. They are the subjects of this Kingdom, equally entitled with yourselves to all the natural rights of mankind, and the peculiar privileges of Englishmen: equally bound by its law and equally participating of the constitution of this free country. The Americans are the sons, not the bastards of England. As subjects they are entitled to the common right of representation and cannot be bound to pay taxes without their consent.

Taxation is no part of the governing power. The taxes are a voluntary gift and grant of the Commons alone. When, therefore, in this House we give and grant, we give what is our own. But in an American tax what do we do? We, your Majesty's Commons of Great Britain, give and grant to your Majesty—what? our own property? No. We give and grant to your Majesty the property of your Majesty's Commons in America. It is an absurdity in terms.

There is an idea, in some, that the colonies are virtually represented in this House. They never have been represented at all in Parliament; they were not even virtually represented at the time when this law, as captious as it is iniquitous, was passed to deprive them of the most inestimable of their privileges. I would fair know by whom an American is represented here? Is he represented by any knight of the shire? in any county of this Kingdom? Would to God that respectable representation was augmented to a greater number! Or will you tell him that he is represented by any representative of a borough—a borough which, perhaps, no man ever saw? That is what is called the "rotten part of the constitution." It cannot endure the century. If it does not drop, it must be amputated. The idea of a virtual representation of America in this House is the most contemptible that ever entered into the head of a man. It does not deserve a serious refutation.

The Commons of America, represented in their several assemblies, have ever been in possession of the exercise of their constitutional right, of giving and granting their own money. They would have been slaves if they had not enjoyed it. And how is the right of taxing the colonies internally compatible with that of framing regulations without number for their trade? The laws of this kind, which Parliament is daily making, prove that they form a body separate from Great Britain. While you hold their manufactures in the most servile restraint, will you add a new tax to deprive them of the last remnants of their liberty? This would be to plunge them into the most odious slavery, against which their charters should protect them. If this House suffers the Stamp Act to continue in force, France will gain more by your colonies than she ever could have done if her arms in the last war had been victorious.

Gentlemen, Sir, have been charged with giving birth to sedition in America. They have spoken their sentiments with freedom against this unhappy act, and that freedom has become their crime. Sorry am I to hear the liberty of speech in this House imputed as a crime. But the imputation shall not discourage me. It is a liberty I mean to exercise. No gentleman ought to be afraid to exercise it. It is a liberty by which a gentleman who calumniates it might have profited. The gentleman tells us, America is obstinate; America is in open rebellion. I rejoice that America has resisted. Three millions of people so dead to all feelings of liberty as voluntarily to submit to be slaves would have been fit instruments to make slaves of the rest.

I come not here armed at all points, with law cases and acts of Parliament, with statute book doubled down in dog's ears, to defend the cause of liberty: if I had, I myself would have cited the two cases of Chester and Durham. I would have cited them, to have shown that, even under former arbitrary reigns, Parliaments were ashamed of taxing a people without their consent and allowed them representatives. Why did the gentleman confine himself to Chester and Durham? He might have taken a higher example in Wales; Wales, that never was taxed by Parliament until it was incorporated.

If the gentleman does not understand the difference between external and internal taxes, I cannot help it; but there is a plain distinction between taxes levied for the purpose of raising a revenue, and duties imposed for the regulation of trade, for the accommodation of the subject; although, in the consequences, some revenue might incidentally arise from the latter.

The gentleman asks, when were the colonies emancipated? But I desire to know when were they made slaves? But I dwell not upon words.

I never shall own the justice of taxing America internally until she enjoys the right of representation. In every other point of legislation, the authority of Parliament is, like the North Star, fixed for the reciprocal benefit of the parent country and her colonies. The British Parliament, as the supreme governing and legislative power, has always bound them by her laws, by her regulations, of their trade and manufactures, and even in a more absolute interdiction of both.

The power of Parliament, like the circulation from the human heart, active, vigorous, and perfect in the smallest fibre of the arterial system, may be known in the colonies by the prohibition of their carrying a hat to market over the line of one province into another, or by breaking down a loom in the most distant corner of the British Empire in America; and if this power were denied, I would not permit them to manufacture a lock of wool or a horseshoe or a hobnail.

In everything you may bind them except that of taking their money out of their pockets without their consent. Here I would draw the line

> sunt certi denique fines,
> Quos ultra citreque nequit consistere rectum

But I repeat, the House has no right to lay an internal tax upon America, that country not being represented.

I know not what we may hope or fear from those now in place; but I have confidence in their good intentions. I could not refrain from expressing the reflections I have made in my retirement, which I hope long to enjoy, beholding, as I do, ministries changed one after another, and passing away like shadows.

Edmund Burke

1729–1797

Edmund Burke, British statesman and orator of great power, was born and educated in Dublin and, after graduating without distinction from Trinity College, went to London and entered the Middle Temple with the intention of studying law. He became involved in various political causes and began writing for publications. After his election to Parliament, he astonished his listeners with a new style of eloquence clear in its logic and full of fire in its delivery. All that Burke had within him to give to a cause, he gave. He did have some dramatic points of delivery for which his contemporaries criticized him, but the fundamental honesty of the man and the long view he had of immediate conditions has made him an orator not for his own day but for all time.

The speech on "Conciliation" took over three hours. (His speech on the impeachment of Warren Hastings took four days.) It is not possible, therefore, in a short space here to give the complete view of this great mind and how it developed a speech. At the end of the speech on "Conciliation" he presented thirteen motions, all aimed to conciliate the colonists and give them proper representation in Parliament. Great orator though he was, he had addressed a Parliament biased against the American cause as he saw it. He was popular but his ideas were not. None of the thirteen motions carried. Before the report of the speech reached American shores, the embattled farmers at Concord had "fired the shot heard round the world."

In the speech delivered to the electors at Bristol at the Guildhall on September 6, 1780, Burke gives an eighteenth-century campaign speech. Before a candidate was chosen to run, he had to present himself to the people of his town and be selected by them. Burke had served the city of Bristol for a long time and he had returned to give *an accounting of his stewardship. Two others were seeking his position, and there was considerable feeling that Burke had not truly represented Bristol. This audience is different from that of the members of Parliament; we find here a political gathering, and this is the manner in which Burke met his critics. They elected him to run for office, but three days after they had selected him, Burke made a canvass of his friends there and believed that it would be wiser if he withdrew from the race. This he did in another, but brief, speech to the citizens of Bristol.*

CONCILIATION WITH AMERICA

The proposition is peace. Not peace through the medium of war; not peace to be hunted through the labyrinth of intricate and endless negotiations; not peace to arise out of universal discord, fomented from principle, in all parts of the empire; not peace to depend on the juridical determination of perplexing questions, or the precise marking of the shadowy boundaries of a complex government. It is simple peace, sought in its natural course and its ordinary haunts. It is peace sought in the spirit of peace, and laid in principles purely pacific. I propose, by removing the ground of the difference, and by restoring *the former unsuspecting confidence of the colonies in the mother country,* to give permanent satisfaction to your people; and, far from a scheme of ruling by discord, to reconcile them to each other in the same act, and by the bond of the very same interest, which reconciles them to British government.

My idea is nothing more. Refined policy ever has been the parent of confusion, and ever will be so long as the world endures. Plain good intention, which is as easily discovered at the first view as fraud is surely detected at last, is (let me say) of no mean force in the government of mankind. Genuine simplicity of heart is a healing and cementing principle. My plan, therefore, being formed upon the most simple grounds imaginable, may disappoint some people when they hear it. It has nothing to recommend it to the pruriency of curious ears. There is nothing at all new and captivating in it. It has nothing of the splendor of the project which has been lately laid upon your table by the noble lord in the blue ribbon. It does not propose to fill your lobby with squabbling colony agents, who will require the interposition of your mace at every instant to keep the peace among them. It does not institute a magnificent auction of finance, where captivated provinces come to general ransom by bidding against each other, until you knock down the hammer, and determine a proportion of payments beyond all the powers of algebra to equalize and settle.

The plan which I shall presume to suggest derives, however, one great advantage from the proposition and registry of that noble lord's project. The idea of conciliation is admissible. First, the House, in accepting the resolution moved by the noble lord, has admitted, notwithstanding the menacing front of our address, notwithstanding our heavy bill of pains and penalties, that we do not think ourselves precluded from all ideas of free grace and bounty.

The House has gone further: it has declared conciliation admissible, *previous* to any submission on the part of America. It has even shot a good deal beyond that mark, and has admitted that the complaints of our former mode of exerting the right of taxation were not wholly unfounded. That right, thus exerted, is allowed to have had something reprehensible in it, something unwise, or something grievous; since, in the midst of our heat and resentment, we, of ourselves, have proposed a capital alteration, and, in order to get rid of what seemed so very exceptional, have instituted a mode that is altogether new; one that is, indeed wholly alien from all the ancient methods and forms of parliament.

The *principle* of this proceeding is large enough for my purpose. The means proposed by the noble lord for carrying his ideas into execution, I think, indeed, are very indifferently suited to the end; and this I shall endeavor to show you before I sit down. But, for the present, I take my ground on the admitted principle. I mean to give peace. Peace implies reconciliation; and, where there has been a material dispute, reconciliation does in a manner always imply concession on the one part or on the other. In this state of things I make no difficulty in affirming that the proposal ought to originate from us. Great and acknowledged force is not impaired, either in effect or in opinion, by an unwillingness to exert itself. The superior power may offer peace with honor and with safety. Such an offer from such a power will be attributed to magnanimity. But the concessions of the weak are the concessions of fear. When such a one is disarmed, he is wholly at the mercy of his superior, and he loses forever that time and those chances which, as they happen to all men, are the strength and resources of all inferior power.

The capital leading questions on which you must this day decide, are these two: *First, whether you ought to concede; and, secondly, what your concession ought to be.*

On the first of these questions we have gained, as I have just taken the liberty of observing to you, some ground. But I am sensible that a good deal more is still to be done. Indeed, sir, to enable us to determine both on the one and the other of these great questions with a firm and precise judgment, I think it may be necessary to consider distinctly: The true *nature* and the peculiar *circumstances* of the object which we have before us; because, after all our struggle, whether we will or not, we must govern America according to that nature and to those circumstances, and not according to our imaginations; not according to abstract ideas of right; by no means according to mere general theories of government, the resort to which appears to me, in our present situation, no better than arrant trifling. I shall therefore endeavor, with your leave, to lay before you some of the most material of these circumstances in as full and as clear a manner as I am able to state them.

[Burke then dwelt (1) on the large and growing population of the colonies, and (2) on the profitable commerce with the home country and (3) on the development of agriculture which is destined to feed the old world. To

such great colonies he is willing to pardon something to
the spirit of liberty.]

I am sensible, sir, that all which I have asserted in my
detail is admitted in the gross; but that quite a different
conclusion is drawn from it. America, gentlemen say, is a
noble object. It is an object well worth fighting for. Certainly it is, if fighting a people be the best way of gaining
them. Gentlemen in this respect will be led to their choice
of means by their complexions and their habits. Those
who understand the military art will, of course, have some
predilection for it. Those who wield the thunder of the
state may have more confidence in the efficacy of arms.
But I confess, possibly for want of this knowledge, my
opinion is much more in favor of prudent management
than of force; considering force not as an odious, but a
feeble instrument for preserving a people so numerous,
so active, so growing, so spirited as this, in a profitable
and subordinate connection with us.

First, sir, permit me to observe, that the use of force
alone is but temporary. It may subdue for a moment, but
it does not remove the necessity of subduing again; and a
nation is not governed which is perpetually to be conquered.

My next objection is its uncertainty. Terror is not always
the effect of force; and an armament is not a victory. If
you do not succeed, you are without resource; for, conciliation failing, force remains; but, force failing, no further
hope of reconciliation is left. Power and authority are
sometimes bought by kindness, but they can never be
begged as alms by an impoverished and defeated violence.

A further objection to force is that you impair the object by your very endeavors to preserve it. The thing you
fought for is not the thing which you recover; but de-
preciated, sunk, wasted, and consumed in the contest.
Nothing less will content me than *whole* America. I do
not choose to consume its strength along with our own,
because in all parts it is the British strength that I consume. I do not choose to be caught by a foreign enemy at
the end of this exhausting conflict, and still less in the
midst of it. I may escape; but I can make no insurance

against such an event. Let me add, that I do not choose wholly to break the American spirit, because it is the spirit that has made the country.

Lastly, we have no sort of experience in favor of force as an instrument in the rule of our colonies. Their growth and their utility have been owing to methods altogether different. Our ancient indulgence has been said to be pursued to a fault. It may be so; but we know, if feeling is evidence, that our fault was more tolerable than our attempt to mend it; and our sin far more salutary than our penitence.

These, sir, are my reasons for not entertaining that high opinion of untried force, by which many gentlemen, for whose sentiments in other particulars I have great respect, seem to be so greatly captivated.

But there is still behind a third consideration concerning this object, which serves to determine my opinion on the sort of policy which ought to be pursued in the management of America, even more than its population and its commerce—I mean its temper and character. In this character of the Americans a love of freedom is the predominating feature which marks and distinguishes the whole; and, as an ardent is always a jealous affection, your colonies become suspicious, restive, and untractable, whenever they see the least attempt to wrest from them by force, or shuffle from them by chance, what they think the only advantage worth living for. This fierce spirit of liberty is stronger in the English colonies, probably, than in any other people of the earth, and this from a variety of powerful causes, which, to understand the true temper of their minds, and the direction which this spirit takes, it will not be amiss to lay open somewhat more largely.

First, the people of the colonies are descendants of Englishmen. England, sir, is a nation which still, I hope, respects, and formerly adored, her freedom. The colonists emigrated from you when this part of your character was most predominant; and they took this bias and direction the moment they parted from your hands. They are, therefore, not only devoted to liberty, but to liberty according to English ideas and on English principles. Abstract liberty, like other mere abstractions, is not to be found. Liberty inheres in some sensible object; and every nation has formed to itself some favorite point which, by way of eminence, becomes the criterion of their happiness. It happened, you know, sir, that the great contests for freedom in this country were, from the earliest times, chiefly upon the question of taxing. Most of the contests in the ancient commonwealths turned primarily on the right of election of magistrates, or on the balance among the several orders of the state. The question of money was not with them so immediate. But in England it was otherwise. On this point of taxes the ablest pens and most eloquent tongues have been exercised; the greatest spirits have acted and suffered. In order to give the fullest satisfaction concerning the importance of this point, it was not only necessary for those who in argument defended the excellence of the English Constitution, to insist on this privilege of granting money as a dry point of fact, and to prove that the right had been acknowledged in ancient parchments and blind usages to reside in a certain body called the House of Commons. They went much further: they attempted to prove (and they succeeded) that in theory it ought to be so, from the particular nature of a House of Commons, as an immediate representative of the people, whether the old records had delivered this oracle or not. They took infinite pains to inculcate, as a fundamental principle, that in all monarchies the people must, in effect, themselves, mediately or immediately, possess the power of granting their own money, or no shadow of liberty could subsist. The colonies draw from you, as with their life-blood, those ideas and principles, their love of liberty, as with you, fixed and attached on this specific point of taxing. Liberty might be safe or might be endangered in twenty other particulars, without their being much pleased or alarmed. Here they felt its pulse; and, as they found that beat, they thought themselves sick or sound. I do not say whether they were right or wrong in applying your general arguments to their own case. It is not easy, indeed, to make a monopoly of theorems and corollaries. The fact is, that they did thus apply those general arguments; and your mode of governing them, whether through lenity or indolence, through wisdom, or mistake, confirmed them in the imagination that they, as well as you, had an interest in these common principles.

They were further confirmed in these pleasing errors by the form of their provincial legislative assemblies. Their governments are popular in a high degree; some are merely popular; in all, the popular representative is the most weight; and this share of the people in their ordinary government never fails to inspire them with lofty sentiments, and with a strong aversion from whatever tends to deprive them of their chief importance.

If anything were wanting to this necessary operation of the form of government, religion would have given it a complete effect. Religion, always a principle of energy, in this new people is no way worn out or impaired; and their mode of professing it is also one main cause of this free spirit. The people are Protestants; and of that kind which is the most averse to all implicit submission of mind and opinion. This is a persuasion not only favorable to liberty, but built upon it. I do not think, sir, that the reason of this averseness in the dissenting churches from all that looks like absolute government, is so much to be sought in their religious tenets as in their history. Every one knows that the Roman Catholic Religion is at least coeval with most of the governments where it prevails; that it has generally gone hand in hand with them, and received great favor and every kind of support from authority. The Church of England, too, was formed from her cradle under the nursing care of regular government. But the dissenting interests have sprung up in direct opposition to all the ordinary powers of the world, and could justify that opposition only on a strong claim to natural liberty. Their very existence depended on the powerful and unremitted assertion of that claim. All protestantism, even the most cold and passive, is a kind of dissent. But the religion most prevalent in our northern colonies is a refinement on the principle of resistance; it is the dissidence of dissent and the protestantism of the Protestant Religion. This religion, under a variety of denominations, agreeing in nothing but in the communion of the spirit of liberty, is predominant in most of the northern provinces; where the Church of England, notwithstanding its legal rights, is in reality no more than a sort of private sect, not composing, most probably, the tenth of the people. The colonists left England when this spirit was high, and in the emigrants was the highest of all; and even that stream of foreigners, which has been constantly flowing into these colonies, has, for the greatest part, been composed of dissenters from the establishments of their several countries, who have brought with them a temper and character far from alien to that of the people with whom they mixed.

Sir, I can perceive by their manner that some gentlemen object to the latitude of this description, because in the southern colonies the Church of England forms a large body, and has a regular establishment. It is certainly true. There is, however, a circumstance attending these colonies which, in my opinion, fully counterbalances this difference, and makes the spirit of liberty still more high and haughty than in those to the northward. It is that in Virginia and the Carolinas they have a vast multitude of *slaves.* Where this is the case in any part of the world, those who are free are by far the most proud and jealous of their freedom. Freedom is to them not only an enjoyment, but a kind of rank and privilege. Not seeing there that freedom, as in countries where it is a common blessing, and as broad and general as the air, may be united with much abject toil, with great misery, with all the exterior of servitude, liberty looks, among them, like something that is more noble and liberal. I do not mean, sir, to commend the superior morality of this sentiment, which has at least as much pride as virtue in it; but I cannot alter the nature of man. The fact is so; and these people of the southern colonies are much more strongly, and with a higher and more stubborn spirit, attached to liberty than those to the northward. Such were all the ancient commonwealths; such were our Gothic ancestors; such, in our days, were the Poles, and such will be all masters of slaves, who are not slaves themselves. In such a people the haughtiness of domination combines with the spirit of freedom, fortifies it, and renders it invincible.

Permit me, sir, to add another circumstance in our colonies, which contributes no mean part toward the growth and effect of this untractable spirit—I mean their education. In no other country, perhaps, in the world is the law so general a study. The profession itself is numerous and powerful, and in most provinces it takes the lead. The greater number of the deputies sent to Congress were lawyers. But all who read, and most do read, endeavor to obtain some smattering in that science. I have been told by an eminent bookseller that in no branch of his business, after tracts of popular devotion, were so many books as those on the law exported to the plantations. The colonists have now fallen into the way of printing them for their own use. I hear that they have sold nearly as many of "Blackstone's Commentaries" in America as in England. General Gage marks out this disposition very particularly in a letter on your table. He states that all the people in his government are lawyers, or smatterers in law; and that in Boston they have been enabled, by successful chicane, wholly to evade many parts of one of your capital penal constitutions. The smartness of debate will say that this knowledge ought to teach them more clearly the rights of legislature, their obligations to obedience, and the penalties of rebellion. All this is mighty well. But my honorable and learned friend [the Attorney-General, afterward Lord Thurlow] on the floor, who condescends to mark what I say for animadversion, will disdain that ground. He has heard, as well as I, that when great honors and great emoluments do not win over this knowledge to the service of the state, it is a formidable adversary to government. If the spirit be not tamed and broken by these happy methods, it is stubborn and litigious. *Abeunt studia in mores.* This study renders men acute, inquisitive, dexterous, prompt in attack, ready in defense, full of resources. In other countries, the people, more simple and of a less mercurial cast, judge of an ill principle in government only by an actual grievance. Here they anticipate the evil, and judge of the pressure of the grievance by the badness of the principle. They augur misgovernment at a distance, and snuff the approach of tyranny in every tainted breeze.

The last cause of this disobedient spirit in the colonies is hardly less powerful than the rest, as it is not merely moral, but laid deep in the natural constitution of things. Three thousand miles of ocean lie between you and them. No contrivance can prevent the effect of this distance in weakening government. Seas roll and months pass between the order and the execution; and the want of a speedy explanation of a single point is enough to defeat the whole system. You have, indeed, "winged ministers" of vengeance, who carry your bolts in their pouches to the remotest verge of the sea. But there a power steps in that limits the arrogance of raging passion and furious elements, and says: "So far shalt thou go, and no farther." Who are you, that should fret and rage and bite the chains of nature? Nothing worse happens to you than does to all nations who have extensive empire; and it happens in all the forms into which empire can be thrown. In large bodies the circulation of power must be less vigorous at the extremities. Nature has said it. The Turk cannot govern Egypt, and Arabia, and Koordistan as he governs Thrace; nor has he the same dominion in Crimea and Algiers which he has at Brusa and Smyrna. Despotism itself is obliged to truck and huckster. The sultan gets such obedience as he can. He governs with a loose rein, that he may govern at all; and the whole of the force and vigor of his authority in his center is derived from a prudent relaxation in all his borders. Spain, in her provinces, is, perhaps, not so well obeyed as you are in yours. She complies too; she submits; she watches times. This is the immutable condition, the eternal law, of extensive and detached empire.

Then, sir, from these six capital sources of descent, of form of government, of religion in the northern provinces, of manners in the southern, of education, of the remoteness of situation from the first mover of government—from all these causes a fierce spirit of liberty has grown up. It has grown with the growth of the people in your colonies, and increased with the increase of their wealth; a spirit that, unhappily meeting with an exercise of power in England, which, however lawful, is not reconcilable to any ideas of liberty, much less with theirs, has kindled this flame, that is ready to consume us.

I do not mean to commend either the spirit in this excess, or the moral causes which produce it. Perhaps a more smooth and accommodating spirit of freedom in them would be more acceptable to us. Perhaps ideas of liberty might be desired, more reconcilable with an arbitrary and boundless authority. Perhaps we might wish the colonists to be persuaded that their liberty is more secure when held in trust for them by us, as guardians during a perpetual minority, than with any part of it in their own hands. But the question is not whether their spirit deserves praise or blame. What, in the name of God, shall we do with it? You have before you the object, such as it is, with all its glories, with all its imperfections on its head. You see the magnitude, the importance, the temper, the habits, the disorders. By all these considerations we are strongly urged to determine something concerning it. We are called upon to fix some rule and line for our future conduct which may give a little stability to our politics, and prevent the return of such unhappy deliberations as the present. Every such return will bring the matter before us in a still more untractable form. For, what astonishing and incredible things have we not seen already? What monsters have not been generated from this unnatural contention? While every principle of authority and resistance has been pushed upon both sides, as far as it would go, there is nothing so stolid and certain, either in reasoning or in practice, that it has not been shaken. Until very lately, all authority in America seemed to be nothing but an emanation from yours. Even the popular part of the colony constitution derived all its activity, and its first vital movement, from the pleasure of the crown. We thought, sir, that the utmost which the discontented colonists could do was to disturb authority. We never dreamed they could of themselves supply it, knowing in general what an operose business it is to establish a government absolutely new. But having, for our purposes in this contention, resolved that none but an obedient assembly should sit, the humors of the people there, finding all passage through the legal channel stopped, with great violence broke out another way. Some provinces have tried their experiment as we have tried ours; and theirs has succeeded. They have formed a government sufficient for its purposes, without the bustle of a revolution, or the troublesome formality of an election. Evident necessity and tacit consent have done the business in an instant. So well they have done it, that Lord Dunmore (the account is among the fragments on your table) tells you, that the new institution is infinitely better obeyed than the ancient government ever was in its most fortunate periods. Obedience is what makes government, and not the names by which it is called; nor the name of governor, as formerly, or committee, as at present. This new government has originated directly from the people, and was not transmitted through any of the ordinary artificial media of a positive constitution. It was not a manufacture ready formed, and transmitted to them in that condition from England. The evil arising from hence is this: that the colonists having once found the possibility of enjoying the advantages of order in the midst of a struggle for liberty, such struggles will not henceforward seem so terrible to the settled and sober part of mankind as they had appeared before the trial.

Pursuing the same plan of punishing by the denial of the exercise of government to still greater lengths, we wholly abrogated the ancient government of Massachusetts. We are confident that the first feeling, if not the very prospect of anarchy, would instantly enforce a complete submission. The experiment was tried. A new, strange, unexpected face of things appeared. Anarchy is found tolerable. A vast province has now subsisted, and subsisted in a considerable degree of health and vigor, for near a twelvemonth, without governor, without public council, without judges, without executive magistrates. How long it will continue in this state, or what may arise out of this unheard-of situation, how can the wisest of us conjecture? Our late experience has taught us, that many of those fundamental principles formerly believed infallible, are either not of the importance they were imagined to be, or that we have not at all adverted to some other far more important and far more powerful principles, which entirely overrules those we had considered as omnipotent.

I am much against any further experiments which tend to put to the proof any more of these allowed opinions which contribute so much to the public tranquillity. In effect, we suffer as much at home by this loosening of all ties, and this concussion of all established opinions, as we do abroad. For, in order to prove that the Americans have no right to their liberties, we are every day endeavoring to subvert the maxims which preserve the whole spirit of our own. To prove that the Americans ought not to be free, we are obliged to depreciate the value of freedom itself; and we never seem to gain a paltry advantage over them in debate, without attacking some of those principles, or deriding some of those feelings, for which our ancestors have shed their blood.

[Burke next proceeds to examine various schemes for the taxation of the colonies or repressing their liberties. He exposes the difficulties of such schemes and returns to his proposal of conciliation.]

Instead of a standing revenue, you will therefore have a perpetual quarrel. Indeed, the noble lord who proposed this project of a ransom by auction, seemed himself to be of that opinion. His project was rather designed for breaking the union of the colonies than for establishing a revenue. He confessed that he apprehended that his proposal would not be to their taste. I say this scheme of disunion seems to be at the bottom of the project; for I will not suspect that the noble lord meant nothing but merely to delude the nation by an airy phantom which he never intended to realize. But, whatever his views may be, as I propose the peace and union of the colonies at the very foundation of my plan, it cannot accord with one whose foundation is perpetual discord.

Compare the two. This I offer to give you is plain and simple. The other, full of perplexed and intricate mazes. This is mild; that, harsh. This is found by experience effectual for its purposes; the other is a new project. This is universal; the other, calculated for certain colonies only. This is immediate in its conciliatory operation; the other, remote, contingent, full of hazard. Mine is what becomes the dignity of a ruling people; gratuitous, unconditional, and not held out as a matter of bargain and sale. I have done my duty in proposing it to you. I have indeed tried you by a long discourse; but this is the misfortune of those to whose influence nothing will be conceded, and who must win every inch of their ground by argument. You have heard me with goodness. May you decide with wisdom! For my part, I feel my mind greatly disburdened by what I have done today. I have been the less fearful of trying your patience, because on this subject I mean to spare it altogether in future. I have this comfort, that in every stage of the American affairs, I have steadily opposed the measures that have produced the confusion, and may bring on the destruction of this empire. I now go so far as to risk a proposal of my own. If I cannot give peace to my country, I give it to my conscience.

But what, says the financier, is peace to us without money? Your plan gives us no revenue. No! But it does—for it secures to the subject the power of REFUSAL—the first of all revenues. Experience is a cheat, and fact a liar, if this power in the subject of proportioning his grant, or of not granting at all, has not been found the richest mine of revenue ever discovered by the skill or by the fortune of man. It does not indeed vote you £152,750 11s. 2¾d., nor any other paltry limited sum, but it gives the strong box itself, the fund, the bank, from whence only revenues can arise among a people sensible of freedom: *Posita lauditur arca.*

Cannot you in England; cannot you at this time of day; cannot you—a House of Commons—trust to the principle which has raised so mighty a revenue, and accumulated a debt of near one hundred and forty millions in this country? Is this principle to be true in England and false everywhere else? Is it not true in Ireland? Has it not hitherto been true in the colonies? Why should you presume that in any country, a body duly constituted for any functions will neglect to perform its duty, and abdicate its trust. Such a presumption would go against all government in all modes. But, in truth, this dread of penury of supply, from a free assembly, has no foundation in nature. For first observe, that, besides the desire, which all men have naturally, of supporting the honor of their own government, that sense of dignity, and that security of property, which ever attends freedom, has a tendency to increase the stock of the free community. Most may be taken where most is accumulated. And what is the soil or climate where experience has not uniformly proved that the voluntary flow of heaped-up plenty, bursting from the weight of its own rich luxuriance, has ever run with a more copious stream of revenue, than could be squeezed from the dry husks of oppressed indigence, by the straining of all the politic machinery in the world?

Next, we know that parties must ever exist in a free country. We know, too, the emulations of such parties, their contradictions, their reciprocal necessities, their hopes and their fears, must send them all in their turns to him that holds the balance of the state. The parties are the gamesters, but government keeps the table, and is sure to be the winner in the end. When this game is played, I really think it is more to be feared that the people will be exhausted than that government will not be supplied; whereas, whatever is got by acts of absolute power, ill obeyed, because odious or by contracts ill kept because constrained, will be narrow, feeble, uncertain, and precarious.

> "Ease would retract.
> Vows made in pain, as violent and void."

I, for one, protest against compounding our demands. I declare against compounding, for a poor, limited sum, the immense, ever-growing, eternal debt which is due to generous government from protected freedom. And so may I speed in the great object I propose to you, as I think it would not only be an act of injustice, but would be the worst economy in the world, to compel the colonies to a sum certain, either in the way of ransom or in the way of compulsory compact.

But to clear up my ideas on this subject: A revenue from America transmitted hither—do not delude yourselves—you never can receive it—no, not a shilling. We have experienced that from remote countries it is not to be expected. If, when you attempted to extract revenue from Bengal, you were obliged to return in loan what you had taken in imposition, what can you expect from North America? for certainly, if ever there was a country qualified to produce wealth, it is India; or an institution fit for the transmission, it is the East India Company. America has none of these aptitudes. If America gives you taxable objects on which you lay your duties here, and gives you, at the same time, a surplus by a foreign sale of her commodities to pay the duties on these objects which you tax at home, she has performed her part to the British revenue. But with regard to her own internal establishments, she may, I doubt not she will, contribute in moderation; I say in moderation, for she ought not to be permitted to exhaust herself. She ought to be reserved to a war, the weight of which, with the enemies that we are most likely to have, must be considerable in her quarter of the globe. There she may serve you, and serve you essentially.

For that service, for all service, whether of revenue, trade or empire, my trust is in her interest in the British Constitution. My hold of the colonies is in the close affection which grows from common names, from kindred blood, from similar privileges, and equal protection. These are ties which, though light as air, are as strong as links of iron. Let the colonies always keep the idea of their civil rights associated with your government; they will cling and grapple to you, and no force under heaven will be of power to tear them from their allegiance. But let it be once understood that your government may be one thing, and their privileges another; that these two things may exist without any mutual relation; the cement is gone; the cohesion is loosened; and everything hastens to decay and dissolution. As long as you have the wisdom to keep the sovereign authority of this country as the sanctuary of liberty, the sacred temple consecrated to our common faith, wherever the chosen race and sons of England worship freedom, they will turn their faces toward you. The more they multiply, the more friends you will have. The more ardently they love liberty, the more perfect will be their obedience. Slavery they can have anywhere. It is a weed that grows in every soil. They may have it from Spain; they may have it from Prussia; but, until you become lost to all feeling of your true interest and your natural dignity, freedom they can have from none but you. This is the commodity of price, of which you have the monopoly. This is the true Act of Navigation, which binds to you the commerce of the colonies, and through them secures to you the wealth of the world. Deny them this participation of freedom, and you break that sole bond which originally made, and must still preserve, the unity of the empire. Do not entertain so weak an imagination as that your registers and your bonds, your affidavits and your sufferances, your cockets and your clearances, are what form the great securities of your commerce. Do not dream that your letters of office, and your instructions, and your suspending clauses, are the things that hold together the great contexture of this mysterious whole. These things do not make your government. Dead instruments, passive tools as they are, it is the spirit of the English communion that gives all their life and efficacy to them. It is the spirit of the English Constitution which, infused through the mighty mass, pervades, feeds, unites, invigorates, vivifies every part of the empire, even down to the minutest member.

Is it not the same virtue which does everything for us here in England?

Do you imagine, then, that it is the land tax which raises your revenue, that it is the annual vote in the committee of supply which gives you your army? or that it is the mutiny bill which inspires it with bravery and discipline? No! surely no! It is the love of the people; it is their attachment to their government, from the sense of the deep stake they have in such a glorious institution, which gives you your army and your navy, and infuses into both that liberal obedience, without which your army would be a base rabble, and your navy nothing but rotten timber.

All this, I know well enough, will sound wild and chimerical to the profane herd of those vulgar and mechanical politicians, who have no place among us; a sort of people who think that nothing exists but what is gross and material, and who, therefore, far from being qualified to be directors of the great movement of empire, are not fit to turn a wheel in the machine. But to men truly initiated and rightly taught, these ruling and master principles, which, in the opinion of such men as I have mentioned, have no substantial existence, are in truth everything and all in all. Magnanimity in politics is not seldom the truest wisdom; and a great empire and little minds go ill together. If we are conscious of our situation, and glow with zeal to fill our place as becomes our station and ourselves, we ought to auspicate all our public proceeding on America with the old warning of the church, *sursum corda!* We ought to elevate our minds to the greatness of that trust to which the order of Providence has called us. By adverting to the dignity of this high calling, our ancestors have turned a savage wilderness into a glorious empire, and have made the most extensive and only honorable conquests, not by destroying, but by promoting, the wealth, the number, the happiness of the human race. Let us get an American revenue as we have got an American empire. English privileges have made it all that it is; English privileges alone will make it all it can be.

In full confidence of this unalterable truth, I now, *quod felix faustumque sit,* lay the first stone in the temple of peace; and I move you,

1. That the colonies and plantations of Great Britain in North America, consisting of fourteen separate governments, and containing two millions and upwards of free inhabitants, have not had the liberty and privilege of electing and sending any knights and burgesses, or others, to represent them in the high court of parliament.

[This is the first of thirteen resolutions Burke then presented to Parliament. All of them aimed to bring American representation into Parliament and proper treatment for the colonies. None of these resolutions was carried.]

To the Electors of Bristol

Mr. Mayor and Gentlemen:—

I am extremely pleased at the appearance of this large and respectable meeting. The steps I may be obliged to take will want the sanction of a considerable authority; and in explaining anything which may appear doubtful in my public conduct, I must naturally desire a very full audience.

I have been backward to begin my canvass. The dissolution of the Parliament was uncertain; and it did not become me, by an unseasonable importunity, to appear diffident of the fact of my six years' endeavor to please you. I had served the city of Bristol honorably; and the city of Bristol had no reason to think, that the means of honorable service to the public were become indifferent to me.

I found, on my arrival here, that three gentlemen had been long in eager pursuit of an object which but two of us can obtain. I found, that they had all met with encouragement. A contested election in such a city as this is no light thing. I paused on the brink of the precipice.

I am not come by a false and counterfeit show of deference to your judgment, to seduce it in my favor. I ask it seriously and unaffectedly. If you wish that I should retire I shall not consider that advice as a censure upon my conduct, or an alteration in your sentiments; but as a rational submission to the circumstances of affairs. If, on the contrary, you should think it proper for me to proceed on my canvass, if you will risk the trouble on your part, I will risk it on mine. My pretentions are such as you cannot be ashamed of, whether they succeed or fail.

Do you think, gentlemen, that every public act in the six years since I stood in this place before you—that all the arduous things which have been done in this eventful period, which has crowded into a few years' space the revolutions of an age, can be opened to you on their fair grounds in half an hour's conversation?

But it is no reason, because there is a bad mode of inquiry, that there should be no examination at all. Look, gentlemen, to the whole tenor of your member's conduct. Try whether his ambition or his avarice have justled him out of the straight line of duty; or whether that grand foe of the offices of active life, that master-vice in men of business, a degenerate and inglorious sloth, has made him flag and languish in his course? This is the object of our inquiry. If our member's conduct can bear this touch, mark it for sterling. He may have fallen into errors; he must have faults; but our error is greater, and our fault is radically ruinous to ourselves, if we do not bear, if we do not even applaud, the whole compound and mixed mass of such a character. He censures God, who quarrels with the imperfections of man.

Let me say with plainness, I who am no longer in a public character, that if by a fair, by an indulgent, by a gentlemanly behavior to our representatives, we do not give confidence to their minds, and a liberal scope to their understandings; if we do not permit our members to act upon a *very* enlarged view of things; we shall at length infallibly degrade our national representation into a confused and scuffling bustle of local agency. When the popular member is narrowed in his ideas, and rendered timid in his proceedings, the service of the Crown will be the sole nursery of statesmen. On the side of the people there will be nothing but impotence: for ignorance is impotence; narrowness of mind is impotence; timidity is itself impotence, and makes all other qualities that go along with it, impotent and useless.

At present it is the plan of the Court to make its servants insignificant. If the people should fall into the same humor, and should choose their servants on the same principles of mere obsequiousness, and flexibility, and total vacancy or indifference of opinion in all public matters, then no part of the State will be sound; and it will be in vain to think of saving it.

I thought it very expedient at this time to give you this candid counsel, and with this counsel I would willingly close, if matters, which at various times have been objected to me in this city, concerned only myself, and my own election. These charges, I think, are four in number: —my neglect of a due attention to my constituents, the not paying more frequent visits here; my conduct on the affairs of the first Irish Trade Acts; my opinion and mode of proceeding on Lord Beauchamp's debtor's bill; and my votes on the late affairs of the Roman Catholics. All of these (except, perhaps, the first) relate to matters of very considerable public concern; and it is not lest you should censure me improperly, but lest you should form improper opinions on matters of some moment to you, that I trouble you at all upon the subject. My conduct is of small importance.

With regard to the first charge, my friends have spoken to me of it in the style of amicable expostulation; not so much blaming the thing, as lamenting the effects. Others, less partial to me, were less kind in assigning the motives. But, gentlemen, I live at a hundred miles' distance from Bristol; and at the end of the Session I come to my own house, fatigued in body and mind, to a little repose, and to a very little attention to my family and my private concerns. A visit to Bristol is always a sort of canvass; else it would do more harm than good. To pass from the toils of a Session to the toils of a canvass is the furthest thing in the world for repose. I could hardly serve you *as I have done*, and court you too. Most of you have heard, that I do not remarkably spare myself in *public* business; and in the *private* business of my constituents, I have done very near as much as those who have nothing else to do. My canvass of you was not on the 'Change, nor in the county meetings, nor in the clubs of the city; it was in the House of Commons; it was at the Custom-house; it was at the council; it was at the Treasury; it was at the Admiralty. I canvassed you through your affairs, and not your persons. I was not only your representative as a body; I was the agent, the solicitor of individuals; I ran about wherever your affairs could call me; and in acting for you I often appeared rather as a shipbroker, than as a member of Parliament. There was nothing too laborious or too low for me to undertake. If some lesser matters have slipped through my fingers, it was because I filled my hands too full; and in my eagerness to serve you, took in more than any hands could grasp.

Since I have touched upon this matter, let me say, gentlemen, that if I had a disposition or a right to complain, I have some cause of complaint on my side. With a petition of this city in my hand, passed through the corporation without a dissenting voice, a petition in unison with almost the whole voice of the kingdom (with whose formal thanks I was covered over) while I labored on no less than five bills for a public reform, and fought against the opposition of great abilities, and of the greatest power, every clause and every word of the largest bills almost to the very last day of a very long Session; at this time a canvass in Bristol was as calmly carried on as if I were dead. I was considered as a man wholly out of the question. Whilst I watched, and fasted, and sweated in the House of Commons—but the most easy and ordinary arts of election, by dinners and visits, by "How do you do's" and "My worthy friends," I was to be quietly moved out of my seat—and promises were made, and engagements entered into, without any exception or reserve, as if my laborious zeal in my duty had been a regular abdication of my trust.

It has been said, and it is the second charge, that in the questions of the Irish trade, I did not consult the interests of my constituents, or, to speak out strongly, that I rather acted as a native of Ireland, than as an English member of Parliament.

I certainly have very warm good wishes for the place of my birth. But the sphere of my duties is in my true country. It was as a man attached to your interests, and zealous for the conservation of your power and dignity, that I acted on that occasion, and on all occasions. You were involved in the American War. A new world of policy was opened, to which it was necessary that we should conform, whether we would or not; and my only thought was how to conform to our situation in such a manner as to unite to this kingdom, in prosperity and in affection, whatever remained of the empire.

The whole kingdom of Ireland was instantly in a flame. Threatened by foreigners, and, as they thought, insulted by England, they resolved at once to resist the power of France, and to cast off yours. Forty thousand men were raised and disciplined without commission from the Crown. Two illegal armies were seen with banners displayed at the same time in the same country. In this unexampled state of things, which the least error, the least trespass on the right or left, would have hurried down the precipice into an abyss of blood and confusion.

A sudden light broke in upon us all. It broke in, not through well-contrived and well disposed windows, but through flaws and breaches; through the yawning chasms of our ruin. We were taught wisdom by humiliation. This scene of shame and disgrace has, in a manner, whilst I am speaking, ended by the perpetual establishment of a military power in the dominions of this Crown without consent of the British legislature, contrary to the policy of the constitution, contrary to the declaration of right: and, by this, your liberties are swept away along with your supreme authority—and both linked together from the beginning, have, I am afraid, both together perished forever.

I was an Irishman in the Irish business, just as much as I was an American, when, on the same principles, I wished to concede to America at a time when she prayed concession at our feet. Just as much was I an American, when I wished Parliament to offer terms in victory, and not to wait the hour of defeat, for making good, by weakness and by supplication, a claim of prerogative, pre-eminence, and authority.

The next article of charge on my public conduct, and that which I find rather the most prevalent of all, is Lord Beauchamp's bill. I mean his bill of last session, for reforming the law-process concerning imprisonment. It is said, to aggravate the offence, that I treated the petition of this city with contempt even in presenting it to the House, and expressed myself in terms of marked disrespect. Had this latter part of the charge been true, no merits on the side of the question which I took could possibly excuse me. But I am incapable of treating this city with disrespect. Very fortunately, at this minute, (if my bad eye-sight does not deceive me,) the worthy gentleman deputed on this business, stands directly before me. To him I appeal, whether I did not, though it militated with my oldest and most recent public opinions, deliver the petition with a strong and more than usual recommendation to the consideration of the House, on account of the character and consequence of those who signed it. I believe the worthy gentleman will tell you that, the very day I received it, I applied to the Solicitor, now the Attorney-General, to give it an immediate consideration; and he most obligingly and immediately consented to employ a great deal of his very valuable time to write an explanation of the bill.

But what will you say to those who blame me for supporting Lord Beauchamp's bill, as a disrespectful treatment of your petition, when you hear, that out of respect to you, I myself was the cause of the loss of that very bill? for the noble lord who brought it in, and who, I must say, has much merit for this and some other measures, at my request consented to put it off for a week, which the Speaker's illness lengthened to a fortnight; and then the frantic tumult about popery drove that and every rational business from the House. So that, if I chose to make a defense of myself, on the little principles of a culprit pleasing in his exculpation, I might not only secure my acquittal, but make merit with the opposers of the bill. But I shall do no such thing. The truth is, that I did occasion the loss of the bill, and by a delay caused by my respect to you.

Nothing now remains to trouble you with, but the fourth charge against me—the business of the Roman Catholics. It is a business closely connected with the rest. They are all on one and the same principle. My little scheme of conduct, such as it is, is all arranged. I could do nothing but what I have done on this subject, without confounding the whole train of my ideas, and disturbing the whole order of my life.

In explaining to you the proceedings of Parliament which have been complained of, I will state to you,—first, the thing that was done; next, the persons who did it; and, lastly, the grounds and reasons upon which the legislature proceeded in this deliberate act of public justice and public prudence.

Gentlemen, bad laws are the worst sort of tyranny. In such a country as this they are, of all bad things, the worst; worse by far than anywhere else; and they derive a particular malignity even from the wisdom and soundness of the rest of our institutions. For very obvious reasons, you cannot trust the Crown with a dispensing power over any of your laws. However, a government, be it as bad as it may, will in the exercise of a discretionary power, discriminate times and persons; and will not ordinarily pursue any man, when its own safety is not concerned. A mercenary informer knows no distinction. Under such a system, the obnoxious people are slaves, not only to the government, but they live at the mercy of every individual; they are at once the slaves of the whole community, and of every part of it; and the worst and most unmerciful men are those on whose goodness they most depend.

I find that it has been industriously given out in this city (from kindness to me unquestionably) that I was the mover [of this bill] or the seconder. The fact is, I did not once open my lips on the subject during the whole progress of the bill. I do not say this as disclaiming my share in the measure. Very far from it. I inform you of this fact, lest I seem to arrogate to myself the merits which belong to others. To have been the man chosen out to redeem one fellow-citizen from slavery, to purify our laws from absurdity and injustice, and to cleanse our religion from the blot and stain of persecution, would be an honor and happiness to which my wishes would undoubtedly aspire; but to which nothing but my wishes could have possibly entitled me.

Long before this act, indeed, the spirit of toleration began to gain ground in Europe. In Holland, the third part of the people are Catholics; they live at ease, and are a sound part of the state. In many parts of Germany, Protestants and Papists partake the same cities, the same councils, even the same churches. A worthy Protestant gentleman of this country now fills, and fills it with credit, a high office in the Austrian Netherlands. Even the Lutheran obstinacy of Sweden has thawed at length, and opened a toleration to all religions. I know myself, that in France the Protestants begin to be at rest. The first minister of finance in that country is a Protestant!

I must fairly tell you, that so far as my principles are concerned, (principles, that I hope will only depart with my last breath,) that I have no idea of a liberty unconnected with honesty and justice. Nor do I believe, that any good constitutions of government or of freedom, can find it necessary for their security to doom any part of the people to a permanent slavery.

Now, gentlemen, on this serious day, when I come, as it were to make up my account with you, let me take to myself some degree of honest pride on the nature of the charges that are against me. I do not here stand before you accused of venality, or of neglect of duty. It is not said, that, in the long period of my service, I have, in a single instance, sacrificed the slightest of your interests to my ambition, or to my fortune. It is not alleged, that, to gratify any anger, or revenge of my own, or of my party, I have had a share in wronging or oppressing any description of men, or any one man in any description, No! the charges against me are all of one kind, that I have pushed the principles of general justice and benevolence too far; further than a cautious policy would warrant; and further than the opinions of many would go along with me. In every accident which may happen through life, in pain, in sorrow, in depression, and distress—I will call to mind this accusation, and be comforted.

Gentlemen, I submit the whole to your judgment. Mr. Mayor, I thank you for the trouble you have taken on this occasion. In your state of health it is particularly obliging. If this company should think it advisable for me to withdraw, I shall resectfully retire; if you think otherwise, I shall go directly to the Council-house and to the 'Change, and, without a moment's delay, begin my canvass.

Patrick Henry

1736–1799

*Patrick Henry, a Virginian, self- or family-educated, be-
came a foremost American statesman and orator. He
delved into the history of Greece and Rome, England, and
of the American Colonies. He was admitted to the practice
of law reading by himself, but his examiners suggested that
he read further before he practiced. In 1763, when he was
twenty-seven, he delivered a speech in "The Parson's
Case," which drew to him many clients and great renown.
He won, for the parson, a large amount of money, and
Henry became the idol of the common people of Virginia.
In 1765 they sent him to the Virginia legislature. There
he made his first statement—to be quoted by the people for
generations. In support of the Virginia Resolutions he said,
"Tarquin and Caesar each had his Brutus, Charles the
First his Cromwell, and George the Third [here he was
interrupted by cries of "Treason!"]—may profit by their ex-
ample! If this be treason, make the most of it."*

*In 1775, in the second revolutionary convention of Vir-
ginia, Henry regarded the war as inevitable and presented
his plans for arming the Virginia militia. There in the capitol at Williamsburg he uttered the words which have rung
through the centuries: "Give me liberty, or give me
death!"*

GIVE ME LIBERTY, OR GIVE ME DEATH!

Mr. President:—No man thinks more highly than I do of
the patriotism, as well as abilities, of the very worthy
gentlemen who have just addressed the House. But different men often see the same subject in different lights;
and, therefore, I hope that it will not be thought disrespectful to those gentlemen, if, entertaining as I do,

opinions of a character very opposite to theirs, I shall speak forth my sentiments freely and without reserve. This is no time for ceremony. The question before the House is one of awful moment to this country. For my own part I consider it as nothing less than a question of freedom or slavery; and in proportion to the magnitude of the subject ought to be the freedom of the debate. It is only in this way that we can hope to arrive at truth, and fulfil the great responsibility which we hold to God and our country. Should I keep back my opinions at such a time, through fear of giving offence, I should consider myself as guilty of treason towards my country, and of an act of disloyalty towards the majesty of heaven, which I revere above all earthly kings.

Mr. President, it is natural to man to indulge in the illusions of hope. We are apt to shut our eyes against a painful truth, and listen to the song of that siren, till she transforms us into beasts. Is this the part of wise men, engaged in a great and arduous struggle for liberty? Are we disposed to be of the number of those who, having eyes, see not, and having ears, hear not, the things which so nearly concern their temporal salvation? For my part, whatever anguish of spirit it may cost, I am willing to know the whole truth; to know the worst and to provide for it.

I have but one lamp by which my feet are guided; and that is the lamp of experience. I know of no way of judging of the future but by the past. And judging by the past, I wish to know what there has been in the conduct of the British ministry for the last ten years, to justify those hopes with which gentlemen have been pleased to solace themselves and the House? Is it that insidious smile with which our petition has been lately received? Trust it not, sir; it will prove a snare to your feet. Suffer not yourselves to be betrayed with a kiss. Ask yourselves how this gracious reception of our petition comports with these war-like preparations which cover our waters and darken our land. Are fleets and armies necessary to a work of love and reconciliation? Have we shown ourselves so unwilling to be reconciled, that force must be called in to win back our love? Let us not deceive ourselves, sir. These are the implements of war and subjugation; the last arguments to which kings resort. I ask gentlemen, sir, what means this martial array, if its purpose be not to force us to submission? Can gentlemen assign any other possible motives for it? Has Great Britain any enemy, in this quarter of the world, to call for all this accumulation of navies and armies? No, sir, she has none. They are meant for us; they can be meant for no other. They are sent over to bind and rivet upon us those chains which the British ministry have been so long forging. And what have we to oppose to them? Shall we try argument? Sir, we have been trying that for the last ten years. Have we anything new to offer on the subject? Nothing. We have held the subject up in every light of which it is capable; but it has been all in vain. Shall we resort to entreaty and humble supplication? What terms shall we find which have not been already exhausted? Let us not, I beseech you, sir, deceive ourselves longer. Sir, we have done everything that could be done, to avert the storm which is now coming on. We have petitioned; we have remonstrated; we have supplicated; we have prostrated ourselves before the throne, and have implored its interposition to arrest the tyrannical hands of the ministry and Parliament. Our petitions have been slighted; our remonstrances have produced additional violence and insult; our supplications have been disregarded; and we have been spurned, with contempt, from the foot of the throne. In vain, after these things, may we indulge the fond hope of peace and reconciliation. There is no longer any room for hope. If we wish to be free—if we mean to preserve inviolate those inestimable privileges for which we have been so long contending—if we mean not basely to abandon the noble struggle in which we have been so long engaged, and which we have pledged ourselves never to abandon until the glorious object of our contest shall be obtained, we must fight! I repeat it, sir, we must fight! An appeal to arms and to the God of Hosts is all that is left us!

They tell us, sir, that we are weak; unable to cope with so formidable an adversary. But when shall we be stronger? Will it be the next week, or the next year? Will it be when we are totally disarmed, and when a British guard shall be stationed in every house? Shall we acquire the means of effectual resistance, by lying supinely on our backs, and hugging the delusive phantom of hope, until our enemies shall have bound us hand and foot? Sir, we are not weak, if we make a proper use of the means which the God of nature hath placed in our power. Three millions of people, armed in the holy cause of liberty, and in such a country as that which we possess, are invincible by any force which our enemy can send against us. Besides, sir, we shall not fight our battles alone. There is a just God who presides over the destinies of nations; and who will raise up friends to fight our battles for us. The battle, sir, is not to the strong alone; it is to the vigilant, the active, the brave. Besides, sir, we have no election. If we were base enough to desire it, it is now too late to retire from the contest. There is no retreat, but in submission and slavery! Our chains are forged! Their clanking may be heard on the plains of Boston! The war is inevitable—and let it come! I repeat it, sir, let it come!

It is in vain, sir, to extenuate the matter. Gentlemen may cry peace, peace—but there is no peace. The war is actually begun! The next gale that sweeps from the north will bring to our ears the clash of resounding arms! Our brethren are already in the field! Why stand we here idle? What is it that gentlemen wish? What would they have? Is life so dear, or peace so sweet, as to be purchased at the price of chains and slavery? Forbid it, Almighty God! I know not what course others may take; but as for me, give me liberty, or give me death!

William Jennings Bryan
1860–1925

*William Jennings Bryan held a position in the national
mind which few men have enjoyed. He was followed
blindly by masses of Americans, especially in the West,
and held up as a superior intellectual leader who would
carry the United States to unimagined glories in every
field of human and political experience. He was a man of
great integrity, a masterful orator with a magnetic, magnificent, and imposing appearance.*

*The speech here presented out of innumerable speeches
he made at every crossroads in America in his many
campaigns for the presidency of the United States is a
prime example of Bryan's style. This speech in 1896 led
to his nomination for the office of President; here he advocated the free coinage of silver, always an important
position to take with the miners of silver in the West. He
spoke in twenty-seven different states (at a time when
travel was not easy) and made six hundred speeches without the benefit of any microphone; but his voice could be
heard in the largest convention hall without straining either
his voice or the ears of his auditors. William McKinley,
the Republican candidate, however, was elected. Yet no
speech of McKinley remains impressed on the oratory of
the United States, but "The Cross of Gold" speech will
remain forever.*

THE CROSS OF GOLD

I would be presumptuous, indeed, to present myself
against the distinguished gentlemen to whom you have
listened if this were a mere measuring of abilities; but this
is not a contest between persons. The humblest citizen in
all the land, when clad in the armor of a righteous cause,

is stronger than all the hosts of error. I come to speak to you in defense of a cause as holy as the cause of liberty —the cause of humanity.

When this debate is concluded, a motion will be made to lay upon the table the resolution offered in commendation of the Administration, and also the resolution offered in condemnation of the Administration. We object to bringing this question down to the level of persons. The individual is but an atom; he is born, he acts, he dies; but principles are eternal; and this has been a contest over a principle.

Never before in the history of this country has there been witnessed such a contest as that through which we have just passed. Never before in the history of American politics has a great issue been fought out as this issue has been, by the voters of a great party. On the fourth of March, 1895, a few Democrats, most of them members of Congress, issued an address to the Democrats of the nation, asserting that the money question was the paramount issue of the hour; declaring that a majority of the Democratic party had the right to control the action of the party on this paramount issue; and concluding with the request that the believers in the free coinage of silver in the Democratic party should organize, take charge of, and control the policy of the Democratic party. Three months later, at Memphis, an organization was perfected, and the silver Democrats went forth openly and courageously proclaiming their belief, and declaring that, if successful, they would crystallize into a platform the declaration which they had made. Then began the conflict. With a zeal approaching the zeal which inspired the Crusaders who followed Peter the Hermit, our silver Democrats went forth from victory unto victory until they are now assembled, not to discuss, not to debate, but to enter up the judgment already rendered by the plain people of this country. In this contest brother has been arrayed against brother, father against son. The warmest ties of love, acquaintance, and association have been disregarded; old leaders have been cast aside when they have refused to give expression to the sentiments of those whom they would lead, and new leaders have sprung up to give direction to this cause of truth. Thus has the contest been waged, and we have assembled here under as binding and solemn instructions as were ever imposed upon representatives of the people.

We say to you that you have made the definition of a business man too limited in its application. The man who is employed for wages is as much a business man as his employer; the attorney in a country town is as much a business man as the corporation counsel in a great metropolis; the merchant at the crossroads store is as much a business man as the merchant of New York; the farmer who goes forth in the morning and toils all day, who begins in spring and toils all summer, and who by the application of brain and muscle to the natural resources of the country creates wealth, is as much a business man as the man who goes upon the Board of Trade and bets upon the price of grain; the miners who go down a thousand feet into the earth, or climb two thousand feet upon the cliffs, and bring forth from their hiding places the precious metals to be poured into the channels of trade are as much business men as the few financial magnates who, in a back room, corner the money of the world. We come to speak of this broader class of business men.

Ah, my friends, we say not one word against those who live upon the Atlantic Coast, but the hardy pioneers who have braved all the dangers of the wilderness, who have made the desert to blossom as the rose—the pioneers away out there [*pointing to the West*], who rear their children near to Nature's heart, where they can mingle their voices with the voices of the birds—out there where they have erected schoolhouses for the education of their young, churches where they praise their creator, and cemeteries where rest the ashes of their dead—these people, we say, are as deserving of the consideration of our party as any people in this country. It is for these that we speak. We do not come as aggressors. Our war is not a war of conquest; we are fighting in the defense of our homes, our families, and posterity. We have petitioned, and our petitions have been scorned; we have entreated, and our entreaties have been disregarded; we have begged, and they have mocked when our calamity came. We beg no longer; we entreat no more; we petition no more. We defy them!

The gentleman from Wisconsin has said that he fears a Robespierre. My friends, in this land of the free you need not fear that a tyrant will spring up from among the people. What we need is an Andrew Jackson to stand, as Jackson stood, against the encroachments of organized wealth.

They tell us that this platform was made to catch votes. We reply to them that changing conditions make new issues; that the principles upon which Democracy rests are as everlasting as the hills, but that they must be applied to new conditions as they arise. Conditions have arisen, and we are here to meet those conditions. They tell us that the income tax ought not to be brought in here; that is a new idea. They criticize us for our criticism of the Supreme Court of the United States. My friends, we have not criticized; we have simply called attention to what you already know. If you want criticisms, read the dissenting opinions of the court. There you will find criticisms. They say that we passed an unconstitutional law; we deny it. The income tax law was not unconstitutional when it was passed; it was not unconstitutional when it went before the Supreme Court for the first time; it did not become unconstitutional until one of the judges changed his mind, and we cannot be expected to know when a judge will change his mind. The income tax is just. It simply intends to put the burdens of government justly upon the backs of the people. I am in favor of an income tax. When I find a man who is not willing to bear his share of the burdens of the government which protects him, I find a man who is unworthy to enjoy the blessings of a government like ours.

They say that we are opposing national bank currency; it is true. If you will read what Thomas Benton said, you will find he said that, in searching history, he could find but one parallel to Andrew Jackson; that was Cicero, who destroyed the conspiracy of Catiline and saved Rome. Benton said that Cicero only did for Rome what Jackson did for us when he destroyed the bank conspiracy and saved America. We say in our platform that we believe that the right to coin and issue money is a function of government. We believe it. We believe that it is a part of sovereignty, and can no more with safety be delegated to private individuals than we could afford to delegate to private individuals the power to make penal statutes or levy taxes. Mr. Jefferson, who was once regarded as good Democratic authority, seems to have differed in opinion from the gentleman who has addressed us on the part of the minority. Those who are opposed to this proposition tell us that the issue of paper money is a function of the bank, and that the government ought to go out of the banking business. I stand with Jefferson rather than with them, and tell them, as he did, that the issue of money is a function of government, and that the banks ought to go out of the governing business.

They complain about the plank which declares against life tenure in office. They have tried to strain it to mean that which it does not mean. What we propose by that plank is the life tenure which is being built up in Washington, and which excludes from participation in official benefits the humbler members of society.

Let me call your attention to two or three important things. The gentleman from New York says that he will propose an amendment to the platform providing that the proposed change in our monetary system shall not affect contracts already made. Let me remind you that there is no intention of affecting those contracts which, according to present laws, are made payable in gold; but if he means to say that we cannot change our monetary system without protecting those who have loaned money before the change was made, I desire to ask him where, in law or in morals, he can find justification for not protecting the debtors when the act of 1873 was passed, if he now insists that we must protect the creditors.

He says he will also propose an amendment which will provide for the suspension of free coinage if we fail to maintain a parity within a year. We reply that when we advocate a policy which we believe will be successful, we are not compelled to raise a doubt as to our own sincerity by suggesting what we shall do if we fail. I ask him, if he would apply his logic to us, why he does not apply it to himself. He says he wants this country to try to secure an international agreement. Why does he not tell us what he is going to do if he fails to secure an international agreement? There is more reason for him to do that than there is for us to provide against the failure to maintain the parity. Our opponents have tried for twenty years to secure an international agreement, and those are waiting for it most patiently who do not want it at all.

And now, my friends, let me come to the paramount issue. If they ask us why it is that we say more on the money question than we say upon the tariff question, I reply that, if protection has slain its thousands, the gold standard has slain its tens of thousands. If they ask us why we do not embody in our platform all the things that we believe in, we reply that when we have restored the money of the Constitution all other necessary reforms will be possible; but that until this is done there is no other reform that can be accomplished.

Why is it that within three months such a change has come over the country? Three months ago when it was confidently asserted that those who believe in the gold standard would frame our platform and nominate our candidates, even the advocates of the gold standard did not think that we could elect a President. And they had good reason for their doubt, because there is scarcely a State here today asking for the gold standard which is not in the absolute control of the Republican party. But note the change. Mr. McKinley was nominated at St. Louis upon a platform which declared for the maintenance of the gold standard until it can be changed into bimetallism by international government. Mr. McKinley was the most popular man among the Republicans, and three months ago everybody in the Republican party prophesied his election. How is it today? Why, the man who was once pleased to think that he looked like Napoleon—that man shudders today when he remembers that he was nominated on the anniversary of the battle of Waterloo. Not only that, but as he listens he can hear with ever-increasing distinctness the sound of the waves as they beat upon the lonely shores of St. Helena.

Why this change? Ah, my friends, is not the reason for the change evident to any one who will look at the matter? No private character, however pure, no personal popularity, however great, can protect from the avenging wrath of an indignant people a man who will declare that he is in favor of fastening the gold standard upon this country, or who is willing to surrender the right of self-government and place the legislative control of our affairs in the hands of foreign potentates and powers.

We go forth confident that we shall win. Why? Because upon the paramount issue of this campaign there is not a spot of ground upon which the enemy will dare to challenge battle. If they tell us that the gold standard is a good thing, we shall point to their platform and tell them that their platform pledges the party to get rid of the gold standard and substitute bimetallism. If the gold standard is a good thing, why try to get rid of it? I call your attention to the fact that some of the very people who are in this Convention today and who tell us that we ought to declare in favor of international bimetallism—thereby declaring that the gold standard is wrong and that the principle of bimetallism is better—these very people four months ago were open and avowed advocates of the gold standard, and were then telling us that we could not legislate two metals together, even with the aid of all the world. If the gold standard is a good thing, we ought to declare in favor of its retention and not in favor of abandoning it; and if the gold standard is a bad thing why should we wait until other nations are willing to help us to let go? Here is the line of battle, and we care not upon which issue they force the fight; we are prepared to meet them on either issue or on both. If they tell us that the gold standard is the standard of civilization, we reply to them that this, the most enlightened of all the nations of the earth, has never declared for a gold standard and that both the great parties this year are declaring against it. If the gold standard is the standard of civilization, why, my friends, should we not have it? If they come to meet us on that issue we can present the history of our nation. More than that; we can tell them that they will search the pages of history in vain to find a single instance where the common people of any land have ever declared themselves in favor of the gold standard. They can find where the holders of fixed investments have declared for a gold standard, but not where the masses have. Mr. Carlisle said in 1878 that this was a struggle between "the idle holders of idle capital" and "the struggling masses, who produce the wealth and pay the taxes of the country"; and, my friends, the question we are to decide is: Upon which side will the Democratic party fight; upon the side of "the idle holders of idle capital" or upon the side of "the struggling masses"? That is the question which the party must answer first, and then it must be answered by each individual hereafter. The sympathies of the Democratic party, as shown by the platform, are on the side of the struggling masses who have ever been the foundation of the Democratic party. There are two ideas of government. There are those who believe that, if you will only legislate to make the well-to-do prosperous, their prosperity will leak through on those below. The Democratic idea, however, has been that if you legislate to make the masses prosperous, their prosperity will find its way up through every class which rests upon them.

You come to us and tell us that the great cities are in favor of the gold standard; we reply that the great cities rest upon our broad and fertile prairies. Burn down your cities and leave our farms, and your cities will spring up again as if by magic; but destroy our farms and the grass will grow in the streets of every city in the country.

My friends, we declare that this nation is able to legislate for its own people on every question, without waiting for the aid or consent of any other nation on earth; and upon that issue we expect to carry every state in the Union. I shall not slander the inhabitants of the fair state of Massachusetts nor the inhabitants of the state of New York by saying that, when they are confronted with the proposition, they will declare that this nation is not able to attend to its own business. It is the issue of 1776 over again. Our ancestors, when but three millions in number, had the courage to declare their political independence of every other nation; shall we, their descendants, when we have grown to seventy millions, declare that we are less independent than our forefathers?

No, my friends, that will never be the verdict of our people. Therefore, we care not upon what lines the battle is fought. If they say bimetallism is good, but that we cannot have it until other nations help us, we reply that, instead of having a gold standard because England has, we will restore bimetallism, and then let England have bimetallism because the United States has it. If they dare to come out in the open field and defend the gold standard as a good thing, we will fight them to the uttermost. Having behind us the producing masses of this nation and the world, supported by the commercial interests, the laboring interests and the toilers everywhere, we will answer their demand for a gold standard by saying to them: You shall not press down upon the brow of labor this crown of thorns, you shall not crucify mankind upon a cross of gold.

Frederick Douglass
1817–1895

Frederick Douglass, born in slavery in Talbot County, Maryland, escaped at the age of twenty-one and went to New York, then New Bedford, Massachusetts, where he supported himself as a day laborer. Though he was self-taught, his mind and imagination were aflame with the injustices he had witnessed as a child and growing young man. In the summer of 1841 at an antislavery convention at Nantucket he attracted attention to himself and his ideas demonstrating the makings of a really great orator for his causes.

In a short time he became the spokesman for his race and was in demand throughout the North. He traveled to England and there he was manumitted through the generosity of English friends. Back in the United States as a free man, he continued his campaign for his race and a contemporary said that "few men have spoken oftener, or more effectively, or to a larger number of the American people, than Frederick Douglass."

The first speech here was delivered at the National Hall, Philadelphia, Pennsylvania, on July 6, 1863, and in it he encouraged the enlistment of Negroes in the United States Army. The second address he delivered in the presence of President Grant, members of his Cabinet, senators, and representatives at the unveiling of the Emancipation Monument in memory of the Emancipation Proclamation of Abraham Lincoln. It resembles, in many ways, "I Have a Dream" of the Reverend Dr. Martin Luther King, Jr., delivered at the March on Washington. The latter part of the speech is omitted because it is almost entirely in praise of Abraham Lincoln and does not deal with Douglass' theme of civil rights.

NEGROES AND THE NATIONAL WAR EFFORT

Mr. President and Fellow Citizens:—

I shall not attempt to follow Judge Kelley [William D. Kelley, Republican Congressman of Philadelphia] and Miss Dickinson [Anna Dickinson, poet and abolitionist orator who had advocated the dividing of the large southern plantations among the Negroes] in their eloquent and thrilling appeals to the colored men to enlist in the service of the United States. They have left nothing to be desired on that point. I propose to look at the subject in a plain and practical common-sense light. There are obviously two versions to be taken of such enlistments—a broad view and a narrow view. I am willing to take both, and consider both. The narrow view of this subject is that which respects the matter of dollars and cents. There are those among us who say they are in favor of taking a hand in this tremendous war, but they add they wish to do so on terms of equality with white men. They say if they enter the service, endure all the hardships, perils and suffering—if they make bare their breasts, and with strong arms and courageous hearts confront rebel cannons, and wring victory from the jaws of death, they should have the same pay, the same rations, the same bounty, and the same favorable conditions every way offered to other men.

I shall not oppose this view. There is something deep down in the soul of every man present which assents to the justice of the claim thus made, and honors the manhood and self-respect which insists upon it. [*Applause*] I say at once, in peace and in war, I am content with nothing for the black man short of equal and exact justice. The only question I have, and the point which I differ from those who refuse to enlist, is whether the colored man is more likely to obtain justice and equality while refusing to assist in putting down this tremendous rebellion than he would be if he should promptly, generously and earnestly give his hand and heart to the salvation of the country in this its day of calamity and peril. Nothing can be more plain, nothing more certain than that the speediest and best possible way open to us to manhood, equal rights and elevation, is that we enter this service. For my own part, I hold that if the Government of the United States offered nothing more, as inducement to colored men to enlist, than bare subsistence and arms, considering the moral effect of compliance upon ourselves, it would be the wisest and best thing for us to enlist. [*Applause*] There is something ennobling in the possession of arms, and we of all other people in the world stand in need of their ennobling influence.

The case presented in the present war, and the light in which every colored man is bound to view it, may be stated thus. There are two governments struggling now for the possession of and endeavoring to bear rule over the United States—one has its capital in Richmond and is represented by Mr. Jefferson Davis, and the other has its capital in Washington, and is represented by "Honest Old Abe." [*Cheers and long-continued applause*] These two governments are today face to face, confronting each other with vast armies, and grappling each other upon many a bloody field, north and south, on the banks of the Mississippi, and under the shadow of the Alleghenies. Now, the question for every colored man is, or ought to be, what attitude is assumed by these respective governments and armies towards the rights and liberties of the colored race in this country; which is for us, and which is against us! [*Cries of "That's the question"*]

Now, I think there can be no doubt as to the attitudes of the Richmond or Confederate Government. Wherever else there has been concealment, here all is frank, open, and diabolically straight forward. Jefferson Davis and his government make no secret as to the cause of this war, and they do not conceal the purpose of the war. That purpose is nothing more or less than to make slavery of the African race universal and perpetual on this continent. It is not only evident from the history and logic of events, but the declared purpose of the atrocious war now being waged against the country. Some, indeed, have denied that slavery has anything to do with the war, but the very same men who do this affirm it in the same breath in which they deny it, for they tell you that the abolitionists are the cause of the war. Now, if the abolitionists are the cause of the war, they are the cause of it only because they have sought the abolition of slavery. View it in any way you please, therefore, the rebels are fighting for the existence of slavery—they are fighting for the privilege, the horrid privilege of sundering the dearest ties of human nature—of trafficking in slaves and the souls of men—for the ghastly privilege of scourging women and selling innocent children. [*Cries of "That's true"*]

I say this is not the concealed object of the war, but the openly confessed and shamelessly proclaimed object of the war. Vice President Stephens has stated, with the utmost clearness and precision, the difference between the fundamental ideals of the Confederate Government and those of the Federal Government. One is based upon the idea that colored men are an inferior race, who may be enslaved and plundered forever and to the heart's content of any man of a different complexion, while the Federal Government recognizes the natural and fundamental equality of all men. [*Applause*]

I say, again, we all know that this Jefferson Davis Government holds out to us nothing but fetters, chains, auction-blocks, bludgeons, branding irons, and eternal slavery and degradation. If it triumphs in this contest, woe, woe, ten thousand woes, to the black man! Such of us as are free, in all the likelihoods of the case, would be given over to the most excruciating tortures, while the last hope of the long-crushed bondman would be extinguished forever. [*Sensation*]

Now, what is the attitude of the Washington Government toward the colored race? What reason have we to desire its triumph in the present contest? Mind, I do not ask what was its attitude towards us before this bloody rebellion broke out. I do not ask what was its disposition when it was controlled by the very men who are now fighting to destroy it when they could no longer control it. I do not even ask what it was two years ago, when McClellan [George B. McClellan, major general in the

United States Army in 1861. He was opposed to the emancipation of the Negro and ordered his soldiers to return fugitive slaves to their owners. When Lincoln removed him from command he determined to run against him for the Presidency in 1864 on the Democratic ticket.] shamelessly gave out that in a war between loyal slaves and disloyal masters, he would take the side of the masters against the slaves—when he openly proclaimed his purpose to put down slave insurrections with an iron hand when glorious Ben Butler [*Cheers and applause*] [Benjamin F. Butler was at first a pro-slavery Democrat of Massachusetts; but in the course of the Civil War, he became a staunch anti-slavery man.] proffered his services to the Governor of Maryland to suppress a slave insurrection, while treason ran riot in that State, and the warm, red blood of Massachusetts soldiers still stained the pavements of Baltimore.

I do not ask what was the attitude of this government when many of the officers and men who had undertaken to defend it, openly threatened to throw down their arms and leave the service if men of color should step forward to defend it, and be invested with the dignity of soldiers. Moreover, I do not ask what was the position of this government when our loyal camps were made slave hunting grounds, and United States officers performed the disgusting duty of slave dogs to hunt down slaves for rebel masters. These were all dark and terrible days for the republic. I do not ask you about the dead past. I bring you the living present. Events more mighty than men, eternal Providence, all-wise and all-controlling, have placed us in new relation to the government and the government to us. What that government is to us today, and what it will be tomorrow, is made evident by a very few facts. Look at them, colored man. Slavery in the District of Columbia is abolished forever; the foreign slave trade, with its ten thousand revolting abominations, is rendered impossible; slavery in ten States of the Union is abolished forever; slavery in the five remaining States is to follow the same fate as the night is to follow the day. The independence of Haiti is recognized; her Minister sits beside our Prime

Minister, Mr. Seward, and dines at his table in Washington, while colored men are excluded from the cars in Philadelphia; showing that a blackman's complexion in Washington, in the presence of the Federal Government, is less offensive than in the city of brotherly love. Citizenship is no longer denied us under this government.

Under the interpretation of our rights by Attorney General Bates, we are American citizens. We can import goods, own and sail ships, and travel in foreign countries with American passports in our pockets; and now, so far from there being any opposition, so far from excluding us from the Army as soldiers, the President at Washington, the Cabinet and the Congress, the generals commanding and the whole army of the nation unite in giving us one thunderous welcome to share with them in the honor and glory of suppressing treason and upholding the star-spangled banner. The revolution is tremendous, and it becomes us as wise men to recognize the change and to shape our action accordingly. [*Cheers and cries of "We will"*]

I hold that the Federal Government was never in its essence, anything but an anti-slavery government. Abolish slavery tomorrow, and not a sentence or syllable of the Constitution need be altered. It was purposely so framed as to give no claim, no sanction to the claim of property in man. If in its origin slavery had any relation to the government, it was only as the scaffolding to the magnificent structure, to be removed as soon as the building was completed. There is in the Constitution no East, no West, no North, no South, no black, no white, no slaves, no slaveholder, but all are citizens who are of American birth.

Such is the government, fellow citizens, you are now called upon to uphold with your arms. Such is the government that you are called upon to cooperate with in burying rebellion and slavery in a common grave. [*Applause*] Never since the world began was a better chance offered to a long enslaved and oppressed people. The opportunity is given us to be men. With one courageous resolution we may blot out the handwriting of ages against us. Once let the black man get upon his person the brass letters U.S.; let him get an eagle on his button, and a musket on his shoulder, and bullets in his pocket, and there is no power on earth or under the earth which can deny that he has earned the right of citizenship in the United States. [*Laughter and applause*] I say again, this is our chance, and woe betide if we fail to embrace it. The immortal bard hath told us:

> "There is a tide in the affairs of men,
> Which, taken at the flood, leads to fortune.
> Omitted, all the voyage of their life
> Is bound in shallows and in miseries.
> We must take the current when it serves.
> Or lose our ventures."

Depend upon it, this is no time for hesitation. Do you say you want the same pay white men get? I believe that the justice and magnanimity of your country will speedily grant it. But will you be overnice in this matter? Do you get as good wages now as white men get by staying out of the service? Don't you work for less every day than white men get? You know you do. Do I hear you say you want black officers? Very well, and I have not the slightest doubt that in the progress of this war we shall see black officers, black colonels, and generals even. But is it not ridiculous in us in all at once refusing to be commanded by white men in time of war, when we are everywhere commanded by white men in time of peace? Do I hear you say still that you are a son, and want your mother provided for in your absence?—a husband, and want your wife cared for?—a brother, and want your sister secured against what? I honor you for your solicitude. Your mother, your wives and your sisters ought to be cared for, and an association of gentlemen, composed of responsible white and colored men, is now being organized in this city for this very purpose.

Do I hear you say you offered your services to Pennsylvania and were refused? I know it. But what of that? The State is not more than the Nation. The greater includes the lesser. Because the State refuses, you should all the more readily turn to the United States. [*Applause*] When the children fall out, they should refer their quarrels to the parents. "You came unto your own, and your own received you not." But the broad gates of the United States stand open night and day. Citizenship in the United States will, in the end, secure your citizenship in the State.

Young men of Philadelphia, you are without excuse. The hour has arrived, and your place is in the Union army. Remember that the musket—the United States musket with its bayonet of steel—is better than all mere parchment guarantees of liberty; and should your constitutional right at the close of the war be denied, which, in the nature of things, it cannot be, your brethren are safe while you have a Constitution which proclaims your right to keep and bear arms. [*Immense applause.*]

ORATION DELIVERED AT THE UNVEILING OF THE
EMANICIPATION MONUMENT IN LINCOLN SQUARE,
WASHINGTON, D.C., APRIL 14, 1876

Friends and Fellow Citizens:—

I warmly congratulate you upon the highly interesting object which has caused you to assemble in such numbers and spirit as you have today. This occasion is in some respects remarkable. Wise and thoughtful men of our race, who shall come after us, and study the lesson of our history in the United States; who shall survey the long and dreary spaces over which we have travelled; who shall count the links in the great chain of events by which we have reached our present position, will make note of this occasion; they will think of it and speak of it with a sense of manly pride and complacency.

I congratulate you, also, upon the very favorable circumstances in which we meet today. They are high, inspiring, and uncommon. They lend grace, glory, and significance to the object for which we have met. Nowhere else in this great country, with its uncounted towns and cities, unlimited wealth, and immeasurable territory extending from sea to sea, could conditions be found more favorable to the success of this occasion than here.

We stand today at the national centre to perform like a national act—an act which is to go into history; and we are here where every pulsation of the national heart can be heard, felt, and reciprocated. A thousand wires, fed with thought and winged with lightning, put us in instantaneous communication with the loyal and true men over this country.

Few facts could better illustrate the vast and wonderful change which has taken place in our condition as a people than the fact of our assembling here for the purpose we have today. Harmless, beautiful, proper, and praiseworthy as this demonstration is, I cannot forget that no such demonstration would have been tolerated here twenty years ago. The spirit of slavery and barbarism, which still lingers to blight and destroy in some dark and distant parts of our country, would have made our assembly here the signal and excuse for opening upon us all the flood-gates of wrath and violence. That we are here in peace today is a compliment and a credit to American civilization, and a prophecy of still greater national enlightenment and progress in the future. I refer to the past not in malice, for this is no day for malice; but simply to place more distinctly in front the gratifying and glorious change which has come both to our white fellow-citizens and ourselves, and—to congratulate all upon the contrast between now and then; the new dispensation of freedom with its thousand blessings to both races, and the old dispensation of slavery with its ten thousand evils to both races—white and black. In view, then, of the past, the present, and the future, with the long and dark history of our bondage behind us, and with liberty, progress, and enlightenment before us, I again congratulate you upon this auspicious day and hour.

[He then developed his speech reviewing the life and actions of Abraham Lincoln.]

Martin Luther King, Jr.

1928–

The Reverend Dr. Martin Luther King, Jr., founder and president of the Southern Christian Leadership Conference, received the Nobel Peace Prize in 1964 for his work in the cause of civil rights in the United States.

He is the son of a clergyman and co-pastor of the Ebenezer Baptist Church in Atlanta, Georgia. In Crozer Theological Seminary in Chester, Pennsylvania, he was an outstanding student and was so voted by his classmates. He received his Ph.D. from Boston College in 1955.

Every year he travels over two hundred thousand miles teaching, preaching, and conferring on the complicated problems of the Negro, but his most exciting national address was the following one given at the Lincoln Memorial on August 28, 1963, during the March on Washington.

I HAVE A DREAM

Five score years ago, a great American, in whose symbolic shadow we stand, signed the Emancipation Proclamation. This momentous decree came as a great beacon light of hope to millions of Negro slaves who had been seared in the flames of withering injustice. It came as a joyous daybreak to end the long night of captivity.

But one hundred years later, we must face the tragic fact that the Negro is still not free. One hundred years later, the life of the Negro is still crippled by the manacles of segregation and the chains of discrimination. One hundred years later, the Negro lives on a lonely island of poverty in the midst of a vast ocean of material prosperity. One hundred years later, the Negro is still languished in the corners of American society and finds himself an exile in his own land. So we have come here today to dramatize an appalling condition.

In a sense we have come to our nation's Capital to cash a check. When the architects of our republic wrote the magnificent words of the Constitution and the Declaration of Independence, they were signing a promissory note to which every American was to fall heir. This note was a promise that all men would be guaranteed the unalienable rights of life, liberty, and the pursuit of happiness.

It is obvious today that America has defaulted on this promissory note insofar as her citizens of color are concerned. Instead of honoring this sacred obligation, America has given the Negro people a bad check; a check which has come back marked "insufficient funds." But we refuse to believe that the bank of justice is bankrupt. We refuse to believe that there are insufficient funds in the great vaults of opportunity of this nation. So we have come to cash this check—a check that will give us upon demand the riches of freedom and the security of justice. We have also come to this hallowed spot to remind America of the fierce urgency of *now*. This is no time to engage in the luxury of cooling off or to take the tranquilizing drug of gradualism. *Now* is the time to make real the promises of Democracy. *Now* is the time to rise from the dark and desolate valley of segregation to the sunlit path of racial justice. *Now* is the time to open the doors of opportunity to all of God's children. *Now* is the time to lift our nation from the quicksands of racial injustice to the solid rock of brotherhood.

It would be fatal for the nation to overlook the urgency of the moment and to underestimate the determination of the Negro. This sweltering summer of the Negro's legitimate discontent will not pass until there is an invigorating autumn of freedom and equality. Nineteen sixty-three is not an end, but a beginning. Those who hope that the Negro needed to blow off steam and will now be content will have a rude awakening if the Nation returns to business as usual. There will be neither rest nor tranquility in America until the Negro is granted his citizenship rights. The whirlwinds of revolt will continue to shake the foundations of our Nation until the bright day of justice emerges.

But there is something that I must say to my people who stand on the warm threshold which leads into the palace of justice. In the process of gaining our rightful place we must not be guilty of wrongful deeds. Let us not seek to satisfy our thirst for freedom by drinking from the cup of bitterness and hatred.

We must forever conduct our struggle on the high plane of dignity and discipline. We must not allow our creative protest to degenerate into physical violence. Again and again we must rise to the majestic heights of meeting physical force with soul force. The marvelous new militancy which has engulfed the Negro community must not lead us to a distrust of all white people, for many of our white brothers, as evidenced by their presence here today, have come to realize that their destiny is tied up with our destiny and their freedom is inextricably bound to our freedom. We cannot walk alone.

And as we walk, we must make the pledge that we shall march ahead. We cannot turn back. There are those who are asking the devotees of civil rights, "when will you be satisfied?" We can never be satisfied as long as the Negro is the victim of unspeakable horrors of police brutality. We can never be satisfied as long as our bodies, heavy with the fatigue of travel, cannot gain lodging in the motels of the highways and the hotels of the cities. We cannot be satisfied as long as the Negro's basic mobility is from a smaller ghetto to a larger one. We can never be satisfied as long as a Negro in Mississippi cannot vote and a Negro in New York believes he has nothing for which to vote. No, no we are not satisfied, and we will not be satisfied until justice rolls down like waters and righteousness like a mighty stream.

I am not unmindful that some of you have come here out of great trials and tribulations. Some of you have come fresh from narrow cells. Some of you have come from areas where your quest for freedom left you battered by the storms of persecution and staggered by the winds of police brutality. You have been the veterans of creative suffering. Continue to work with the faith that unearned suffering is redemptive.

Go back to Mississippi, go back to Alabama, go back to South Carolina, go back to Georgia, go back to Louisiana, go back to the slums and ghettos of our northern cities, knowing that somehow this situation can and will be changed. Let us not wallow in the valley of despair.

I say to you today, my friends, that in spite of the difficulties and frustrations of the moment I still have a dream. It is a dream deeply rooted in the American dream.

I have a dream that one day this nation will rise up and live out the true meaning of its creed: "We hold these truths to be self-evident; that all men are created equal."

I have a dream that one day on the red hills of Georgia the sons of former slaves and the sons of former slave-owners will be able to sit down together at the table of brotherhood.

I have a dream that one day even the state of Mississippi, a desert state sweltering with the heat of injustice and oppression, will be transformed into an oasis of freedom and justice.

I have a dream that my four little children will one day live in a nation where they will not be judged by the color of their skin but by the content of their character.

I have a dream today.

I have a dream that one day the state of Alabama, whose governor's lips are presently dripping with the words of interposition and nullification, will be transformed into a situation where little black boys and black girls will be able to join hands with little white boys and white girls and walk together as sisters and brothers.

I have a dream today.

I have a dream that one day every valley shall be exalted, every hill and mountain shall be made low, and rough places will be made plains, and the crooked places will be made straight, and the glory of the Lord shall be revealed, and all flesh shall see it together.

This is our hope. This is the faith with which I return to the South. With this faith we will be able to hew out of the mountain of despair a stone of hope. With this faith we will be able to transform the jangling discords of our nation into a beautiful symphony of brotherhood. With this faith we will be able to work together, to pray together, to struggle together, to go to jail together, to stand up for freedom together, knowing that we will be free one day.

This will be the day when all of God's children will be able to sing with a new meaning "My country 'tis of thee, sweet land of liberty, of thee I sing. Land where my fathers died, land of the pilgrim's pride, from every mountainside, let freedom ring."

And if America is to be a great nation this must become true. So let freedom ring from the prodigious hilltops of New Hampshire. Let freedom ring from the mighty mountains of New York. Let freedom ring from the heightening Alleghenies of Pennsylvania!

Let freedom ring from the snowcapped Rockies of Colorado!

Let freedom ring from the curvaceous peaks of California!

But not only that; let freedom ring from Stone Mountain in Georgia!

Let freedom ring from Lookout Mountain of Tennessee!

Let freedom ring from every hill and molehill of Mississippi. From every mountainside, let freedom ring.

When we let freedom ring, when we let it ring from every village and every hamlet, from every state and every city, we will be able to speed up that day when all of God's children, black men and white men, Jews and Gentiles, Protestants and Catholics, will be able to join hands and sing the words of the old Negro spiritual, "Free at last! free at last! thank God Almighty, we are free at last!"

John Fitzgerald Kennedy

1917–1963

This speech was made by Senator Kennedy to the Greater Houston (Texas) Ministerial Association on September 12, 1960. As the Democratic nominee for the presidency, Kennedy was obliged to confront much strong feeling against a Catholic becoming President. The remarks here are the result of his effort to combine with dignity a statement of personal belief with a political purpose.

RELIGION IN GOVERNMENT

I am grateful for your generous invitation to state my views.

While the so-called religious issue is necessarily and properly the chief topic here tonight, I want to emphasize from the outset that I believe that we have far more critical issues in the 1960 election: the spread of Communist influence, until it now festers only ninety miles off the coast of Florida—the humiliating treatment of our President and Vice President by those who no longer respect our power—the hungry children I saw in West Virginia, the old people who cannot pay their doctor's bills, the families forced to give up their farms—an America with too many slums, with too few schools, and too late to the moon and outer space.

These are the real issues which should decide this campaign. And they are not religious issues—for war and hunger and ignorance and despair know no religious barrier.

But because I am a Catholic, and no Catholic has ever been elected President, the real issues in this campaign have been obscured—perhaps deliberately in some quarters less responsible than this. So it is apparently necessary for me to state once again—not what kind of church I believe in, for that should be important only to me, but what kind of America I believe in.

I believe in an America where the separation of church and state is absolute—where no Catholic prelate would tell the President (should he be a Catholic) how to act and no Protestant minister would tell his parishioners for whom to vote—where no church or church school is granted any public funds or political preference—and where no man is denied public office merely because his religion differs from the President who might appoint him or the people who might elect him.

I believe in an America that is officially neither Catholic, Protestant nor Jewish—where no public official either requests or accepts instructions on public policy from the Pope, the National Council of Churches or any other ecclesiastical source—where no religious body seeks to impose its will directly or indirectly upon the general populace or the public acts of its officials—and where religious liberty is so indivisible that an act against one church is treated as an act against all.

For while this year it may be a Catholic against whom the finger of suspicion is pointed, in other years it has been, and may someday be again, a Jew—or a Quaker—or a Unitarian—or a Baptist. It was Virginia's harassment of Baptist preachers, for example, that led to Jefferson's statute of religious freedom. Today, I may be the victim—but tomorrow it may be you—until the whole fabric of our harmonious society is ripped apart at a time of great national peril.

Finally, I believe in an America where religious intolerance will someday end—where all men and all churches are treated as equal—where every man has the same right to attend or not attend the church of his choice—where there is no Catholic vote, no anti-Catholic vote, no bloc voting of any kind—and where Catholics, Protestants and Jews, both the lay and the pastoral level, will refrain from those attitudes of disdain and division which have so often marred their works in the past, and promote instead the American ideal of brotherhood.

That is the kind of America in which I believe. And it represents the kind of Presidency in which I believe—a great office that must be neither humbled by making it the instrument of any religious group, nor tarnished by arbitrarily withholding it, its occupancy, from the member of any religious group. I believe in a President whose views on religion are his own private affair, neither imposed upon him by the nation or imposed by the nation upon him as a condition to holding that office.

I would not look with favor upon a President working to subvert the First Amendment's guarantees of religious liberty (nor would our system of checks and balances permit him to do so). And neither do I look with favor upon those who would work to subvert Article VI of the Constitution by requiring a religious test—even by indirection—for if they disagree with that safeguard, they should be openly working to repeal it.

I want a Chief Executive whose public acts are responsible to all and obligated to none—who can attend any ceremony, service or dinner his office may appropriately require him to fulfill—and whose fulfillment of his Presidential office is not limited or conditioned by any religious oath, ritual or obligation.

This is the kind of America I believe in—and this is the kind of America I fought for in the South Pacific and the kind my brother died for in Europe. No one suggested then that we might have a "divided loyalty," that we did "not believe in liberty" or that we belonged to a disloyal group that threatened "the freedom for which our forefathers died."

And in fact this is the kind of America for which our forefathers did die when they fled here to escape religious test oaths, that denied office to members of less favored churches, when they fought for the Constitution, the Bill of Rights, the Virginia Statute of Religious Freedom—and when they fought at the shrine I visited today—the Alamo. For side by side with Bowie and Crockett died Fuentes and McCafferty and Bailey and Bedillo and Carey—but no one knows whether they were Catholics or not. For there was no religious test there.

I ask you tonight to follow in that tradition, to judge me on the basis of fourteen years in the Congress—on my declared stands against an ambassador to the Vatican, against unconstitutional aid to parochial schools, and against any boycott of the public schools (which I attended myself)—instead of judging me on the basis of these pamphlets and publications we have all seen that carefully select quotations out of context from the statements of Catholic Church leaders, usually in other countries, frequently in other centuries, and rarely relevant to any situation here—and always omitting, of course, that statement of the American bishops in 1948 which strongly endorsed church-state separation.

I do not consider these other quotations binding upon my public acts—why should you? But let me say, with respect to other countries, that I am wholly opposed to the state being used by any religious group, Catholic or Protestant, to compel, prohibit or persecute the free exercise of any other religion. And that goes for any persecution at any time, by anyone, in any country.

And I hope that you and I condemn with equal fervor those nations which deny their Presidency to Protestants and those which deny it to Catholics. And rather than cite the misdeeds of those who differ, I would also cite the record of the Catholic Church in such nations as France and Ireland—and the independence of such statesmen as de Gaulle and Adenauer.

But let me stress again that these are my views—for contrary to common newspaper usage, I am not the Catholic candidate for President. I am the Democratic Party's candidate for President, who happens also to be a Catholic.

I do not speak for my church on public matters—and the church does not speak for me.

Whatever issue may come before me as President, if I should be elected—on birth control, divorce, censorship, gambling, or any other subject—I will make my decision in accordance with these views, in accordance with what my conscience tells me to be in the national interest, and without regard to outside religious pressure or dictate. And no power or threat of punishment could cause me to decide otherwise.

But if the time should ever come—and I do not concede any conflict to be remotely possible—when my office would require me to either violate my conscience, or violate the national interest, then I would resign the office, and I hope any other conscientious public servant would do likewise.

But I do not intend to apologize for these views to my critics of either Catholic or Protestant faith, nor do I intend to disavow either my views or my church in order to win this election. If I should lose on the real issues, I shall return to my seat in the Senate, satisfied that I tried my best and was fairly judged.

But if this election is decided on the basis that forty million Americans lost their chance of being President on the day they were baptized, then it is the whole nation that will be the loser in the eyes of Catholics and non-Catholics around the world, in the eyes of history, and in the eyes of our own people.

But if, on the other hand, I should win the election, I shall devote every effort of mind and spirit to fulfilling the oath of the Presidency—practically identical, I might add, with the oath I have taken for fourteen years in the Congress. For, without reservation, I can, and I quote, "solemnly swear that I will faithfully execute the office of President of the United States and will to the best of my ability preserve, protect and defend the Constitution, so help me God."

Learned Hand
1872–1961

Learned Hand has been called "one of the greatest American jurists," equal in many respects to Marshall, Holmes, Brandeis, and Cardozo. This high rating comes from the fact that the Supreme Court cited his opinions more often than those of any other lower-court jurist in the nation. He served fifteen years on the Federal District Court and was appointed by President Coolidge to the Circuit Court of Appeals. He was known as a "liberal" in the best sense of that word for decisions such as that against the suppression of the communistic magazine, New Masses and his declaration that James Joyce's Ulysses was not obscene. He was noted for his short, pithy speeches, of which this is one of the best. The speech was given on "I Am an American Day" in New York, N.Y., May 21, 1944.

THE SPIRIT OF LIBERTY

We have gathered here to affirm a faith, a faith in a common purpose, a common conviction, a common devotion. Some of us have chosen America as the land of our adoption; the rest have come from those who did the same. For this reason we have some right to consider ourselves a picked group, a group of those who had the courage to break from the past and brave the dangers and the loneliness of a strange land. What was the object that nerved us, or those who went before us, to this choice? We sought liberty: freedom from oppression, freedom from want, freedom to be ourselves. This we then sought; this we now believe that we are by way of winning. What do we mean when we say that first of all we seek liberty? I often wonder whether we do not rest our hopes too much upon constitutions, upon laws and upon courts. These are false hopes; believe me, these are false hopes. Liberty lies in the hearts of men and women; when it dies there, no constitution, no law, no court can save it; no constitution, no law, no court can even do much to help it. While it lies there, it needs no constitution, no law, no court to save it. And what is this liberty which must lie in the hearts of men and women? It is not the ruthless, the unbridled will; it is not freedom to do as one likes. That is the denial of liberty, and leads straight to its overthrow. A society in which men recognize no check upon their freedom, soon becomes a society where freedom is the possession of only a savage few; as we have learned to our sorrow.

What then is the spirit of liberty? I cannot define it; I can only tell you my own faith. The spirit of liberty is the spirit which is not too sure that it is right; the spirit of liberty is the spirit which seeks to understand the minds of other men and women; the spirit of liberty is the spirit which weighs their interests alongside its own without bias; the spirit of liberty remembers that not even a sparrow falls to earth unheeded; the spirit of liberty is the spirit of Him who, near two thousand years ago, taught mankind that lesson it has never learned, but has never quite forgotten: that there may be a kingdom where the least shall be heard and considered side by side with the greatest. And now in that spirit, that spirit of an America which has never been, and which may never be; nay, which never will be, except as the conscience and the courage of Americans create it; yet in the spirit of that America which lies hidden in some form in the aspirations of us all; in the spirit of that America for which our young men are at this moment fighting and dying; in the spirit of liberty and of America I ask you to rise and with me to pledge our faith in the glorious destiny of our beloved country.

I pledge allegiance to the flag of the United States of America and to the Republic for which it stands, one nation indivisible, with liberty and justice for all.

PART FIVE

SERMONS

Girolamo Savonarola
1452–1498

Savonarola, Dominican monk, orator, religious reformer of the Italian Renaissance, saw in the life of the people of Florence luxury, poverty, idleness, and sin. As a result of his observations he began a series of sermons in 1494 against the laxity of standards of life in the Church, the city, and the people. They were outstanding examples of eloquence for that day and this. The people listened speechless and after a sermon were fired with such zeal that they would have done whatever he suggested.

When the Medici were exiled from Florence in 1494 by the republicans under the dominance of Savonarola, the monk became the virtual ruler of the city, and put into execution a rule of life that would have endeared him to our own Puritan forefathers. In his evangelism he dared to speak against the kind of life that existed at the court of Pope Alexander VI. The Pope, for a period, silenced him, and then in 1497 excommunicated Savonarola.

Rioting filled the city of Florence, and city officials dared to arrest the monk and put him to torture, where, it was said, he confessed to have been a false prophet. He was hanged on a cross in the public square, then burned; but the flames he kindled in men's minds continued to rage for generations, so great was the impression his words had made on the people. This sermon was delivered to some 20,000 people on All Saints' Day, in the Duomo in Florence, November 1, 1494.

DO PENANCE, PENANCE, PENANCE

Poenitentiam agite: appropinquabit regnum coelorum, etc. . . .

Everyone who wishes to find his own salvation must

make an effort to do penance in this life, and I do not refrain from exclaiming: *agite poenitentiam,* do penance, for the kingdom of heaven shall thereby draw near to you; and I have called on everyone to enter the Ark. In the previous sermons I have spoken of the tokens possessed by those who have done true penance. The first token is that of gladness in understanding; to be seen in the true penitent in his happiness in everything that is enduring. The second token is that of enlightenment because he realizes that the simplicity of Christ's life and of all true Christians is the supreme happiness; and, thus, so much knowledge does the true penitent have that he recognizes the vanity of the entire world and its pleasures. The third token is the token of praise, for God is always praised in the true penitent's life and his speech is ever concerned with things divine and with the praise of God's glory. The fourth token is the conversation of the true penitent is the conversation of one with the good: one does not see the true penitent converse any longer with evil friends nor with worldly society but rather with the modest, the self-restrained, and the devout.

Know you, then, beloved friends, that our Ark has been completed and many good penitents have entered it. I had wished this morning to give you some moral admonitions to those who have entered, but it seems that I am not allowed to do so yet, and I will declare the reason to you.

But first I turn to you, My Almighty God, confessing my ignorance. You have truly conquered me, Oh Lord, and before your Presence, I am bewildered. I had believed, Oh Lord, how sublime your goodness was and how infinite your mercy, but my imagination could not soar so high as to comprehend your mercy. I saw the great and grave sins of the masses of people; I saw and considered the obstinacy so entrenched within their hearts that I supposed, Oh Lord, that they could not receive from you any further mercy but were only awaiting their punishment, and I felt that one should look after only those who are converted and have entered the Ark of moral living. And I wished to give them the instructions necessary for their preservation, and I imagined that the earth would open up and swallow the wicked and obstinate ones because they would not find further mercy in you. But I was told: "Wait; speak yet to them, and call to penance those who are full of corruption and sin." For this reason, Oh Lord, have I said that you have conquered me and that my imagination did not soar so high.

Therefore, my beloved, I shall not preach this morning, but we shall speak to and call to repentance all who desire to return.

Oh sinners, Oh obstinate ones, Oh half-hearted ones, Oh all who wait until the last moment to repent, *agite poenitentiam* do penance; do it immediately; do no longer put if off for the Lord Himself awaits you and He calls. Harken to my words, not as if they came from me, but as if they came from God Himself. I can do no more than say, *agite poenitentiam.* See how good and how full of mercy God is and how He wants to lead you to the Ark and thus to save you. Come you sinners, come, for God calls you. I have great sorrow and great compassion for you. Come in this solemn Festival of All Saints, which we celebrate to-day. When I think of it, my own sorrow increases fearfully because whenever I compare the joy and blessed state that the Saints enjoy to your misery I cannot but feel woe-fully sorry for you for the sake of charity. So great is their joy and contentment that not only one cannot speak of it, but one cannot even picture it in his mind . . . Oh insen-sate men who in their sinning are yet willing to lose so much peace and rest, *agite poenitentiam,* do penance; re-turn to God and there you will find repose; repent you of your sins; confess; make firm your intention never to sin again; receive the Holy Sacrament which will make you, also, to be blessed! When we consider those who are con-verted and who follow the way of living the good Christian life and who confess and receive Holy Communion often, we see in them almost a divinity, a modesty, a spiritual joy. Their faces have assumed an almost angelic appearance. And, *e converso,* on the other side, looking upon the faces of the wicked and perversely obstinate and especially upon the faces of certain religious ecclesiastics when they are unlimited in their vices, these people we see as demons, and worse than members of the church. And, *tamen*, these ecclesiastics use the Sacrament every day! See what a difference is the effect upon them. This Sacrament softens the hearts of the good people and causes perfect modesty in them; the contrary is seen in the actions of the sinful. Thus I thought and have spoken; if this Sacrament in which one has placed his faith in what is invisible to him, will thus give so much joy to one who, well disposed, takes it, and Oh how much greater will be and is this happiness among those blessed spirits who *facie* [sic] *ad faciem*, that is, face to face, see Him and rejoice in Him. Oh human heart, who do you not thaw and melt in so much sweetness and in so great a love. . . .

Super flumina Babylonis illic sedimus, flevimus. The Israelites, deploring and remembering their Babylonian captivity, said: "Upon the rivers of Babylon we sat down and wept," and thought back upon the country whence they had been uprooted, and thereupon mourned, wept and said: *applicavimus organa salicibus,* that is, "We do not rejoice any longer with song and music but we have hung our musical instruments on willow trees, and we weep by the rivers of Babylon." Oh Florence, you are sitting on the rivers of your sins! Make a river of your tears to wash them away; remember the celestial abode whence your soul came; seek through penance to return to that abode, just as did the Israelites. One cannot sing but can only weep in an alien land, that is, in you who, through sins, are become strangers and removed from God . . .

Oh you rich, Oh you poor, do penance; and you rich ones, give alms to the poor ones from your wealth. *Peccata tua elemosinis redime.* Oh you who fear God, be charitable and do not fear tribulations, because even in your tribulations God will bring you much consolation. Penance is the only remedy; and if you will do penance, you will remove a great portion of the tribulations. *Agite poenitentiam* and remove the sins that are the cause of your tribulations.

It is still your ingratitude, on the other hand, Oh Florence, that is the cause of your tribulations: *ingratitudo extinguit fontem divinae pietatis.* Oh ungrateful Florence!

God has spoken and you refuse to hear Him. Had the Turks heard what you heard, they would have done penance for their sins. On my part, I have shouted and declaimed so much that I know not what more to say . . .

Remember what I used to tell you: God shall take away your mind and understanding; and you shall seem drunk and shall not know what to do. Oh Florence, God had many blessings ready for you, and blessed would you be had you believed them. *Praeterea*, do you not recall my telling you that God wished to revive His Church and His Christian people by the sword and very soon? Do you not recall that I told you that God foretold you that these governments were not pleasing to Him? You now see how everything is accomplished as I predicted for all the matters that I announced *in verbo Domini* not a single iota shall fail to pass. You know how contradicted I was by others regarding the things that I uttered on the renewal of the Church; and although there were many oppositions, I did not remain silent . . .

Would that at least you might be moved to compassion because I am much grieved in the very fact of you yourselves and your salvation. What do I want from you, Oh Florence, if not that you be saved and do well, and nothing more? Other cities have told me that if I had done and accomplished for them what I have done and accomplished within you, they would have acquired a moral quality other than yours. Thus I plead with you all that you be no longer obstinate, but that you be converted to the Lord and soon do penance; for I do not tell you this without reason . . .

Oh priests of the Church, hear my words, Oh priests, Oh prelates of the Church of Christ give up your benefices that you are not able to serve; give up your pomp and your riotous meetings and banquets that you give so magnificently . . . Say your mass with devotion; if you do not, if you are not willing to fathom what God wishes, you will finally lose both the benefices and life itself . . .

Oh monks, give up the extravagance of your wardrobe and your vessels of silver and the full-bellied fatness of your abbeys and benefices. Give yourselves to simplicity and work with your hands as did the ancestral monks, your fathers, your predecessors; otherwise if you do not do it voluntarily, there will come the time when you will be made to do it by force.

Oh nuns, give up, give up you, also, your extravagances; give up your simonies when you accept in the place of nuns those who come to stay in your nunneries; give up such decorations and unnecessary pomp at the time when your sisters are made nuns; give up your elaborate songs, weep, I say, as quickly as possible for your failings and your faults. If you do not, I say that soon will come the time of weeping and not singing.

Oh my brothers, to you I say, give up your extravagances, your paintings, and your ornaments. Make your wearing apparel not with such fullness and make it of material less thickly woven. Do you not realize that your extravagances are taking alms away from the destitute? Oh brothers, Oh children, it is necessary to speak frankly in this way, that no one may say, "I did not know about it," and thus make excuse. I am required to speak thus *et vae mihi si non evangeliz a vero*. Woe to me were I not to say it! I say to you that if you will not listen to the voice of God, He will punish you.

Oh merchants, give up your usuries; give back other people's goods and the things that in truth belong to others; otherwise, I say, you will lose everything.

You who have everything in excess, give it to the poor, for it is not yours. Bring it to the Society of Santo Martino, so that they may distribute it to the poor, timid persons, because they often die of hunger while you are living with more than you need. Give it, I entreat you, to the good people of Santo Martino, bring it to them; I do not say to me or to my brother monks for it is not our duty to distribute alms to the poor. You poor ones, go to those who distribute the city's alms and you shall be helped. I say that he who has in excess should give it to the poor, and even more, I tell you that it is now time to give of your superfluity.

Oh priests, I must come back to you; I mean the bad priests, because I am always full of reverence for the good ones. Give up, I say, that unspeakable vice, give up that accursed vice that has so greatly provoked the wrath of God upon you; if not, woe, woe to you! Oh lustful creatures, dress yourselves in haircloth and do that penance which you need! Oh you who have your house full of vanities, pictures, statues and indecent things and evil books and poetry contrary to the faith, bring them to me to make a bonfire or a sacrifice to God. And you, mother, who adorns your daughter with so much vanity and extravagance and fancy hair ornaments, bring all those things here to us to throw into the fire, so that when the wrath of God comes, He will not find them in your houses. And then, I command you as a father, if you will do thus in these things, as I have told you, you will be acceptable, you alone who do this, to satisfy the wrath of God; otherwise, I should regret to have to bring you bad tidings.

Vox dicentis: clama, a voice that says, cry aloud. *O Italia, propter peccata tua venient tibi adversa.* Oh all you cities of Italy, the time has come to punish you for your sins. Oh Italy because of your lust and lechery, avarice, pride, ambition and your robberies and extortions, you shall be visited by many misfortunes and scourges.

Vox dicentis: clama, a voice that says, cry aloud. Oh Florence! Oh Florence! Oh Florence! Because of your sins, cruelty, avarice, lust, ambition, you shall receive many misfortunes and many anguishes.

Vox dicentis: clama, and what does the voice cry aloud? Oh tonsured heads of the priesthoood and brotherhoods, Oh clergy, you who are the principal cause of all these evils, through your wicked doing comes all this tempest, and because of your sins many tribulations have been made ready for all of us. Woe, woe I say to whomever has a tonsured head.

Oh Florence I have wished to speak to you this morning and to everyone in particular and openly for I could not do otherwise. And yet again a voice cried aloud *vox dicentis: clama,* the voice of one saying "I cry aloud" I have cried aloud to everyone to repent: *clama ad Dominum Deum tuum* I cried and shouted to your Lord God. I turned to you, Oh Lord, that we be in a state of death through our love of ourselves and through our sins. *Parce, Domine, popula tuo,* pardon, Oh Lord, the Florentine people who desire to be your own. I commit to your charge this people.

We are all celebrating the Festival of All Saints. I pray you, blessed Saints, through the virtue of your festival that you entreat the Lord God for this people. And you, Oh God, that you give of your mercy to all those who have taken part in this day's festival . . . give to this people a true recognition of yourself and a true penitence for their sins.

Translated by Sandro Sticca

Cotton Mather
1663–1728

Cotton Mather, a Congregational minister of Boston, Massachusetts, in his life and writings presented the image of the righteous minister. He exemplified also the tyranny of that time in upholding the Puritan idea, yet his religious pronouncements and writings had great influence. He had the power of eloquence fired with the zeal of a crusader against evil, as he understood it. He had an important part in the Salem witch trials of 1692–93, wherein he saw evil spread across the country and set his power to remove it forever from the face of America, if not the world.

THE JOYFUL SOUND OF SALVATION

Blessed is the people that know the joyful sound. *Psalms* 89:15

In the Gospel, and the ordinances of it, there is a joyful sound, which we are made partakers of. A true knowledge of this joyful sound, will render the people that have it, *a blessed people.*

Let us proceed more distinctly, in three propositions, to consider what we have before us.

First, there is a *joyful sound,* which is to be heard among the children of men, where the Gospel is published, and where the ordinances of it are established. The sound of silver trumpets which entertained the ancient Israelites, in and for their solemn assemblies, was no less typical than musical.

There is a *sound* in the Gospel, and the ordinances thereof; and it is, first, a *great sound.* Oh! were we so much "in the spirit on the Lord's Day" as to hear, what is to be heard in the Gospel that brought unto us, we should be able to say, I heard a great voice as of a trumpet. There is a famous prophecy "The great trumpet shall be blown, and they that were ready to pass, shall come and worship the Lord." Whatever other accomplishments this prophecy may have, it is very gloriously accomplished in the proclamation which our Savior in His Gospel makes unto us. The Gospel, as with the sound of a trumpet, invites the sinners ready to perish. O come and worship, and obey, and enjoy the Lord. And when this great trumpet is blown, *great, great* is the sound thereof. The sound of the trumpet is great in the *extent* of it. We read, "The sound goes into all the earth." In less than forty years, it reached into the utmost bounds of the vast Roman Empire; and though Satan seduced numbers of miserables into America, that they might be out of its hearing, it has now reached hither also. The silver trumpets were at first but a couple, for the two sons of Aaron; but afterward, in Solomon's time, we find an hundred and twenty silver trumpets all sounding together. Before the incarnation of our Savior, His Gospel was heard but a little way. Afterwards, it sounded far and near, and the Gospel was *preached unto every creature:* it might be said, it *sounds in every place.* The sound of the trumpet is also *great* in the *effect* of it. A loud sound, indeed; so loud, as to awaken them that have a dead sleep upon them! So loud, as to convey life unto them that lie dead in trespass and sin: "The hour now is, when the dead hear the voice of the Son of God and live." The sound of the trumpet fetches back the lost souls of all the elect from the power of Satan unto God. They are not silver trumpets that are now sounding unto us; but they are saving trumpets! Faith comes, the love of God comes, by the hearing of them. What are they, but the power of God unto Salvation.

Secondly. 'Tis a good sound as well as a great one. No trumpet can give so good, so grateful, so lovely a sound as the trumpets of the Gospel do. Fame often in her trumpet, has a sound, which may not be relied upon; but every trumpet of the Gospel gives a sound, of none but faithful sayings, and worthy of all acceptation. We are told: "As cold water to a thirsty soul, so is good news from a far country." In the trumpets of the Gospel, we have the sound of nothing but good news "from a far country." The sound which we hear in the trumpets of the Gospel, is what was once heard from the mouth of an angel: "Behold I bring you good tidings of great joy, that unto you there is born a Savior." . . . The joyful sound, which here distinguishes a blessed people, may carry allusion to the trumpets of jubilee, heard once in fifty years among the Israelites. Once in fifty years, there was that custom observed: "Then shalt thou cause the trumpets of jubilee to sound, and ye shall proclaim liberty throughout the land." Certainly the trumpets of September, proclaiming the acceptable year of the Lord, made a very good sound unto the poor people that were now to see a release from various miseries: a good sound unto the servants, who were now to call for and to take up their indentures: a good sound unto the debtors, whose mortgages were now expired, and whose tenements returned to them. Thus where the Gospel arrives, it brings a jubilee with it. It proclaims a liberty for the captives; a redemption for the miserable; a recovery of what we sinned away.

No wonder, then, if *thirdly*, it be a glad sound, when we find it such a good one. A joyful sound! the souls that are effectually called by the sound of the Gospel, how joyful does it render them! The trumpets of the Gospel do to the soul as the harps of David did to Saul: they drive away the evil spirit of sorrow, of sadness, of despair. The Psalmist could say, "I was glad when they said unto me, Let us go into the house of the Lord." The trumpets which gave a joyful sound unto the blessed people, had among other intentions of them; they were for calling the assembly. Glad, glad at heart, was that Israelite indeed, when he heard the trumpets give that call: "Come away to the sacrifices!" The trumpets of the Gospel call us to those appointments of God wherein we are to glorify Him with the sacrifices of righteousness; and how glad will a sincere Christian be of such invitations! . . . when the Gospel was preached with success: "There was great joy in the city." Well might there be so, as such a joyful sound! How joyful is the soldier when the trumpet invites him "to the spoil! to the spoil!" The joyful sound of the Gospel carried this in it: else it had not been said, "I rejoice at thy word, as one that findeth great spoil." The blessings which the word of God lead us to, are matchless treasures.

The blessedness of the people who thus know this joyful sound is very glorious blessedness.

But more particularly, *First,* In the joyful sound, we have the guide to blessedness. The silver trumpets put us into the way, unto the "rest that remaineth for the people of God." We are ignorant of the way to blessedness; and the way of peace we have not known. But where the trumpets of the Gospel sound, there is a fulfillment of that word: "Thine ears shall hear a word behind thee, saying, this is the way, walk in it."

Secondly. In the joyful sound we have the cause of blessedness. The silver trumpets are like the golden pipes of Zechariah, which convey the golden oil of grace into the souls of men. 'Tis by them that God fetches men out of the graves, in which they lie sinfully and woefully putrefying; and infuses a principle of piety into them; and inclines them to the things that are holy, and just, and good. That effectual calling which brings men into blessedness, 'tis in the trumpets of the Gospel that the spirit of God gives it unto His chosen ones; men hear the word of the Gospel and believe.

John Wesley

1703–1791

John Wesley with his younger brother, Charles, was the founder of a "Methodist" society. Charles had really established the society as a student at Christ Church, Cambridge. John, also a student at the same college, became the leader of the society in 1729. John had been ordained a priest in the Church of England, and his work with the group derisively called Methodists did not at that time interfere with his own ordination. He was interested, primarily, in "field preaching," that is, out-of-doors meetings, or preachings in buildings not necessarily churches. Charles was never the great preacher that John became, but was, rather, the writer of many hymns that are still sung in many churches.

Wesley is said to have preached some forty thousand sermons and traveled many thousands of miles in his ministry. He became detached from the Church of England; he and George Whitehead held the peasantry of England attentive to their message of salvation through faith in Christ alone. John Wesley was a man of deep learning and autocratic temper but with a powerful attraction to his listeners. The auditors were for the most part the workers, young apprentices, housewives, and laborers in England; his message had a freshness which the sermons of the Church of England did not have. Each sermon was a personal appeal to each individual, and the listeners were moved by such intensity and individuality.

GOD'S LOVE TO FALLEN MAN

How innumerable are the benefits which God conveys to the children of men through the channel of sufferings, so that it might well be said, "What are termed afflictions in the language of men are in the language of God styled blessings." Indeed, had there been no suffering in the world, a considerable part of religion, yea, and in some respects, the most excellent part, could have had no place therein: since the very existence of it depends on our suffering: so that had there been no pain it could have had no being. Upon this foundation, even our suffering, it is evident all our passive graces are built; yea, the noblest of all Christian graces, love enduring all things. Here is the ground for resignation to God, enabling us to say from the heart, in every trying hour, "It is the Lord: let him do what seemeth Him good." "Shall we receive good at the hand of the Lord, and shall we not receive evil?" And what a glorious spectacle is this! Did it not constrain even a heathen to cry out, *"Ecce spectaculum Deo dignum!"* See a sign worthy of God: a good man struggling with adversity, and superior to it. Here is the ground for confidence in God, both with regard to what we feel and with regard to what we should fear, were it not that our soul is calmly stayed on him. What room could there be for trust in God if there was no such thing as pain or danger? Who might not say then, "The cup which my Father had given me, shall I not drink it?" It is by sufferings that our faith is tried, and, therefore, made more acceptable to God. It is in the day of trouble that we have occasion to say, "Though he slay me, yet will I trust in him." And this is well pleasing to God, that we should own him in the face of danger; in defiance of sorrow, sickness, pain or death.

Again: Had there been neither natural nor moral evil in the world, what must have become of patience, meekness, gentleness, long-suffering? It is manifest they could have had no being: seeing all these have evil for their object. If, therefore, evil had never entered into the world, neither could these have had any place in it. For who could have returned good for evil, had there been no evildoer in the universe? How had it been possible, on that supposition, to overcome evil with good?

Will you say, "But all these graces might have been divinely infused into the hearts of men." Undoubtedly they might: but if they had, there would have been no use or exercise for them. Whereas in the present state of things we can never long want occasion to exercise them. And the more they are exercised, the more all our graces are strengthened and increased. And in the same proportion as our resignation, our confidence in God, our patience and fortitude, our meekness, gentleness, and long-suffering, together with our faith and love of God and man increase, must our happiness increase, even in the present world.

Yet again: As God's permission of Adam's fall gave all his posterity a thousand opportunities of suffering, and thereby of exercising all those passive graces which increase both their holiness and happiness: so it gives them opportunities of doing good in numberless instances, of exercising themselves in various good works, which otherwise could have had no being. And what exertions of benevolence, of compassion, of godlike mercy, had been totally prevented! Who could then have said to the lover of men,—

> "Thy mind throughout my life be shown,
>   While listening to the wretches' cry,
> The widow's or the orphan's groan;
>   On Mercy's wings I swiftly fly,
> The poor and needy to relieve;
> Myself, my all for them to give"?

It is the just observation of a benevolent man,—

> "All worldly joys are less
> Than that one of joy doing kindnesses."

Surely in keeping this commandment, if no other, there is great reward. "As we have time, let us do good unto all men"; good of every kind and in every degree. Accordingly the more good we do (other circumstances being equal), the happier we shall be. The more we deal our bread to the hungry, and cover the naked with garments; the more we relieve the stranger, and visit them that are sick or in prison: the more kind offices we do to those that groan under the various evils of human life,—the more com-

fort we receive even in the present world; the greater the
recompense we have in our own bosom.

To sum up what has been said under this head: As the
more holy we are upon earth, the more happy we must
be (seeing there is an inseparable connection between
holiness and happiness); as the more good we do to others, the more of present reward redounds into our own
bosom: even as our sufferings for God lead us to rejoice in
him "with joy unspeakable and full of glory": therefore the
fall of Adam first, by giving us an opportunity of being far
more holy; secondly, by giving us the occasions of doing
innumerable good works which otherwise could not have
been done; and, thirdly, by putting it into our power to
suffer for God, whereby "the Spirit of glory and of God
rests upon us"; may be of such advantage to the children
of men even in the present life, as they will not thoroughly
comprehend till they attain life everlasting.

It is then we shall be enabled fully to comprehend, not
only the advantages which accrue at the present time to
the sons of men by the fall of their first parent, but the
infinitely greater advantages which they may reap from
it in eternity. In order to form some conception of this we
may remember the observation of the Apostle, "As one star
differeth from another star in glory, so also in the resurrec-
tion of the dead." The most glorious stars will undoubtedly be those who are the most holy; who bear most of
that image of God wherein they were created. The next in
glory to these will be those who have been most abundant
in good works: and next to them, those that have suffered
most, according to the will of God.

But what advantages in every one of these respects will
the children of God receive in heaven by God's permitting
the introduction of pain upon earth in consequence of sin?
By occasion of this they attained many holy tempers which
otherwise could have had no being: resignation to God,
confidence in him in times of trouble and danger, patience,
meekness, gentleness, long-suffering, and the whole train
of passive virtues. And on account of this superior holiness
they will then enjoy superior happiness.

Again: every one will then "receive his own reward, according to his own labor." Every individual will be "rewarded according to his work." But the fall gave rise to innumerable good works which could otherwise never have existed, such as ministering to the necessities of the saints, yea, relieving the distressed in every kind. And hereby innumerable stars will be added to their eternal crown. Yet again: there will be an abundant reward in heaven, for suffering, as well as for doing, the will of God: "these light afflictions, which are but for a moment, work out for us a far more exceeding and eternal weight of glory." Therefore that event which occasioned the entrance of suffering ino the world has thereby occasioned to all the children of God an increase of glory to all eternity. For although the sufferings themselves will be at an end: although—

> "The pain of life shall then be o'er,
>   The anguish and distracting care;
> The sighing grief shall weep no more;
>   And sin shall never enter there:"

—yet the joys occasioned thereby shall never end, but flow at God's right hand forevermore.

There is one advanage more that we reap from Adam's fall, which is not unworthy our attention. Unless in Adam all had died, being in the loins of their first parent, every descendant of Adam, every child of man, must have personally answered for himself to God: it seems to be a necessary consequence of this, that if he had once fallen, once violated any command of God, there would have been no possibility of his rising again; there was no help, but he must have perished without remedy. For that covenant knew not to show mercy: the word was, "The soul that sinneth, it shall die." Now who would not rather be on the footing he is now; under a covenant of mercy? Who would wish to hazard a whole eternity upon one stake? Is it not infinitely more desirable to be in a state wherein, though encompassed with infirmities, yet we do not run such a desperate risk, but if we fall we may rise again? Wherein we may say,—

"My trespass is grown up to heaven!
But, far above the skies,
In Christ abundantly forgiven,
I see thy mercies rise!"

In Christ! Let me entreat every serious person once more to fix his attention here. All that has been said, all that can be said, on these subjects, centers in this point. The fall of Adam produced the death of Christ! Hear, O heavens, and given ear, O earth! Yea,—

"Let earth and heaven agree,
Angels and men be joined,
To celebrate with me,
The Savior of mankind;
To adore the all-atoning Lamb,
And bless the sound of Jesu's Name!"

If God had prevented the fall of man, the Word had never been made flesh; nor had we ever "seen his glory, the glory as of the only begotten of the Father." Those mysteries had never been displayed "which the very angels desire to look into." Methinks this consideration swallows up all the rest, and should never be out of our thoughts. Unless "by one man judgment had come upon all men to condemnation," neither angels nor men could ever have known "the unsearchable riches of Christ."

See then, upon the whole, how little reason we have to repine at the fall of our first parent, since herefrom we may derive such unspeakable advantages both in time and eternity. See how small pretense there is for questioning the mercy of God in permitting that event to take place, since, therein, mercy, by infinite degrees, rejoices over judgment! Where, then, is the man that presumes to blame God for not preventing Adam's sin? Should we not rather bless him from the ground of the heart, for therein laying the grand scheme of man's redemption and making way for that glorious manifestation of his wisdom, holiness, justice, and mercy? If, indeed, God had decreed, before the foundation of the world, that millions of men should dwell in everlasting burnings because Adam sinned hundreds or thousands of years before they had a being; I know not who could thank him for this, unless the devil and his angels: seeing on this supposition, all those millions of unhappy spirits would be plunged into hell by Adam's sin without any possible advantage from it. But, blessed be God, this is not the case. Such a decree never existed. On the contrary, every one born of a woman may be an unspeakable gainer thereby: and none ever was or can be a loser but by his own choice.

We see here a full answer to that plausible account "of the origin of evil," published to the world some years since, and supposed to be unanswerable: that it "necessarily resulted from the nature of matter, which God was not able to alter." It is very kind in this sweet-tongued orator to make an excuse for God! But there is really no occasion for it: God hath answered for himself. He made man in his own image, a spirit endued with understanding and liberty. Man, abusing that liberty, produced evil; brought sin and pain into the world. This God permitted, in order to a fuller manifestation of his wisdom, justice, and mercy by bestowing on all who would receive it an infinitely greater happiness than they could possibly have attained if Adam had not fallen.

"O the depth of the riches both of the wisdom and knowledge of God!" Although a thousand particulars of "his judgments, of his ways are unsearchable" to us, and past our finding out, yet we may discern the general scheme, running through time into eternity. "According to the council of his own will," the plan he had laid before the foundation of the world, he created the parent of all mankind in his own image. And he permitted all men to be made sinners by the disobedience of this one man, that, by the obedience of one, all who receive the free gift may be infinitely holier and happier to all eternity!

PART SIX

WAR AND PEACE

William Shakespeare
1564–1616

While we have no evidence that Shakespeare himself was an active rhetorician, these speeches from Henry V, Richard III, *and* Henry VIII *could only have been written by a man with an intuitive grasp of the structure and psychology of effective oration.*

KING HENRY V EXHORTS HIS SOLDIERS BEFORE HARFLEUR

KING HENRY. Once more unto the breach, dear friends,
    once more,
Or close the wall up with our English dead.
In peace there's nothing so becomes a man
As modest stillness and humility;
But when the blast of war blows in our ears,
Then imitate the action of the tiger;
Stiffen the sinews, summon up the blood,
Disguise fair nature with hard-favour'd rage;
Then lend the eye a terrible aspect;
Let it pry through the portage of the head
Like the brass cannon; let the brow o'erwhelm it
As fearfully as doth a galled rock
O'erhang and jutty his confounded base,
Swill'd with the wild and wasteful ocean.
Now set the teeth and stretch the nostril wide,
Hold hard the breath, and bend up every spirit
To his full height. On, on, you noblest English,
Whose blood is fet from fathers of war-proof!
Fathers that, like so many Alexanders,
Have in these parts from morn till even fought,
And sheath'd their swords for lack of argument.
Dishonour not your mothers; now attest

That those whom you call'd fathers did beget you.
Be copy now to men of grosser blood,
And teach them how to war. And you, good yeomen,
Whose limbs were made in England, show us here
The mettle of your pasture; let us swear
That you are worth your breeding, which I doubt not;
For there is none of you so mean and base
That hath not noble lustre in your eyes.
I see you stand like greyhounds in the slips,
Straining upon the start. The game's afoot!
Follow your spirit, and upon this charge
Cry, "God for Harry! England and Saint George!"

Henry V, III, i, 1–34

KING HENRY V AND THE ENGLISH ARMY

KING HENRY.   Thou dost thy office fairly. Turn thee back,
And tell thy King I do not seek him now,
But could be willing to march on to Calais
Without impeachment; for, to say the sooth,
Though 'tis no wisdom to confess so much
Unto an enemy of craft and vantage,
My people are with sickness much enfeebled,
My numbers lessen'd, and those few I have
Almost no better than so many French;
Who when they were in health, I tell thee, herald,
I thought upon one pair of English legs
Did march three Frenchmen. Yet, forgive me, God,
That I do brag thus! This your air of France
Hath blown that vice in me. I must repent.
Go therefore, tell thy master here I am;
My ransom is this frail and worthless trunk,
My army but a weak and sickly guard;
Yet, God before, tell him we will come on,
Though France himself and such another neighbour
Stand in our way. There's for thy labour, Montjoy.
Go, bid thy master well advise himself.
If we may pass, we will; if we be hind'red,

We shall your tawny ground with your red blood
Discolour; and so, Montjoy, fare you well.
The sum of all our answer is but this:
We would not seek a battle, as we are;
Nor, as we are, we say we will not shun it.
So tell your master.

Henry V, III, vi, 148–75

KING HENRY V BEFORE AGINCOURT

KING HENRY.   What's he that wishes so?
My cousin Westmoreland? No, my fair cousin.
If we are mark'd to die, we are enow
To do our country loss; and if to live,
The fewer men, the greater share of honour.
God's will! I pray thee, wish not one man more.
By Jove, I am not covetous for gold,
Nor care I who doth feed upon my cost;
It yearns me not if men my garments wear;
Such outward things dwell not in my desires;
But if it be a sin to covet honour,
I am the most offending soul alive.
No, faith, my coz, wish not a man from England.
God's peace! I would not lose so great an honour
As one man more, methinks, would share from me
For the best hope I have. O, do not wish one more!
Rather proclaim it, Westmoreland, through my host,
That he which hath no stomach to this fight,
Let him depart. His passport shall be made,
And crowns for convoy put into his purse.
We would not die in that man's company
That fears his fellowship to die with us.
This day is call'd the feast of Crispian.
He that outlives this day, and comes safe home,
Will stand tip-toe when this day is named,
And rouse him at the name of Crispian.
He that shall live this day, and see old age,
Will yearly on the vigil feast his neighbours,

And say, "To-morrow is Saint Crispian."
Then will he strip his sleeve and show his scars,
And say, "These wounds I had on Crispin's day."
Old men forget; yet all shall be forgot,
But he'll remember with advantages
What feats he did that day. Then shall our names,
Familiar in his mouth as household words,
Harry the King, Bedford, and Exeter,
Warwick and Talbot, Salisbury and Gloucester,
Be in their flowing cups freshly rememb'red.
This story shall the good man teach his son;
And Crispin Crispian shall ne'er go by,
From this day to the ending of the world,
But we in it shall be remembered,
We few, we happy few, we band of brothers.
For he today that sheds his blood with me
Shall be my brother; be he ne'er so vile,
This day shall gentle his condition;
And gentlemen in England now a-bed
Shall think themselves accurs'd they were not here,
And hold their manhoods cheap whiles any speaks
That fought with us upon Saint Crispin's day.

Henry V, IV, iii, 18–67

KING RICHARD III'S ORATION TO HIS ARMY

KING RICHARD.   What shall I say more than I have in-
        ferr'd?
Remember whom you are to cope withal;
A sort of vagabonds, rascals, and runaways,
A scum of Bretons and base lackey peasants,
Whom their o'er-cloyed country vomits forth
To desperate ventures and assur'd destruction.
You sleeping safe, they bring you to unrest;
You having lands, and blest with beauteous wives,
They would restrain the one, distain the other.
And who doth lead them but a paltry fellow,
Long kept in Bretagne at our mother's cost?

A milk-sop, one that never in his life
Felt so much cold as over shoes in snow?
Let's whip these stragglers o'er the seas again;
Lash hence these overweening rags of France,
These famish'd beggars, weary of their lives,
Who, but for dreaming on this fond exploit,
For want of means, poor rats, had hang'd themselves.
If we be conquered, let men conquer us
And not these bastard Bretons whom our fathers
Have in their own land beaten, bobb'd and thump'd,
And on record, left them the heirs of shame.
Shall these enjoy our lands? lie with our wives?
Ravish our daughters? Hark! I hear their drum.
Fight, gentlemen of England! fight, bold yeomen!
Draw, archers, draw your arrows to the head!
Spur your proud horses hard and ride in blood;
Amaze the welkin with your broken staves!

. . . .

A thousand hearts are great within my bosom.
Advance our standards, set upon our foes;
Our ancient word of courage, fair Saint George,
Inspire us with the spleen of fiery dragons!
Upon them! Victory sits on our helms.

Richard III, V, iii, 314–41; 347–51

CARDINAL WOLSEY FORESEES HIS FALL

WOLSEY.   So farewell to the little good you bear me.
Farewell! a long farewell, to all my greatness!
This is the state of man: today he puts forth
The tender leaves of hopes; tomorrow blossoms,
And bears his blushing honours thick upon him;
The third day comes a frost, a killing frost,
And, when he thinks, good easy man, full surely
His greatness is a-ripening, nips his root,
And then he falls, as I do. I have ventur'd
Like little wanton boys that swim on bladders,
This many summers in a sea of glory,

But far beyond my depth. My high-blown pride
At length broke under me, and now has left me,
Weary and old with service, to the mercy
Of a rude stream that must for ever hide me.
Vain pomp and glory of this world, I hate ye!
I feel my heart new open'd. O, how wretched
Is that poor man that hangs on princes' favours!
There is, betwixt that smile we would aspire to,
That sweet aspect of princes, and their ruin,
More pangs and fears than wars or women have;
And when he falls, he falls like Lucifer,
Never to hope again.

Henry VIII, III, ii, 356–72

Georges Clemenceau
1841–1929

Georges Clemenceau, a professor of mathematics and French Premier (1906–9, 1917–19) had, obviously, a varied life of the abstract and practical. As a member of the Chamber of Deputies his eloquence was well recognized. In June 1906 he and Jaurès, the equally eloquent exponent of French socialism, carried on a debate concerning socialism. The result of this debate was that the socialists were required to establish a more realistic approach to their problem or face complete political defeat.

Clemenceau was again faced with a socialist problem in 1918. After the German offensive in the spring, an attempt was made by the militant socialists of France to embarrass the government by demanding to know unrevealed matters about the military. Such a revelation had been considered dangerous by the government. On June 4, Clemenceau defied his critics. Although he was Premier at the time, he was harassed by interruptions, yet his powerful command of rhetoric overcame the opposition, and at the end he received an overwhelming vote of confidence.

During the Peace Conference in Paris, Clemenceau was opposed to President Wilson's policies; he called for a more rigid treaty than Wilson was willing to accept. However, in 1919 he was defeated because the French people thought he had become too moderate in his attitude toward Germany.

ONE AIM: VICTORY

When I accepted the premiership offered to me by the President of the Republic I could not ignore the fact that we were at the most critical period of the War. I remember that I told you we should pass together through difficult and exacting times; I remember I spoke of "cruel hours." No one protested when I announced that they would come. They are coming and the only question is whether we can stand them. [*Applause and interruption*]

When Russia's desertion occurred, when men who believed that it was only necessary to will a democratic peace to obtain it from Willian II, had given up their country, unwittingly I prefer to think, to the army of the invader, what one of you here could believe that the million German soldiers who were thus liberated would not turn against us? This and more is what happened. For four years our forces have been wearing themselves out. Our front was guarded by a line of soldiers which was becoming thinner and thinner, with our allies who had themselves enormous losses. And at that moment you saw arrive against you a fresh mass of German divisions in good condition when you were far from your best strength.

Is there any one of you who did not realize that under the shock of this enormous mass our lines had to give way at some points? Certainly not, for in all the conversations which I had with members of this assembly, the question asked me was, how much we had to give way.

The recoil was very serious for the English army, which had suffered formidable losses. It was grave and dangerous for the French army. I said dangerous, serious, but nothing more, and there is nothing in that to shake the confidence we should have in our soldiers. [*Applause and interruptions*]

Our men are engaged in the battle, a terrible one. They fought one against five without sleep for three and four days together. These soldiers, these great soldiers, have good and great leaders: worthy of them in every way. [*Applause and interruptions*] I have seen these leaders at work and some of them against whom I will not deny that I was prejudiced, struck me with admiration. [*Applause*]

Is that saying that there are nowhere mistakes? I cannot maintain that. I know it too well; my duty is to discover these mistakes and correct them. In this I am supported by two great soldiers,—General Foch and General Petain. [*Applause*] General Foch enjoys the confidence of our allies to such a degree that yesterday at the conference of Versailles they wished to have unanimous confidence in him expressed in the communique given to the press. [*Applause and interruptions*]

These men are at this moment fighting the hardest battle of the war, fighting it with a heroism which I can find no phrase worthy to express. And it is we who for a mistake made in such and such a place, or which may not even have been made, demand explanations, on the field of battle of a man worn with fatigue. It is of this man that we demand to know whether on such and such a day he did such and such a thing! Drive me from this place if that is what you ask, for I will not do it. [*Applause*]

I came here with the desire to find simple, brief and measured words to express the sentiment of the French people at the front and at the rear, to show the world a state of mind which cannot be analyzed, but which at this moment is the admiration of all civilized people. [*Applause*]

I accuse no one. I am the leader of these men and it is my duty to punish them if I consider it of general benefit to do so; but it is also my greater duty to protect them if they have been unjustly attacked. [*Applause*]

The army is better than we could ever have expected and when I say "the army" I mean men of all ranks who are under fire. That is one of the elements of our confidence, the main element. Although faith in a cause is an admirable thing, it will not bring victory and our men are dying. We have an army made up of our children and our brothers—what can we say against it? Their leaders too have come from among us; they too are our brothers, they too are good soldiers. They come back covered with wounds when they are not left on the field of battle. What can you say against them? [*Applause*]

We have yielded ground, much more ground than either you or I should have wished. There are men without number who have paid for this and with their blood, without reproach. I know of the deeds of a group of lost men, Bretons, surrounded in a wood all night. The next day, still resisting, they sent a carrier pigeon to their corps to say "We are here. We have promised not to yield. We shall fight to the end. If you can come to find us, come; we can hold out half a day longer." [*Applause*] These men made and safeguard the country of which you are so proud. They die for the greatest and most noble ideal—to continue a history which shall be the foremost among all the histories of civilized peoples.

Our own duty is very simple, very tame. We run no danger. We are at our posts, you here, I with my cabinet —posts which are not dangerous as are those of the soldiers, but which are nevertheless where the capital interests of the country are decided.

As long as you remain calm, confident in yourselves, determined to hold out to the end of this hard struggle, victory is yours. It is yours because our enemies, who are not as intelligent as they are said to be, have only one method—to throw their whole force into the venture and risk everything. They tried it at Verdun and on the Yser, at Dunkirk and at Calais. They were checked—by whom? First by the English and then by the French. After that they appeared in Champagne; they advanced. Do you think it possible to make a war in which you never have to retreat? There is only one thing that matters, the victorious issue, the final success. Our men can only give their lives; but you through patience, firmness and determination can give them what they deserve—victory. [*Applause*]

You have before you a government, which, as it told you at the very beginning, never conceived of the possibility of negotiating without victory. [*Applause*] You know what you are doing. You can keep us in power or send us away; but as long as you keep us, whatever may happen, you can be sure that the country will be defended to the death and that no force will be spared to obtain success. [*Applause*] We will never consent to anything but peace with victory. That is the watchword of our government. [*Applause and interruptions*]

The Germans are once more staking all. The "coup" which they are attempting is to terrorize you, to frighten you so that you will abandon the struggle. [*Applause*] One must be ignorant of German tactics to doubt this.

Why did they suddenly throw all their forces on the Yser? It was to gain Calais, to separate us from England and force us to surrender. For what was the dreadful march on Paris? To take Paris and through terror force us to surrender. Why are they beginning again today? To secure this effect of terror which they have never yet achieved.

The decision is in your hands for the simple reason that it is not a matter of mere reasoning but a question of action. The Americans are coming. The forces of the English and the French, as well as of our enemies, are worn out; but we have Allies who are coming as a decisive factor. I have said from the beginning that American cooperation would decide the issue of the war. The point is this: events in Russia have allowed a million of the enemy's men to appear on the Franco-British front. We have Allies, whom we did not have in 1870, when we yielded because we were alone. We have Allies, who represent the foremost nations of the world, who have pledged themselves to continue the war to the end, to the success which we hold in our grasp, which we are on the point of achieving if we have the necessary tenacity. [*Applause*]

I declare, and it must be my last word, that victory depends upon us. The civil forces must rise to the height of their duty; it is not necessary to make this demand of the soldiers. Send me away if I have been an unworthy servant; drive me out, condemn me, but at least take the trouble to formulate criticisms. As for me, I assert that the French people have in all ways done their full duty. Those who have fallen have not fallen in vain, for they have made French history great. It remains for the living to complete the magnificent work of the dead. [*Applause*]

Benito Mussolini
1883–1945

Benito Mussolini, socialist and then founder of Fascism and dictator of Italy, began his career as editor of Avanti, *a socialist daily newspaper in Milan. Therein he wrote with zeal and vigor and sharp turn of phrase. During World War I, Mussolini broke with socialism and founded his own paper,* Il Popolo d'Italia. *He organized a progressive party and roused its members with his eloquence and the possibility of political conquest. The strikes and protests which were taking place gave him and his followers a pretext for a march on Rome on October 28, 1922. King Victor Emmanuel III saw the march as a show of popular control and called on Mussolini to form a cabinet. Thus Fascism came into actual political power.*

The voice of Mussolini brought this about. He seemed to wear the Roman orator's toga from the beginning. He had an ear for language. For example: "Fascism proclaims the profound hierarchical equality of all individuals in labor and in concept of the Nation;" "Fascism will be the type of this century's and European and world civilization;" "We will be the first to adorn our guns with olive branches."

He failed to establish an Augustan empire, fell to utter disrepute, and was hanged in the public square of Milan.

AIMS OF THE FASCIST PARTY OF ITALY
SPEECH TO THE WORKERS OF MILAN, NOVEMBER 1, 1936

Blackshirts of Milan: By means of the speech which I am about to make to you and for which I ask, and you will give me, a few dozen minutes of your attention, I intend to lay down the position of Fascist Italy with regard to its relations with other peoples in this so turgid and disquieting moment.

The high level of your political education allows me to lay before you those problems which elsewhere are debated in so-called Parliaments, even at so-called democratic banquets.

I shall be extremely brief, but I add that every one of my words has been weighed.

If one wishes to clarify the European atmosphere, it is necessary first to clear the table of all illusions, of all conventional relics of the great shipwreck of Wilsonian ideology.

One of these illusions is already flat, the illusion of disarmament. No one wishes to disarm first, and for all to disarm together is impossible and absurd.

In any event, when a conference for disarmaments meets, the Geneva rule functions in full. This rule consists of blowing up ant hills until they become mountains.

On these mountains is concentrated for some days all the glare of Kleig lights and world publicity. Then, at a certain moment, out from these mountains comes a tiny mouse, which ends running around a labyrinth of procedure which futile invention has no precedent in history.

For us, Fascists, in the habit of examining with cool eye the reality of life in history, another illusion we reject is that which passed by the name of collective security. Collective security never existed, does not exist, and never will exist. A virile people provides within its own borders its collective security and refuses to confide its destiny to uncertain hands of third persons.

Another illusion it is necessary to reject is indivisible peace. Indivisible peace could have only this meaning, indivisible war. Thus, peoples refuse, and justly so, to fight for interests that do not concern them.

Now in order to make a policy of peace it is not necessary to go through the corridors of the League of Nations.

Here I make what in navigation is called the ship's position.

After seventeen years of polemics, recrimination, and

misunderstanding of problems left in suspense, accords with France were reached in January 1935. The accords could and should have opened a new epoch of truly friendly relations between the two countries. But sanctions came along. Naturally, friendship experienced its first freezing.

We were then on the eve of winter. Winter passed; spring came and with spring our triumph and victory.

Sanctions continued to be applied with truly meticulous vigor. For almost two months after we were in Addis Ababa sanctions still continued.

It is a classical case of the letter which kills the spirit; of formalism which strangles the living, concrete reality of life!

France today still holds her finger pointed at the yellowing ledgers of Geneva, saying:

"The empire of the dead ex-lion of Judah [Haile Selassie] is still alive." [*Much laughter*]

The empire of the ex-Negus is more than dead.

One of the countries bordering Italy, with whom our relations were and are and always will be extremely friendly, is Switzerland. It is a little country but of very great importance both for its ethnical composition and for its geographical position, which it occupies at the crossroads of Europe.

By the accord of July 11 a new epoch was opened in the history of modern Austria . . . such accords strengthened the governmental make-up of this State, giving greater guarantee for its independence.

Hungary is truly a great but disabled veteran. Four million Magyars live beyond her present border.

The sentiments of the Italian people towards the Magyar people are marked through recognition—which, moreover, is reciprocal—of their military qualities, their courage, and their spirit of sacrifice.

The fourth country bordering Italy is Yugoslavia. Recently the atmosphere between the two countries was greatly improved.

In addition to these four countries bordering Italy, a

great country recently aroused vast sympathy from the masses of the Italian people. I speak of Germany. The meeting at Berlin had as a result an understanding between the two countries on definite problems, some of which are particularly troublesome these days.

Germany did not adhere to sanctions.

By the accord of July 11 an element of dissension between Berlin and Rome disappeared. May I remind you, even before the meeting in Berlin, Germany had practically recognized the Empire of Rome.

It is no wonder if we today raise the banner of antibolshevism. This is our old banner! We are born under this sign! We have fought against this enemy! We have conquered it through our sacrifice of blood!

This is because what is called bolshevism and communism is today—listen well to me—only super-capitalism of a State carried to its most ferocious extreme. It is not, therefore, the negation of a system, but the development and sublimation of this system, and the time has come to put an end to it. This might be by opposing Fascism and democracy to it.

We are not like true, authentic reactionaries of all countries. We are not embalmers of the past; we are anticipators of the future. We do not carry to its extreme consequences the capitalistic civilization, above all in its mechanical, almost inhuman aspect. We create a new synthesis through which Fascism opens the road to a human, true civilization of work.

I have been occupied up to this point with the continent. But Italy is an island. It is necessary for Italians little by little to take on an insular mentality, because it is the only method for taking all problems of naval defense of the Nation in a true light.

Italy is an island which emerges from the Mediterranean. This sea—I address myself also toward the English, who perhaps at this moment are listening by radio—this sea is the highroad of Great Britain, one of the many highroads by which the British Empire reaches its outlying territory more rapidly.

If the Mediterranean is for others a highroad, for us Italians it is life. We have said a thousand times, and I repeat, that we do not intend to menace this road, we do not intend to interrupt it. But we say, on the other hand, our right and vital interest must be respected.

There are no other alternatives. The reasoning brains of the British Empire must realize the thing is done and is irrevocable. The sooner the better.

Bilateral conflicts are not to be thought of, and even less a conflict which from bilateral would become immediately European. There is, therefore, only one solution direct, rapid, and complete understanding on the basis of recognition of reciprocal interests.

But if this does not come about, if in fact—and I refuse to believe it from today on—one is really thinking of suffocating the life of the Italian people in the sea which was the sea of Rome, very well! Let it be known that the Italian people would spring to their feet like one man, ready for combat with a determination which would have real precedent in history.

Milan comrades, let us turn to our own affairs: marching orders for the fifth year of Fascism are the following:

Peace with all, with those near and far. Armed peace! Therefore, our program of armaments for land, sea, and sky will be regularly developed.

Acceleration of all productive energies of the nation, in agriculture and industrial fields. Development of the corporative system to its definite realization.

But here is a duty I confide to you, O Milanese of the most ardent and most Fascist Milan which has revealed its great soul these days. I confide in you, O Milanese of this generous, working, and untiring Milan, this duty:

You must place yourselves, as you will place yourselves, as an advance guard for the development of the Empire so as to make in the shortest possible period an element of well being, of power, of glory for the nation.

Italy Enters the War
Speech Delivered at Rome June 10, 1940

Fighters of land, sea, and air, Blackshirts of the revolution and of legions, men and women of Italy, of the Empire and of the Kingdom of Albania, listen!

The hour destined by fate is sounding for us. The hour of irrevocable decision has come. A declaration of war already has been handed to the Ambassadors of Great Britain and France.

We take the field against the plutocratic and reactionary democracies who always blocked the march and frequently plotted against the existence of the Italian people.

Our conscience is absolutely clear.

With you, the entire world is witness that the Italy of Fascism has done everything humanly possible to avoid the tempest that envelops Europe, but all in vain.

If today we have decided to take the risks and sacrifices of war, it is because the honor, interests and future firmly impose it; since a great people is truly such, if it considers its obligations sacred and does not avoid the supreme trials that determine the course of history.

We want to break the territorial and military chains that confine us in our sea because a country of forty-five million souls is not truly free if it has not free access to the ocean.

This gigantic conflict is only a phase of the logical development of our revolution. It is the conflict of poor, numerous peoples who labor against starvers who ferociously cling to a monopoly of all riches and all gold on earth. It is a conflict of fruitful, useful people against peoples who are in a decline.

Now the die is cast and our will has burned our ships behind us.

Italians, in a memorable mass meeting in Berlin, I said that according to the rules of Fascist morals when one has a friend one marches with him to the end. This we have done and will continue to do with Germany, her people and her victorious armed forces.

There is only one order. It is categorical and obligatory for everyone. It already wings over and enflames hearts from the Alps to the Indian Ocean: Conquer!

And we will conquer in order, finally, to give a new world of peace and justice to Italy, to Europe and to the universe.

Italian people, rush to arms and show your tenacity, your courage, your valor.

Franklin Delano Roosevelt
1882–1945

Thirty-second President of the United States, educated at Harvard and Columbia University School of Law, Roosevelt early went into the field of politics and in 1913 became the Assistant Secretary of the Navy and held the post through World War I until 1920. He was stricken with poliomyelitis but by determination of will and excellent care he regained his strength but not the use of his legs. His voice was heard in civic work, national service, political debate until he had such political strength that he was nominated for the presidency and won it for four terms.

In this office he was required to speak frequently. Since he was blessed with a warm voice and an engaging sense of style and wit, more Americans heard him than almost any previous President. The speech here given was delivered to both houses of Congress on May 16, 1940. In it he asked for more money for defense. This speech deserves close reading because of the way it is prepared. Notice the short sentence structure; observe how sharply he drew his images and stated what would otherwise be dry statistics. Roosevelt knew he needed money to do the things he foresaw; he wanted Congress to see them through not only his eyes but through his voice and their ears.

REQUEST FOR DEFENSE FUNDS
MAY 16, 1940

Mr. Vice President, Mr. Speaker, members of the Senate and House of Representatives.

These are ominous days—days whose swift and shocking developments force every neutral nation to look to its defenses in the light of new factors. The brutal force of modern offensive war has been loosened in all its horror.

New powers of destruction, incredibly swift and ready have been developed; and those who wield them are ruthless and daring.

No old defense is so strong that it requires no further strengthening, and no attack is so unlikely or impossible that it may be ignored.

Let us examine, without self-deception, the dangers which confront us. Let us measure our strength and our defense without self-delusion.

The clear fact is that the American people must recast their thinking about national problems.

Motorized armies can now sweep through the enemy territories at the rate of 200 miles a day.

Parachute troops are dropped from airplanes in large numbers behind enemy lines. Troops are landed from planes in open fields, or wide highways and at local civil airports.

We have seen the treacherous use of the "fifth column" by which persons supposed to be peaceful visitors were actually a part of an enemy unit of occupation. Lightning attacks, capable of destroying airplane factories and munition works hundreds of miles behind the lines, are part of the new technique of modern war.

The element of surprise which has ever been an important tactic in warfare has become the more dangerous because of the amazing speed with which modern equipment can reach and attack the enemy's country.

Our own interests are widespread. More than ever the protection of the whole American hemisphere against invasion or control or domination by non-American nations has the united support of the twenty-one American republics, including the United States. More than ever in the past this protection calls for ready-at-hand weapons capable of great mobility because of the potential speed of modern attack.

Let me analyse for a moment:

The Atlantic and Pacific Oceans were reasonably adequate defensive barriers when fleets under sail could move at an average speed of five miles an hour. Even in those days by a sudden foray it was possible for an opponent actually to burn our National Capitol. Later, the oceans still gave strength to our defense when fleets and convoys propelled by steam could sail the oceans at fifteen or twenty miles an hour.

But the new element—air navigation—steps up the speed of possible attack to 200 or 300 miles an hour.

Furthermore, it brings the new possibilities of the use of nearer bases from which an attack or attacks on the American Continent could be made. From the fields of Greenland it is four hours by air to Newfoundland, five hours to Nova Scotia, New Brunswick and to the Province of Quebec, and only six hours to New England.

The Azores are only 2,000 miles from parts of our Eastern seaboard, and if Bermuda fell into hostile hands, it is a matter of less than three hours for modern bombers to reach our shores.

From a base in the outer West Indies the coast of Florida could be reached in 200 minutes.

The islands off the West Coast of Africa are only 1,500 miles from Brazil. Modern planes starting from the Cape Verde Islands can be over Brazil in seven hours.

And Para, Brazil, near the mouth of the Amazon River is but four flying hours to Caracas, Venezuela; and Venezuela but two and one-half hours to Tampico, Mexico; and Tampico is two and one-quarter hours to St. Louis, Kansas City and Omaha.

On the other side of the Continent, Alaska, with a white population of only 30,000 people, is within four or five hours of flying distance to Vancouver, Seattle, Tacoma and Portland. The islands of the Southern Pacific are not too far removed from the West Coast of South America to prevent them from becoming bases of enormous strategic advantage to attacking forces.

Surely the developments of the past few weeks have made it clear to all our citizens that the possibility of attack on vital American zones ought to make it essential that we have the physical, the ready ability to meet these attacks and to prevent them from reaching their objectives.

This means military implements—not on paper—which are ready and available to meet any lightning offensive against our American interest. It means also that facilities for the production must be ready to turn out munitions and equipment at top speed.

We have the lesson before us over and over again—nations that were not ready and were unable to get ready found themselves overrun by the enemy. So-called impregnable fortifications no longer exist. A defense which allows an enemy to consolidate his approach without hindrance will lose. A defense which makes no effective effort to destroy the lines of supplies and communications of the enemy will lose.

An effective defense by its very nature requires the equipment to attack the aggressor in his route before he can establish strong bases within the territory of American vital interests.

[There followed a review of the State of the Army, Navy, Air Force. He requested Congress to (1) procure essential equipment for larger arms (2) to replace or modernize old army or navy equipment (3) to increase all production facilities for national defense, and (4) to speed up work to a 24 hour basis on all contracts. He asked for $896,000,000.]

Defense can not be static. Defense must grow and change from day to day. Defense must be dynamic and flexible, an expression of the vital forces of the nation and of its resolute will to meet whatever challenge the future may hold. For these reasons, I need hardly assure you that after the adjournment of this session of Congress, I will not hesitate to call the Congress into special session if at any time the situation of the national defense requires it. . . .

Our ideal—yours and mine, the ideal of almost every man, woman and child in the country—our objective is still peace—peace at home and peace abroad. Nevertheless, we stand ready not only to spend millions for defense but to give our service and even our lives for the maintenance of our American liberties.

Our security is not a matter of weapons alone. The arm that wields them must be strong. The eye that guides them clear; the will that directs them indomitable.

These are the characteristics of a free people, a people devoted to the institutions they themselves have built, a people willing to defend a way of life that is precious to them all, a people who put their faith in God.

Winston Churchill
1874–1965

Winston Churchill represents for the twentieth century the most eloquent speaker among its citizens. As a young man with a hesitancy in speech, he, like Demosthenes, forced himself to overcome his handicap by debating in school and college. Spurred on by an ardent zeal, he developed his skill so that it served his and his nation's purpose in his later magnificent service. His speeches may seem to have come easily, but he took time and great care in their preparation so that when he delivered a speech it seemed to all listeners and observers that he had just thought of it casually.

This speech was delivered in the House of Commons, London, on August 2, 1944.

ALLIED WAR GAINS

At Washington, in January 1942, it was decided that Germany was the prime enemy and that only a minimum of forces necessary for safeguarding vital interests should be diverted to operations against Japan.

Our joint resources, British and American, however, increased so rapidly that it became possible to wage two wars simultaneously with offensive vigor. In the Pacific the immense armadas of the United States are equipped with aircraft and every conceivable form of craft needed on the sea for amphibious warfare, all on the largest scale, armed with science and led with commanding skill both on sea and land under Admiral Nimitz and General MacArthur, who commands not only American but also powerful Australian and New Zealand forces, and we have gained important and expanding success.

New Guinea has been dominated, the Marshalls and

Saipan have been taken. The fleets and other forces of the United States have already advanced through the far-flung outer defenses of Japan, and in some parts have pierced to inner defenses, thus opening to us the prospect of a much more speedy climax in the Far East. Many scores of thousands of Japanese have been bypassed and are starving to death on islands or jungles, with only such aid from Japan as can be given by submarines, which have to be diverted from their normal warlike role. . . .

I must repeat that I am increasingly pleased to feel that the interval between the defeat of Hitler and the defeat of Japan will be much shorter, perhaps much shorter than I at one time supposed. . . .

Now I come to the larger picture. Volumes would be required to recount the story of the crossing of the Channel and the landing of the armies of liberation upon the soil of France. I have only a few minutes, and therefore I must practice a selective method as far as possible.

In April 1943, General Morgan of the British Army became head of the British and American planning staff which surveyed the whole project by decision of the Combined Chief of Staff Committee. They made the plan which I took to Quebec, where it was submitted to the President and combined British and American Chiefs of Staff. This plan selected the beaches for attack and presented the main operations of the scheme, together with a mass of detail to support it. It received in principle complete agreement.

It is rather remarkable that a secret of this character, which had to be entrusted from the beginning to scores, and very soon to hundreds and ultimately to thousands of people, never leaked out, either in the small confines of this island or in the wide expanse of the United States.

At Teheran we promised Marshal Stalin that we should put this plan, or something like it, into operation at the end of May or the beginning of June, and he promised, on his part, that the whole of the Russian armies would be thrown, as indeed they have been, into the general battle in the East.

In January of this year the commanders were appointed.

The Mediterranean became the British command under General Wilson, and General Eisenhower assumed command of the expeditionary forces gathering in Britain.

No man has ever labored more skillfully and more intensively for the unification and good-will of the great forces under his command than General Eisenhower. He has the genius for bringing all of the Allies together and is proud to consider himself the Allied as well as the United States commander. . . .

For more than a year American stores, equipment and men had been moving steadily into this island, and we ourselves had selected from the British armies here an expeditionary force which was practically as large as that of the United States in the opening stage.

The great episode seemed to everyone to be the crossing of the Channel with its stormy waters, swift currents and eighteen-foot rise and fall of tide and, above all, changes of weather, which, when an operation as big as this had to be undertaken, may cut an army off on shore for many days without anyone being able to get at them to reinforce them or withdraw them, and thus leave them to the mercy of a superior enemy.

That was an element, and the possible change in weather conditions certainly did hang like a vulture poised in the sky over the heads of the most sanguine. But in all this matter the work of Combined Operations Headquarters, founded in 1940 under Admiral Keyes for the purpose of amphibious warfare, and its development in 1942 under Admiral Mountbatten, proved its value.

As is well known, I was opposed to making this great invasion across the Channel in 1942, and thereafter it was plainly impossible owing to our having chosen the Mediterranean and our amphibious resources all being concentrated there. But now we were all agreed and the commanders took all the vast mass of knowledge which was accumulated and put their own stamp on it.

I myself saw a few days after the landing was completed six of these medium landing craft charge up in line together until they were stopped by a sloping sandy beach. Down went their drawbridges, out poured their vehicles and in under five minutes the whole heavy battery was drawn up in column of route along the road. In less than fifteen minutes these craft had pushed themselves off shore and were returning to England for another consignment. . . .

At the present time no speech by a prominent politician in any of the various countries could be deemed complete without a full exposition of future organization of the world.

I was severely reproached last time for not having dealt methodically with this considerable topic. One of my difficulties is that it does not rest with me to lay down the law for all our Allies. If that were the general wish I would be ready to offer suggestions. But, odd as it may seem, countries like the United States and Soviet Russia might wish to have their say in that matter. And they may not look at it in exactly the same way or express it in the same terms as would gain the loudest applause in this House. I am sorry about this. Nothing would have given me greater pleasure than to give the House my personal ideas about the general layout.

But it would be very troublesome to all of us here if I made a pronouncement on the subject here and found myself contradicted by our most considerable Allies. From time to time a great many eloquent statements are made about the future organization of the world by the most eminent people. I personally would prefer to hear the opinion of other powerful nations before committing our country to too many details.

Cannot we be content with broad declarations upon which we are all agreed? That there is to be a World Council to preserve peace, which will in the first instance be formed and guided by the major powers who have gained the war and that thereafter other powers, and eventually all powers, will be offered their part in this world organization.

Cannot we be content with that and concentrate our efforts upon winning the victory and bear ourselves so prominently in the conflict that our words will receive honored consideration when we come to the organization of peace? . . .

Let us go on, then, to battle on every front; thrust forward, every man who can be found; arm and equip the forces in bountiful supply; listen to no parleys from the enemy, vie our own gallant allies to intensify the conflict and bear with unflinching fortitude whatever evils, whatever blows we may receive; drive on through the storm, now that it reaches its fury, with the same singleness of purpose and inflexibility of resolve as we showed the world when we were all alone.

Adlai Ewing Stevenson
1900–1965

Adlai E. Stevenson, governor of Illinois from 1948 to 1952, became, in that year, the Democratic candidate for President of the United States. He lost to General Dwight D. Eisenhower, and failed a second time in 1956. Upon the election of President John F. Kennedy in 1960 he was appointed to the position of the United States Representative to the United Nations with the title of Ambassador. In that body he was an alert, intelligent, and forceful speaker for the rights not only of his own country but for mankind throughout the world.

The following speech is taken from his address delivered on United Nations Day at the Memorial Theatre, in Dallas, Texas, October 24, 1963. He was speaking to an audience which was generally ill-disposed to the United Nations. There had been publicity against that body and it was necessary for Ambassador Stevenson to set forth clearly the reasonableness of his position and the rightfulness of the organization to which he was our representative.

THE UNITED NATIONS: PAST AND PRESENT

As I speak to you today, on this, the eighteenth anniversary of the United Nations Charter, it is cheering to note that all the predictions of the early demise for the UN have so far failed to come true. For this millions of us—all of us—have reason to be thankful. Still, there are some who continue to criticize.

Constructive criticism is justified, for we have not yet developed a perfect instrument for peace with justice. But as William Penn said: "They have a right to censure that have a heart to help." The critics I refer to have no heart

to help. Worse, perhaps, they fear to hope. And if anything, this eighteenth anniversary of the United Nations is
an occasion that offers hope.

I don't mean to imply that we are suddenly threatened
in the United Nations—and the world—with harmony or
that the light of sweet reason is about to shine forth everlastingly. I would say such prospects are remote. But I
would say, too, that more and more nations are less and
less flouting the general consensus of what most nations
and men believe to be the law of the Charter.

Nonetheless, if we are to believe our ears on some occasions—when the small vocal opposition to the UN is at
its shrillest—we might think some threat to our independence accompanies our participation in this world-wide
alliance of sovereign nations pledged to preserve the
peace. I understand that some of these fearful groups are
trying to establish a U.S. Day in competition with UN
Day. This is the first time I have heard that the United
States and the United Nations are rivals!

At the House of Burgesses in Williamsburg, Virginia,
a quaintly costumed guide shows visitors a draft prepared
there in 1775 for the new nation's constitutional convention. She tells visitors proudly that the draft was incorporated into the United States Constitution, and that its
principles, in turn, were incorporated into the United Nations Charter. How can we fear our own invention, born
in the original colonies, nurtured in our own city of brotherly love, adopted by the world at our own Golden Gate?
We would hold our principles less dear, if we wanted to
keep them exclusively for ourselves.

In celebrating the ratification of the Charter of the
United Nations, we are paying homage to this universal
adoption of the fundamental principles of the United
States. Moreover, the truth is that our membership in the
United Nations is overwhelmingly in the national interest
—if peace in the world is in our national interest, and I
know of no higher national interest of the United States
than peace and security.

It becomes increasingly difficult, therefore, to understand the logic of those super-patriots who decry the

United Nations; who talk of peace but who object to our only institution for peaceful settlement; who decry every attempt at negotiation and conciliation and offer no alternative save weapons that will destroy friend and foe alike.

Well, we can't afford to prove them wrong—when I consider the possibility my mind goes back to an old Gaelic toast:

> "Here's to us
> And those like us
> Of which there are few
> And they are all dead."

Or, when I consider some of the suicidal fallacies that have been advanced over the years in the name of patriotism, I think about the man who rushed in to see Oscar Hammerstein, the producer, and wanted $50,000 for the greatest act on earth. "What do you do?" asked Mr. Hammerstein. "I stand on stage and blow my brains out," was the answer. "Marvelous," said Mr. Hammerstein. "But what do you do for an encore?"

In a nuclear production, my friends, there won't be any encore. Those of us who hold public office and are involved in life and death responsibilities cannot afford either reckless language or deeds. We have the sobering job of trying to make appraisals which will lead to intelligent, effective policy. And it is in this sensitive area of appraisal that we differ so much with the proponents of the illusion of so-called "instant victory."

I stress this today because victory will not be won in an instant—only mutual annihilation can be attained that fast in our age. And we must not only possess the common sense to recognize the fact—we must also have the courage, the persistence, and the patience to forge ahead even if the progress is slow and frustrative and the goal is far away . . .

In the eighteen years since the United Nations became a viable, vibrant organization, that sense of solidarity has grown, it seems to me, as never before in the history of man. But what responsibilities to assign to an eighteen year old stripling! . . .

The United Nations has aged quickly, in part, because the youngest nations in it are maturing quickly. Peoples long divided by race and political subjugations, with all the lingering resentments that flow from that condition, now meet in a community of equals, they are learning respect for law and order and parliamentary procedure. For they are citizens of our planet and, with few exceptions, they belong to no bloc. Certainly there is no such thing as an Afro-Asian bloc—save on colonial issues—and the sense of community, of interdependence, of common peril and hope they feel weighs heavily on the scales of peace in this dangerous world. Meantime, the older nations are also learning—even as the newer ones—that the most rewarding task of civilized man today is that of reconciling different points of view. And perhaps that is the most valuable of all.

. . . But the great challenge of our time—the challenge the United Nations *is* meeting day in and out—is in striking the proper balance in promoting changes for the better in the condition of mankind . . .

First of all, when one mentions peace-keeping, one thinks immediately of the major confrontations that were averted: Cuba, the Congo, the Middle East, to name only a few. Those of us who are familiar with the history of the First World War know just how senseless and needless that conflict was, beginning as it did with a small incident in the Balkans. We now realize how it could probably have been averted had there been an institution like the United Nations where steam could have been let off, national face saved, mediation instituted, and so on. One remarkable factor is the flexibility the United Nations has developed in dealing differently with different kinds of crises. In some cases it has used troops; in others it has used surveying and observing teams; in others it has turned to mediators; in still others to fact-finders. But regardless of the method, the pervading principle is that the United Nations seeks no victories for itself, only a victory for the rule of law.

And what does all this cost the American taxpayer? Without going into any involved accounting in the eighteen years that the United States has been a member of the United Nations it has cost us slightly over 100 million dollars a year, or one-fourth the cost of the aircraft carrier *Enterprise*. Or to be even more Scotch about it, the cost of the entire operation has been approximately seventy-five cents a year per man, woman and child. Compare that with over 50 billion dollars a year Defense Budget, and one sees how much cheaper it is to prepare for peace than to prepare for war. . . .

The journey of a thousand leagues, we say, begins with a single step. So we must never neglect any work of peace that is within our reach, however small. We have constantly to carry on, or rebegin, the work of building the institutions and practices of a non-violent world, keeping always in mind, beyond the setbacks and disappointments, that a free people should ever be seeking their greatest adventure in the work of peace—that even in the midst of conflict they never surrender the creative and compassionate attitudes proper to a peaceful community. . . .

Our task is to build the Organization to help us master our physical environment, foster peaceful change, and promote human rights.

Our task is to use the Organization—its facilities, its resources, its talents, its procedures—to work at the problems that lie right before us, plain to view. . . .

Our efforts will be erratic, and the world will remain a dangerous place to live. But we have our wits and our resources; we have the United Nations in which to pool them for peace-keeping and nation-building; we have the beginnings of a habit of cooperation on a good many kinds of problems.

And we have a simple conviction: that it is not beyond man's capacity to act human!

On this United Nations Day, therefore, let us renew our hope that, finally, men will learn to live as brothers, to respect each other's differences, heal each other's wounds; promote each other's progress, and benefit from each other's knowledge.

PART SEVEN

HAIL AND FAREWELL

Napoleon Bonaparte
1769–1821

The invasion of Russia had exhausted the French army by the loss of half a million men and in 1815 Bonaparte was soundly defeated at Waterloo. He abdicated on April 6, 1814, and was banished to Elba. In ten months he returned trying to recapture his fame, but 1815 and Waterloo were before him. After his defeat, he was held prisoner on the island of St. Helena by the British until his death on May 15, 1821.

Here is his touching leave of his glorious army, its men and generals, its standard, and all that once was symbolic of the empire he had planned.

FAREWELL TO THE OLD GUARD

Soldiers of my Old Guard: I bid you farewell. For twenty years I have constantly accompanied you on the road to honor and glory. In these latter times, as in the days of our prosperity, you have invariably been models of courage and fidelity. With men such as you our cause could not be lost; but the war would have been interminable; it would have been civil war, and that would have entailed deeper misfortunes on France.

I have sacrificed all my interests to those of the country.

I go, but you, my friends, will continue to serve France. Her happiness was my only thought. It will still be the object of my wishes. Do not regret my fate; if I have consented to survive, it is to serve your glory. I intend to write the history of the great achievements we have performed together.

Adieu, my friends. Would I could press you all to my

heart. I embrace you all in the person of your general. Come, General Petit, that I may press you to my heart! Bring me the eagle that I may embrace it also! Adieu, my children! Be always gallant and good. Do not forget me.

George Washington
1732–1799

George Washington, because of his continuous army experience, his service from 1759–74 in the Virginia House of Burgesses, and in the Continental Congress, undoubtedly had the opportunity to hear the great speakers of his day and to try his own skills at speaking.

Washington grew weary of the political turmoil of his second term as President of the United States and refused a third term. His "Farewell Address" was delivered in September 1796, and contains directives for foreign policy which are invoked even today. On this occasion he was speaking to an assembly whose every heart felt kindly toward him and yet the parting was not as that of Napoleon, with grief, but rather a rest for Washington and a continuing life for the Republic he had helped to build.

FAREWELL ADDRESS

Friends and Fellow Citizens:—The period for a new election of a citizen, to administer the executive government of the United States, being not far distant, and the time actually arrived when your thoughts must be employed in designating the person who is to be clothed with that important trust, it appears to me proper, especially as it may conduce to a more distinct expression of the public voice, that I should now apprise you of the resolution I have formed, to decline being considered among the number of those out of whom a choice is to be made.

I beg you, at the same time, to do me the justice to be assured that this resolution has not been taken without a strict regard to all the considerations appertaining to the relation which binds a dutiful citizen to his country; and that in withdrawing the tender of service which silence, in my situation, might imply, I am influenced by no diminution of zeal for your future interest, no deficiency of grateful respect for your past kindness, but am supported by a full conviction that the step is compatible with both.

The acceptance of, and continuance hitherto, in the office to which your suffrages have twice called me, have been a uniform sacrifice of inclination to the opinion of duty, and to a deference for what appeared to be your desire. I constantly hoped that it would have been much earlier in my power, consistently with motives which I was not at liberty to disregard, to return to that retirement from which I had been reluctantly drawn. The strength of my inclination to do this, previous to the last election, had even led to the preparation of an address, to declare it to you; but mature reflection on the then perplexed and critical posture of our affairs with foreign nations, and the unanimous advice of persons entitled to my confidence, impelled me to abandon the idea.

I rejoice that the state of your concerns, external as well as internal, no longer renders the pursuit of inclination incompatible with the sentiment of duty or propriety, and am persuaded, whatever partiality may be retained for my services, that in the present circumstances of our country, you will not disapprove of my determination to retire.

The impressions with which I first undertook the arduous trust were explained on the proper occasion. In the discharge of this trust I will only say, that I have with good intentions contributed towards the organization and administration of the government, the best exertions of which a very fallible judgment was capable. Not unconscious, in the outset, of the inferiority of my qualifications, experience, in my own eyes, perhaps still more in the eyes of others, has strengthened the motives to diffidence of myself; and every day the increasing weight of years admonishes me more and more that the shade of retirement is as necessary to me as it will be welcome. Satisfied that if any circumstances have given peculiar value to my services they were temporary, I have the consolation to believe, that while choice and prudence invite me to quit the political scene, patriotism does not forbid it.

In looking forward to the moment which is intended to terminate the career of my public life, my feelings do not permit me to suspend the deep acknowledgment of that debt of gratitude which I owe to my beloved country for the many honors it has conferred upon me; still more for the steadfast confidence with which it has supported me; and for the opportunities I have thence enjoyed of manifesting my inviolable attachment, by services, faithful and persevering, though in usefulness unequal to my zeal. If benefits have resulted to our country from these services, let it always be remembered to your praise, and as an instructive example in our annals, that under circumstances in which the passions, agitated in every direction, were liable to mislead, amidst appearances sometimes dubious, vicissitudes of fortune often discouraging, in situations in which not unfrequently want of success has countenanced the spirit of criticism, the constancy of your support was the essential prop of the efforts, and the guarantee of the plans by which they were effected. Profoundly penetrated with this idea, I shall carry it with me to my grave, as a strong incitement to unceasing wishes that heaven may continue to you the choicest tokens of its beneficence; that your union and brotherly affection may be perpetual; that the free constitution, which is the work of your hands, may be sacredly maintained; that its administration, in every department, may be stamped with wisdom and virtue; that, in fine, the happiness of the people of these States, under the auspices of liberty, may be made complete by so careful a preservation and so prudent a use of this blessing as will acquire to them the glory of recommending it to the applause, the affection, and adoption of every nation which is yet a stranger to it.

Here, perhaps, I ought to stop. But a solicitude for your welfare, which cannot end but with my life, and the apprehension of danger, natural to that solicitude, urge me, on an occasion like the present, to offer to your solemn contemplation, and to recommend to your frequent review, some sentiments, which are the result of much reflection, of no inconsiderable observation, and which appear to me all-important to the permanency of your felicity as a people. These will be offered to you with the more freedom, as you can only see in them the disinterested warnings of a parting friend, who can possibly have no personal motive to bias his counsel. Nor can I forget, as an encouragement to it, your indulgent reception of my sentiments on a former and not dissimilar occasion.

Interwoven as is the love of liberty with every ligament of your hearts, no recommendation of mine is necessary to fortify or confirm the attachment.

The unity of government which constitutes you one people is also now dear to you. It is justly so, for it is a main pillar in the edifice of your real independence, the support of your tranquility at home, your peace abroad, of your safety, of your prosperity, of that very liberty which you so highly prize. But as it is easy to foresee, that from different causes and from different quarters, much pains will be taken, many artifices employed, to weaken in your minds the conviction of this truth; as this is the point in your political fortress against which the batteries of internal and external enemies will be most constantly and actively (though often covertly and insidiously) directed, it is of infinite moment that you should properly estimate the immense value of your national union, to your collective and individual happiness; that you should cherish a cordial, habitual, and immovable attachment to it; accustoming yourselves to think and speak of it as of the palladium of your political safety and prosperity, watching for its preservation with jealous anxiety; discountenancing whatever may suggest even a suspicion that it can in any event be abandoned; and indignantly frowning upon the first dawning of every attempt to alienate any portion of our country from the rest, or to enfeeble the sacred ties which now link together the various parts.

For this you have every inducement of sympathy and interest. Citizens, by birth or choice, of a common country, that country has a right to concentrate your affections. The name of American, which belongs to you in your national capacity, must always exalt the just pride of patriotism more than any appellation derived from local discriminations. With slight shades of difference, you have the same religion, manners, habits, and political principles. You have, in a common cause, fought and triumphed together; the independence and liberty you possess are the work of joint councils and joint efforts, of common dangers, sufferings, and successes.

But these considerations, however powerfully they address themselves to your sensibility, are greatly outweighed by those which apply more immediately to your interest. Here every portion of our country finds the most commanding motives for carefully guarding and preserving the union of the whole.

The North, in an unrestrained intercourse with the South, protected by the equal laws of a common government, finds, in the productions of the latter, great additional resources of maritime and commercial enterprise, and precious materials of manufacturing industry. The South, in the same intercourse, benefiting by the agency of the North, sees its agriculture grow and its commerce expand. Turning partly into its own channels the seamen of the North, it finds its particular navigation invigorated; and while it contributes, in different ways, to nourish and increase the general mass of the national navigation, it looks forward to the protection of a maritime strength, to which itself is unequally adapted. The East, in like intercourse with the West, already finds, and in the progressive improvement of interior communications, by land and water, will more and more find a valuable vent for the commodities which it brings from abroad or manufactures at home. The West derives from the East supplies requisite to its growth and comfort, and what is perhaps of still greater consequence, it must of necessity owe the secure enjoyment of indispensable outlets for its own productions to the weight, influence, and the future maritime strength of the Atlantic side of the Union, directed by an indissoluble community of interest as one nation. Any other tenure, by which the West can hold this essential advantage, whether derived from its own separate strength, or from an apostate and unnatural connection with any foreign power, must be intrinsically precarious.

While, then, every part of our country thus feels an immediate and particular interest in union, all the parts combined cannot fail to find, in the united mass of means and efforts, greater strength, greater resource, proportionably greater security, from external danger, a less frequent interruption of their peace by foreign nations; and what is of inestimable value, they must derive from union an exemption from those broils and wars between themselves which so frequently afflict neighboring countries, not tied together by the same government, which their own rivalships alone would be sufficient to produce, but which opposite foreign alliances, attachments, and intrigues, would stimulate and embitter. Hence, likewise, they will avoid the necessity of those overgrown military establishments, which, under any form of government, are inauspicious to liberty, and which are to be regarded as particularly hostile to republican liberty. In this sense it is that your union ought to be considered as a main prop of your liberty, and that the love of the one ought to endear to you the preservation of the other.

These considerations speak a persuasive language to every reflecting and virtuous mind, and exhibit the continuance of the union as a primary object of patriotic desire. Is there a doubt whether a common government can embrace so large a sphere? Let experience solve it. To listen to mere speculation, in such a case, were criminal. We are authorized to hope that a proper organization of the whole, with the auxiliary agency of governments for the respective subdivisions, will afford a happy issue to the experiment. 'Tis well worth a fair and full experiment. With such powerful and obvious motives to union, affecting all parts of our country, while experience shall not have demonstrated its impracticability, there will always be reason to distrust the patriotism of those who, in any quarter, may endeavor to weaken its bands.

In contemplating the causes which may disturb our union, it occurs, as a matter of serious concern, that any ground should have been furnished for characterizing parties by geographical discriminations—Northern and Southern, Atlantic and Western—whence designing men may endeavor to excite a belief that there is a real difference of local interests and views. One of the expedients of party to acquire influence within particular districts is to misrepresent the opinions and aims of other districts. You cannot shield yourselves too much against the jealousies and heart-burnings which spring from these misrepresentations; they tend to render alien to each other those who ought to be bound together by fraternal affection. The inhabitants of our western country have lately had a useful lesson on this head. They have seen, in the negotiation by the executive, and in the unanimous ratification by the Senate, of the treaty with Spain, and in the universal satisfaction of that event throughout the United States, a decisive proof how unfounded were the suspicions propagated among them of a policy in the general government and in the Atlantic States, unfriendly to their interests in regard to the Mississippi; they have been witnesses to the formation of two treaties—that with Great Britain and that with Spain—which secure to them everything they could desire, in respect to our foreign relations, towards confirming their prosperity. Will it not be their wisdom to rely, for the preservation of these advantages, on the union by which they were procured? Will they not henceforth be deaf to those advisers, if such there are, who would sever them from their brethren, and connect them with aliens?

To the efficacy and permanency of your union, a government for the whole is indispensable. No alliances, however strict, between the parts, can be an adequate substitute; they must inevitably experience the infractions and interruptions, which alliances, in all times, have experienced. Sensible of this momentous truth, you have improved upon your first essay by the adoption of a constitution of government better calculated than your former for an intimate union, and for the efficacious management of your common concerns. This government, the offspring of our own choice, uninfluenced and unawed, adopted upon full investigation and mature deliberation, completely free in its principles, in the distribution of its powers, uniting security with energy, and containing within itself a provision for its own amendment, has a just claim to your confidence and your support. Respect for its authority, compliance with its laws, acquiescence in its measures, are duties enjoined by the fundamental maxims of true liberty. The basis of our political systems is the right of the people to make and to alter the constitutions of government. But the constitution, which at any time exists, until changed by an explicit and authentic act of the whole people, is sacredly obligatory upon all. The very idea of the power and the right of the people to establish a government presupposes the duty of every individual to obey the established government.

All obstructions to the execution of the laws, all combinations and associations, under whatever plausible character, with the real design to direct, control, counteract, or awe the regular deliberation and action of the constituted authorities, are destructive of this fundamental principle, and of fatal tendency. They serve to organize faction, to give it an artificial and extraordinary force, to put in the place of the delegated will of the nation, the will of a party, often a small, but artful and enterprising minority of the community; and according to the alternate triumphs of different parties, to make the public administration the mirror of the ill-concerted and incongruous projects of faction, rather than the organ of consistent and wholesome plans, digested by common councils, and modified by mutual interests.

However combinations or associations of the above description may now and then answer popular ends, they are likely, in the course of time and things, to become potent engines, by which cunning, ambitious, and unprincipled men will be enabled to subvert the power of the people, and to usurp for themselves the reins of government; destroying afterward the very engines which have lifted them to unjust dominion.

Toward the preservation of your government and the permanency of your present happy state, it is requisite, not only that you speedily discountenance irregular opposition to its acknowledged authority, but also that you resist with care the spirit of innovation upon its principles, however specious the pretexts. One method of assault may be to effect, in the forms of the constitution, alterations which will impair the energy of the system, and thus to undermine what cannot be directly overthrown. In all the changes to which you may be invited, remember that time and habit are at least as necessary to fix the true character of governments as of other human institutions; that experience is the surest standard by which to test the real tendency of the existing constitution of a country; that facility in changes, upon the credit of mere hypothesis and opinion, exposes to perpetual change, from the endless variety of hypothesis and opinion. And remember especially, that for the efficient management of your common interests, in a country so extensive as ours, a government of as much vigor as is consistent with the perfect security of liberty, is indispensable. Liberty itself will find in such a government, with powers properly distributed and adjusted, its surest guardian. It is, indeed, little else than a name, where the government is too feeble to withstand the enterprises of faction; to confine each member of society within the limits prescribed by the laws, and to maintain all in the secure and tranquil enjoyment of the rights of person and property.

I have already intimated to you the danger of parties in the State, with particular reference to the founding of them on geographical discrimination. Let me now take a more comprehensive view, and warn you, in the most solemn manner, against the baneful effects of the spirit of party, generally.

This spirit, unfortunately, is inseparable from our nature, having its root in the strongest passions of the human mind. It exists under different shapes, in all governments, more or less stifled, controlled, or repressed. But in those of the popular form, it is seen in its greatest rankness, and is truly their worst enemy.

The alternate domination of one faction over another, sharpened by the spirit of revenge, natural to party dissensions, which, in different ages and countries, has perpetrated the most horrid enormities, is itself a frightful despotism. But this leads, at length, to a more formal and permanent despotism. The disorders and miseries, which result, gradually incline the minds of men to seek security and repose in the absolute power of an individual; and sooner or later, the chief of some prevailing faction, more able or more fortunate than his competitors, turns this disposition to the purposes of his own elevation on the ruins of public liberty.

Without looking forward to an extremity of this kind, (which, nevertheless, ought not to be entirely out of sight) the common and continual mischiefs of the spirit of party are sufficient to make it the interest and duty of a wise people to discourage and restrain it.

It serves always to distract the public councils, and enfeeble the public administration. It agitates the community with ill-founded jealousies and false alarms; kindles the animosity of one part against another; foments occasionally riot and insurrection. It opens the door to foreign influence and corruption, which find a facilitated access to the government itself, through the channels of party passion. Thus the policy and the will of one country are subjected to the policy and will of another.

There is an opinion, that parties, in free countries, are useful checks upon the administration of the government, and serve to keep alive the spirit of liberty. This, within certain limits, is probably true; and, in governments of a monarchical cast, patriotism may look with indulgence, if not with favor, upon the spirit of party. But in those of popular character, in governments purely elective, it is a spirit not to be encouraged. From their natural tendency, it is certain there will always be enough of that spirit for every salutary purpose. And there being constant danger of excess, the effort ought to be, by force of public opinion, to mitigate and assuage it. A fire not to be quenched, it demands a uniform vigilance to prevent its bursting into a flame, lest, instead of warming, it should consume.

It is important, likewise, that the habits of thinking, in a free country, should inspire caution in those entrusted with its administration, to confine themselves within their respective constitutional spheres, avoiding, in the exercise of the powers of one department, to encroach upon another. The spirit of encroachment tends to consolidate the powers of all the departments in one, and thus to create, whatever the form of government, a real despotism. A just estimate of that love of power, and proneness to abuse it, which predominate in the human heart, is sufficient to satisfy us of the truth of this position. The necessity of reciprocal checks in the exercise of political power, by dividing and distributing it into different depositaries, and constituting each the guardian of the public weal against invasion by the other, has been evinced by experiments ancient and modern: some of them in our country, and under our own eyes. To preserve them must be as necessary as to institute them. If, in the opinion of the people, the distribution or modification of the constitutional powers, be, in any particular, wrong, let it be corrected by an amendment in the way which the constitution designates. But let there be no change by usurpation; for though this, in one instance, may be the instrument of good, it is the customary weapon by which free governments are destroyed. The precedent must always greatly overbalance, in permanent evil, any partial or transient benefit which the use can at any time yield.

Of all the dispositions and habits, which lead to political prosperity, religion and morality are indispensable supports. In vain would that man claim the tribute of patriotism, who should labor to subvert these great pillars of human happiness, these firmest props of the destinies of men and citizens. The mere politician, equally with the pious man, ought to respect and to cherish them. A volume could not trace all their connection with private and public felicity. Let it simply be asked, where is the security for property, for reputation, for life, if the sense of religious obligation desert the oaths, which are the instruments of investigation in courts of justice? And let us with caution indulge the supposition that morality can be maintained without religion. Whatever may be conceded to the influence of refined education on minds of peculiar structure, reason and experience both forbid us to expect, that national morality can prevail in exclusion of religious principles.

It is substantially true, that virtue or morality is a necessary spring of popular government. The rule, indeed, extends with more or less force to every species of free government. Who, that is a sincere friend to it, can look with indifference upon attempts to shake the foundation of the fabric?

Promote, then, as an object of primary importance, institutions for the general diffusion of knowledge. In proportion as the structure of a government gives force to public opinion, it is essential that public opinion should be enlightened.

As a very important source of strength and security, cherish public credit. One method of preserving it is to use it as sparingly as possible; avoiding occasions of expense by cultivating peace, but remembering also that timely disbursements to prepare for danger frequently prevent much greater disbursements to repel it; avoiding likewise the accumulation of debt, not only by shunning occasions of expense, but by vigorous exertions in time of peace to discharge the debts which unavoidable wars may have occasioned, not ungenerously throwing upon posterity the burden which we ourselves ought to bear. The execution of these maxims belongs to your representatives, but it is necessary that public opinion should co-operate. To facilitate to them the performance of their duty, it is essential that you should practically bear in mind, that towards the payment of debts there must be revenue; that to have revenue there must be taxes; that no taxes can be devised which are not more or less inconvenient and unpleasant; that the intrinsic embarrassment, inseparable from the selection of the proper objects (which is always the choice of difficulties) ought to be a decisive motive for a candid construction of the conduct of the government in making it, and for a spirit of acquiescence in the measures for obtaining revenue which the public exigencies may at any time dictate.

Observe good faith and justice towards all nations;

cultivate peace and harmony with all; religion and morality enjoin this conduct; and can it be that good policy does not equally enjoin it? It will be worthy of a free, enlightened, and, at no distant period, a great nation, to give to mankind the magnanimous and too novel example of a people always guided by an exalted justice and benevolence. Who can doubt that, in the course of time and things, the fruits of such a plan would richly repay any temporary advantages that might be lost by a steady adherence to it? Can it be, that Providence has not connected the permanent felicity of a nation with its virtue? The experiment, at least, is recommended by every sentiment which ennobles human nature. Alas! is it rendered impossible by its vices?

In the execution of such a plan, nothing is more essential than that permanent, inveterate antipathies against particular nations, and passionate attachments for others, should be excluded; and that in place of them just and amicable feelings towards all should be cultivated. The nation which indulges towards another an habitual hatred, or an habitual fondness, is in some degree a slave. It is a slave to its animosity or to its affection, either of which is sufficient to lead it astray from its duty and its interest. Antipathy in one nation against another, disposes each more readily to offer insult and injury, to lay hold of slight causes of umbrage and to be haughty and intractable, when accidental or trifling occasions of dispute occur.

Hence frequent collisions, obstinate, envenomed, and bloody contests. The nation, prompted by ill-will and resentment, sometimes impels to war the government, contrary to the best calculations of policy. The government sometimes participates in the national propensity, and adopts through passion what reason would reject; at other times, it makes the animosity of the nation subservient to projects of hostility instigated by pride, ambition and other sinister and pernicious motives. The peace often, and sometimes, perhaps, the liberty of nations, has been the victim.

So, likewise, a passionate attachment of one nation for another produces a variety of evils. Sympathy for the favorite nation facilitating the illusion of an imaginary common interest in cases where no real common interest exists, and infusing into one the enmities of the other, betrays the former into a participation in the quarrels and wars of the latter, without adequate inducement or justification. It leads also to concessions to the favorite nation of privileges denied to others, which is apt doubly to injure the nation making the concessions; by unnecessarily parting with what ought to have been retained; and by exciting jealousy, ill-will, and a disposition to retaliate, in the parties from whom equal privileges are withheld; and it gives to ambitious, corrupted, or deluded citizens (who devote themselves to the favorite nation) facility to betray, or sacrifice the interests of their own country, without odium, sometimes even with popularity; gilding, with the appearances of a virtuous sense of obligation, a commendable deference for public opinion, or laudable zeal for public good, the base or foolish compliances of ambition, corruption, or infatuation.

As avenues to foreign influence, in innumerable ways, such attachments are particularly alarming to the truly enlightened and independent patriot. How many opportunities do they afford to tamper with domestic factions; to practise the arts of seduction; to mislead public opinion; to influence or awe the public councils! Such an attachment of a small or weak nation, toward a great and powerful one, dooms the former to be the satellite of the latter.

Against the insidious wiles of foreign influence (I conjure you to believe me, fellow-citizens), the jealousy of a free people ought to be constantly awake; since history and experience prove, that foreign influence is one of the most baneful foes of republican government. But that jealousy, to be useful, must be impartial; else it becomes the instrument of the very influence to be avoided, instead of a defence against it. Excessive partiality for one foreign nation, and excessive dislike of another, cause those whom they actuate, to see danger only on one side; and serve to veil and even second the arts of influence on the other. Real patriots, who may resist the intrigues of the favorite, are liable to become suspected and odious; while its tools and dupes usurp the applause and confidence of the people, to surrender their interests.

The great rule of conduct for us, in regard to foreign nations is, in extending our commercial relations, to have with them as little political connection as possible. So far as we have already formed engagements, let them be fulfilled with perfect good faith. Here let us stop.

Europe has a set of primary interests, which to us have none, or a very remote relation. Hence she must be engaged in frequent controversies, the causes of which are essentially foreign to our concerns. Hence, therefore, it must be unwise in us to implicate ourselves, by artificial ties, in the ordinary vicissitudes of her politics, or the ordinary combinations and collisions of her friendships and enmities.

Our detached and distant situation invites and enables us to pursue a different course. If we remain one people, under an efficient government, the period is not far off when we may defy material injury from external annoyance; when we may take such an attitude as will cause the neutrality we may at any time resolve upon, to be scrupulously respected; when belligerent nations, under the impossibility of making acquisitions upon us, will not lightly hazard the giving us provocation; when we may choose peace or war, as our interest, guided by justice, shall counsel.

Why forego the advantages of so peculiar a situation? Why quit our own, to stand upon foreign ground? Why, by interweaving our destiny with that of any part of Europe, entangle our peace and prosperity in the toils of European ambition, rivalship, interest, humor, or caprice?

'Tis our true policy to steer clear of permanent alliances with any portion of the foreign world; so far, I mean, as we are now at liberty to do it; for let me not be understood as capable of patronizing infidelity to existing engagements. I hold the maximum no less applicable to public than to private affairs, that honesty is always the best policy. I repeat it, therefore, let those engagements be observed in their genuine sense. But, in my opinion, it is unnecessary, and would be unwise, to extend them.

Taking care always to keep ourselves, by suitable establishments, in a respectable defensive posture, we may safely trust to temporary alliances for extraordinary emergencies.

Harmony, and a liberal intercourse with all nations, are recommended by policy, humanity, and interest. But even our commercial policy should hold an equal and impartial hand; neither seeking nor granting exclusive favors or preferences; consulting the natural course of things; diffusing and diversifying, by gentle means, the streams of commerce, but forcing nothing; establishing, with powers so disposed, in order to give trade a stable course, to define the rights of our merchants, and to enable the government to support them, conventional rules of intercourse, the best that present circumstances and mutual opinion will permit, but temporary, and liable to be, from time to time, abandoned or varied, as experience and circumstances shall dictate; constantly keeping in view, that it is folly in one nation to look for disinterested favors from another; that it must pay, with a portion of its independence, for whatever it may accept under that character; that, by such acceptance, it may place itself in the condition of having given equivalents for nominal favors, and yet of being reproached with ingratitude for not giving more. There can be no greater error than to expect to calculate upon real favors from nation to nation. It is an illusion, which experience must cure, which a just pride ought to discard.

In offering to you, my countrymen, these counsels of an old and affectionate friend, I dare not hope they will make the strong and lasting impression I could wish; that they will control the usual current of the passions, or prevent our nation from running the course which has hitherto marked the destiny of nations! But, if I may even flatter myself, that they may be productive of some partial benefit, some occasional good; that they may now and then recur to moderate the fury of party spirit; to warn against the mischiefs of foreign intrigues; to guard against the impostures of pretended patriotism; this hope will be a full recompense for the solicitude for your welfare, by which they have been dictated.

How far, in the discharge of my official duties, I have been guided by the principles which have been delineated, the public records and other evidences of my conduct must witness to you and to the world. To myself the assurance of my own conscience is, that I have at least believed myself to be guided by them.

In relation to the still subsisting war in Europe, my proclamation of April 22, 1793, is the index to my plan. Sanctioned by your approving voice, and by that of your representatives in both Houses of Congress, the spirit of that measure has continually governed me, uninfluenced by any attempts to deter or divert me from it.

After deliberate examination, with the aid of the best lights I could obtain, I was well satisfied that our country, under all the circumstances of the case, had a right to take, and was bound in duty and interest to take, a neutral position. Having taken it, I determined, as far as should depend upon me, to maintain it with moderation, perseverance, and firmness.

The considerations which respect the right to hold this conduct, it is not necessary, on this occasion, to detail. I will only observe, that according to my understanding of the matter, that right, so far from being denied by any of the belligerent powers, has been virtually admitted by all.

The duty of holding a neutral conduct may be inferred, without anything more, from the obligation which justice and humanity impose on every nation, in cases in which it is free to act, to maintain inviolate the relations of peace and amity towards other nations.

The inducements of interest for observing that conduct will best be referred to your own reflection and experience. With me, a predominant motive has been to endeavor to gain time to our country to settle and mature its yet recent institutions, and to progress, without interruption, to that degree of strength and consistency which is necessary to give it, humanly speaking, the command of its own fortunes.

Though, in reviewing the incidents of my administration,

I am unconscious of intentional error, I am, nevertheless, too sensible of my defects, not to think it probable that I may have committed many errors. Whatever they may be, I fervently beseech the Almighty to avert or mitigate the evils to which they may tend. I shall also carry with me the hope that my country will never cease to view them with indulgence, and that after forty-five years of my life dedicated to its service, with an upright zeal, the faults of incompetent abilities will be consigned to oblivion, as myself must soon be to the mansions of rest.

Relying on its kindness in this, as in other things, and actuated by that fervent love towards it, which is so natural to a man who views in it the native soil of himself and his progenitors for several generations, I anticipate, with pleasing expectations, that retreat in which I promise myself to realize, without alloy, the sweet enjoyment of partaking, in the midst of my fellow-citizens, the benign influence of good laws under a free government—the ever favorite object of my heart, and the happy reward, as I trust, of our mutual cares, labors, and dangers.

Thomas Jefferson
1743–1826

Thomas Jefferson, third President of the United States, author of the Declaration of Independence, was a believer in the expansion of the United States. He opposed the Federalists and the centralization of power and was called a Republican, a term used for what has become the Democratic Party. He went to the College of William and Mary in Williamsburg, Virginia, and studied law with George Wythe in the same town. He was a member of the Virginia House of Burgesses and then a member of the Continental Congress, where he was assigned the duty to draw up a Declaration of Independence. In 1796 he ran for the presidency but was defeated by John Adams. He became Vice President.

In 1800 Jefferson and Aaron Burr received equal votes for the office of President. The House of Representatives then was empowered to vote, and elected Jefferson President. He was the first President to be inaugurated in the city of Washington. In this speech he declared his policy of expansion, and this was to be exemplified in 1803 with the great Louisiana Purchase and the Lewis and Clarke Expedition to the West.

Jefferson was an eloquent speaker and skillful writer. He was, in many respects, a man who might have come out of the Renaissance.

First Inaugural Address

Friends and Fellow Citizens:—Called upon to undertake the duties of the first executive office of our country, I avail myself of the presence of that portion of my fellow-citizens which is here assembled, to express my grateful thanks for the favor with which they have been pleased to look toward me, to declare a sincere consciousness, that the task is above my talents, and that I approach it with those anxious and awful presentiments, which the greatness of the charge, and the weakness of my powers, so justly inspire. A rising nation, spread over a wide and fruitful land, traversing all the seas with the rich productions of their industry, engaged in commerce with nations who feel power and forget right, advancing rapidly to destinies beyond the reach of mortal eye; when I contemplate these transcendent objects, and see the honor, the happiness and the hopes of this beloved country committed to the issue and the auspices of this day, I shrink from the contemplation, and humble myself before the magnitude of the undertaking. Utterly, indeed, should I despair, did not the presence of many, whom I see here, remind me that, in the other high authorities provided by our constitution, I shall find resources of wisdom, of virtue, and of zeal, on which to rely under all difficulties. To you, then, gentlemen, who are charged with the sovereign functions of legislation, and to those associated with you, I look with encouragement for that guidance and support which may enable us to steer with safety the vessel in which we are all embarked, amidst the conflicting elements of a troubled world.

During the contest of opinion through which we have passed, the animation of discussions and of exertions has sometimes worn an aspect which might impose on strangers unused to think freely, and to speak and to write what they think; but this being now decided by the voice of the nation, announced according to the rules of the constitution, all will of course arrange themselves under the will of the law, and unite in common efforts for the common good. All, too, will bear in mind this sacred principle, that though the will of the majority is in all cases to prevail, that will, to be rightful, must be reasonable; that the minority possess their equal rights, which equal laws must protect, and to violate which would be oppression. Let us then, fellow-citizens, unite with one heart and one mind, let us restore to social intercourse that harmony and affection without which liberty and even life itself are but dreary things. And let us reflect, that having banished from our land that religious intolerance under which mankind so long bled and suffered, we have yet gained little, if we countenance a political intolerance, as despotic, as wicked, and as capable of as bitter and bloody persecutions. During the throes and convulsions of the ancient world, during the agonizing spasms of infuriated man, seeking through blood and slaughter his long-lost liberty, it was not wonderful that the agitation of the billows should reach even this distant and peaceful shore; that this should be more felt and feared by some, and less by others, and should divide opinions as to measures of safety; but every difference of opinion is not a difference of principle. We have called by different names brethren of the same principle. We are all Republicans; we are all Federalists. If there be any among us who wish to dissolve this Union, or to change its republican form, let them stand undisturbed as monuments of the safety with which error of opinion may be tolerated, where reason is left free to combat it. I know, indeed, that some honest men fear that a republican government cannot be strong; that this government is not strong enough. But would the honest patriot, in the full tide of successful experiment, abandon a government which has so far kept us free and firm, on the theoretic and visionary fear, that this government, the world's best hope, may, by possibility, want energy to preserve itself? I trust not. I believe this, on the contrary, the strongest government on earth. I believe it the only one where every man, at the call of the law, would fly to the standard of the law, and would meet invasions of the public order as his own personal concern. Sometimes it is said that man cannot be trusted with the government of himself. Can he then be trusted with the government of others? Or, have we found angels in the form of kings, to govern him? Let history answer this question.

Let us then, with courage and confidence, pursue our own federal and republican principles; our attachment to union and representative government. Kindly separated by nature and a wide ocean from the exterminating havoc of one quarter of the globe; too high-minded to endure the degradation of the others, possessing a chosen country, with room enough for our descendants to the thousandth and thousandth generation, entertaining a due sense of our equal right to the use of our own faculties, to the acquisition of our own industry, to honor and confidence from our fellow-citizens, resulting not from birth, but from our actions and their sense of them, enlightened by a benign religion, professed in deed and practised in various forms, yet all of them inculcating honesty, truth, temperance, gratitude, and the love of man, acknowledging and adoring an overruling Providence, which, by all its dispensations, proves that it delights in the happiness of man here, and his greater happiness hereafter; with all these blessings, what more is necessary to make us a happy and prosperous people? Still one thing more, fellow-citizens, a wise and frugal government, which shall restrain men from injuring one another, shall leave them otherwise free to regulate their own pursuits of industry and improvement, and shall not take from the mouth of labor the bread it has earned. This is the sum of good government; and this is necessary to close the circle of our felicities.

About to enter, fellow-citizens, upon the exercise of duties which comprehend everything dear and valuable to you, it is proper you should understand what I deem the essential principles of our government, and consequently, those which ought to shape its administration. I will compress them within the narrowest compass they will bear, stating the general principle, but not all its limitations. Equal and exact justice to all men, of whatever state or persuasion, religious or political; peace, commerce, and honest friendship with all nations, entangling alliances with none; the support of the State governments in all their rights, as the most competent administrations for our domestic concerns, and the surest bulwarks against anti-republican tendencies; the preservation of the general government in its whole constitutional vigor, as the sheet-anchor of our peace at home and safety abroad; a jealous care of the right of election by the people, a mild and safe corrective of abuses which are lopped by the sword of revolution where peaceable remedies are unprovided;

absolute acquiescence in the decisions of the majority, the vital principle of republics, from which there is no appeal but to force, the vital principle and immediate parent of despotism; a well-disciplined militia, our best reliance in peace, and for the first moments of war, till regulars may relieve them; the supremacy of the civil over the military authority; economy in the public expense, that labor may be lightly burdened; the honest payment of our debts, and sacred preservation of the public faith; encouragement of agriculture, and of commerce as its handmaid; the diffusion of information, and arraignment of all abuses at the bar of the public reason; freedom of religion, freedom of the press, and freedom of person, under the protection of the *habeas corpus,* and trial by juries impartially selected. These principles form the bright constellation which has gone before us, and guided our steps through an age of revolution and reformation. The wisdom of our sages, and blood of our heroes, have been devoted to their attainment; they should be the creed of our political faith, the text of civic instruction, the touchstone by which to try the services of those we trust; and should we wander from them in moments of error or of alarm, let us hasten to retrace our steps, and to regain the road which alone leads to peace, liberty, and safety.

I repair, then, fellow-citizens, to the post you have assigned me. With experience enough in subordinate offices to have seen the difficulties of this, the greatest of all, I have learned to expect that it will rarely fall to the lot of imperfect man, to retire from this station with the reputation and the favor which bring him into it. Without pretensions to that high confidence you reposed in our first and greatest revolutionary character, whose pre-eminent services had entitled him to the first place in his country's love, and destined for him the fairest page in the volume of faithful history, I ask so much confidence only as may give firmness and effect to the legal administration of your affairs. I shall often go wrong through defect of judgment. When right, I shall often be thought wrong by those whose positions will not command a view of the whole ground. I ask your indulgence for my own errors, which will never be intentional; and your support against the errors of others, who may condemn what they would not, if seen in all its parts. The approbation implied by your suffrage, is a great consolation to me for the past; and my future solicitude will be, to retain the good opinion of those who have bestowed it in advance, to conciliate that of others, by doing them all the good in my power, and to be instrumental to the happiness and freedom of all.

Relying then on the patronage of your good-will, I advance with obedience to the work, ready to retire from it whenever you become sensible how much better choices it is in your power to make. And may that infinite power which rules the destinies of the universe, lead our councils to what is best, and give them a favorable issue for your peace and prosperity.

Abraham Lincoln
1809–1865

When Abraham Lincoln left Springfield, Illinois, to take the responsibility of the presidency, he was not unacquainted with responsibility nor did he hesitate to assume it; but the leave-taking from Springfield, his old friends, his law practice, a people to whom, as he says, "I owe all that I am," is as touching a parting as that of Napoleon from his Old Guard. When one looks back at history, we see how great was to be the sorrow of the President in a divided country.

The speech was delivered in Springfield on February 12, 1861.

The Second Inaugural Address was delivered from the steps of the Capitol in Washington, March 4, 1865.

FAREWELL ADDRESS AT SPRINGFIELD

My friends:—No one not in my position can appreciate the sadness I feel at this parting. To this people I owe all that I am. Here I have lived more than a quarter of a century; here my children were born, and here one of them lies buried. I know not how soon I shall see you again. A duty devolves upon me which is, perhaps, greater than that which has devolved upon any other man since the days of Washington. He never could have succeeded except for the aid of Divine Providence, upon which he at all times relied. I feel that I cannot succeed without the same Divine Aid which sustained him; and in the same Almighty Being I place my reliance for support; and I hope you, my friends, will all pray that I may receive that Divine Assistance, without which I cannot succeed, but with which success is certain. Again I bid you all an affectionate farewell.

SECOND INAUGURAL ADDRESS

Fellow Countrymen:—

At this second appearing to take the oath of the Presidential office there is less occasion for an extended address than there was at the first. Then a statement somewhat in detail of a course to be pursued seemed fitting and proper. Now, at the expiration of four years, during which public declarations have been constantly called forth on every point and phase of the great contest which still absorbs the attention and engrosses the energies of the nation, little that is new could be presented. The progress of our arms, upon which all else chiefly depends, is as well known to the public as to myself, and it is, I trust, reasonably satisfactory and encouraging to all. With high hope for the future, no prediction in regard to it is ventured.

On the occasion corresponding to this four years ago all thoughts were anxiously directed to an impending civil war. All dreaded it, all sought to avert it. While the inaugural address was being delivered from this place, devoted altogether to *saving* the Union without war, insurgent agents were in the city seeking to *destroy* it without war—seeking to dissolve the Union and divide effects by negotiation. Both parties deprecated war, but one of them would *make* war rather than let the nation survive, and the other would *accept* war rather than let it perish, and the war came.

One-eighth of the whole population were colored slaves, not distributed generally over the Union, but localized in the southern part of it. These slaves constituted a peculiar and powerful interest. All knew that this interest was somehow the cause of the war. To strengthen, perpetuate, and extend this interest was the object for which the insurgents would rend the Union even by war, while the Government claimed no right to do more than to restrict the territorial enlargement of it. Neither party expected for the war the magnitude or the duration which it has already attained. Neither anticipated that the *cause* of the conflict might cease with or even before the conflict itself should cease. Each looked for an easier triumph, and a result less fundamental and astounding. Both read the same Bible and pray to the same God, and each invokes His aid against the other. It may seem strange that any men should dare to ask a just God's assistance in wringing their bread from the sweat of other men's faces, but let us judge not, that we be not judged. The prayers of both could not be answered. That of neither has been answered fully. The Almighty has His own purposes. "Woe unto the world because of offenses; for it must needs be that offenses come, but woe to that man by whom the offense cometh." If we shall suppose that American slavery is one of those offenses which, in the providence of God, must needs come, but which, having continued through His appointed time, He now wills to remove, and that He gives to both North and South this terrible war as the woe due to those by whom the offense came, shall we discern therein any departure from those divine attributes which the believers in a living God always ascribe to Him? Fondly do we hope, fervently do we pray, that this mighty scourge of war may speedily pass away. Yet, if God wills that it continue until all the wealth piled by the bondsman's two hundred and fifty years of unrequited toil shall be sunk, and until every drop of blood drawn with the lash shall be paid by another drawn with the sword, as was said three thousand years ago, so still it must be said "the judgments of the Lord are true and righteous altogether."

With malice toward none, with charity for all, with firmness in the right as God gives us to see the right, let us strive on to finish the work we are in, to bind up the nation's wounds, to care for him who shall have borne the battle and for his widow and his orphan, to do all which may achieve and cherish a just and lasting peace among ourselves and with all nations.

Franklin Delano Roosevelt

1882–1945

Franklin Delano Roosevelt, thirty-second President of the United States, was elected in 1932. The nation was deep in the Depression, unemployment was high, and discontent with the preceding Hoover administration existed through the country. Unrest, uncertainty, disregard for the law enforcement of the prohibition laws had unsettled everyone.

At his inauguration, Roosevelt by the tone, the assurance, and the firmness of his voice set a new goal and stirred the people. The ring of his rhetoric and eloquence, the new voice in government, strengthened the citizenry of the United States. Here was a moment when oratory was needed and it was given succinctly, well-phrased, and cogently.

First Inaugural Address

I am certain that my fellow Americans expect that on my induction into the Presidency I will address them with a candor and a decision which the present situation of our Nation impels. This is preeminently the time to speak the truth, the whole truth, frankly and boldly. Nor need we shrink from honestly facing conditions in our country today. This great Nation will endure as it has endured, will revive and will prosper. So, first of all, let me assert my firm belief that the only thing we have to fear is fear itself —nameless, unreasoning, unjustified terror which paralyzes needed efforts to convert retreat into advance. In every dark hour of our national life a leadership of frankness and vigor has met with that understanding and support of the people themselves which is essential to victory. I am convinced that you will again give that support to leadership in these critical days.

In such a spirit on my part and on yours we face our common difficulties. They concern, thank God, only material things. Values have shrunken to fantastic levels; taxes have risen; our ability to pay has fallen; government of all kinds is faced by serious curtailment of income; the means of exchange are frozen in the currents of trade; the withered leaves of industrial enterprise lie on every side; farmers find no markets for their produce; the savings of many years in thousands of families are gone.

More important, a host of unemployed citizens face the grim problem of existence, and an equally great number toil with little return. Only a foolish optimist can deny the dark realities of the moment.

Yet our distress comes from no failure of substance. We are stricken by no plague of locusts. Compared with the perils which our forefathers conquered because they believed and were not afraid, we have still much to be thankful for. Nature still offers her bounty and human efforts have multiplied it. Plenty is at our doorstep, but a generous use of it languishes in the very sight of the supply. Primarily this is because the rulers of the exchange of mankind's goods have failed, through their own stubbornness and their own incompetence, have admitted their failure, and abdicated. Practices of the unscrupulous money changers stand indicted in the court of public opinion, rejected by the hearts and minds of men.

True they have tried, but their efforts have been cast in the pattern of an outworn tradition. Faced by failure of credit they have proposed only the lending of more money. Stripped of the lure of profit by which to induce our people to follow their false leadership, they have resorted to exhortations, pleading tearfully for restored confidence. They know only the rules of a generation of self-seekers. They have no vision, and when there is no vision the people perish.

The money changers have fled from their high seats in the temple of our civilization. We may now restore that temple to the ancient truths. The measure of the restoration lies in the extent to which we apply social values more noble than mere monetary profit.

Happiness lies not in the mere possession of money; it lies in the joy of achievement, in the thrill of creative effort. The joy and moral stimulation of work no longer must be forgotten in the mad chase of evanescent profits. These dark days will be worth all they cost us if they teach us that our true destiny is not to be ministered unto but to minister to ourselves and to our fellow men.

Recognition of the falsity of material wealth as the standard of success goes hand in hand with the abandonment of the false belief that public office and high political position are to be valued only by the standards of pride of place and personal profit; and there must be an end to a conduct in banking and in business which too often has given to a sacred trust the likeness of callous and selfish wrongdoing. Small wonder that confidence languishes, for it thrives only on honesty, on honor, on the sacredness of obligations, on faithful protection, on unselfish performance; without them it can not live.

Restoration calls, however, not for changes in ethics alone. This Nation asks for action, and action now.

Our greatest primary task is to put people to work. This is no unsolvable problem if we face it wisely and courageously. It can be accomplished in part by direct recruiting by the Government itself, treating the task as we would treat the emergency of a war, but at the same time, through this employment, accomplishing greatly needed projects to stimulate and reorganize the use of our natural resources.

Hand in hand with this we must frankly recognize the overbalance of population in our industrial centers and, by engaging on a national scale in a redistribution, endeavor to provide a better use of the land for those best fitted for the land. The task can be helped by definite efforts to raise the values of agricultural products and with this the power to purchase the output of our cities. It can be helped by preventing realistically the tragedy of the growing loss through foreclosure of our small homes and our farms. It can be helped by insistence that the Federal, State, and local governments act forthwith on the demand that their cost be drastically reduced. It can be helped by the unifying of relief activities which today are often scattered, uneconomical, and unequal. It can be helped by national planning for and supervision of all forms of transportation and of communications and other utilities which have a definitely public character. There are many ways in which it can be helped, but it can never be helped merely by talking about it. We must act and act quickly.

Finally, in our progress toward a resumption of work we require two safeguards against a return of the evils of the old order; there must be a strict supervision of all banking and credits and investments; there must be an end to speculation with other people's money, and there must be provision for an adequate but sound currency.

There are the lines of attack. I shall presently urge upon a new Congress in special session detailed measures for their fulfillment, and I shall seek the immediate assistance of the several States.

Through this program of action we address ourselves to putting our own national house in order and making income balance outgo. Our international trade relations, though vastly important, are in point of time and necessity secondary to the establishment of a sound national economy. I favor as a practical policy the putting of first things first. I shall spare no effort to restore world trade by international economic readjustment, but the emergency at home can not wait on that accomplishment.

The basic thought that guides these specific means of national recovery is not narrowly nationalistic. It is the insistence, as a first consideration, upon the interdependence of the various elements in and parts of the United States —a recognition of the old and permanently important manifestation of the American spirit of the pioneer. It is the way to recovery. It is the immediate way. It is the strongest assurance that the recovery will endure.

In the field of world policy I would dedicate this Nation to the policy of the good neighbor—the neighbor who resolutely respects himself and, because he does so, respects the rights of others—the neighbor who respects his obligations and respects the sanctity of his agreements in and with a world of neighbors.

If I read the temper of our people correctly, we now realize as we have never realized before our interdependence on each other; that we can not merely take but we must give as well; that if we are to go forward, we must move as a trained and loyal army willing to sacrifice for the good of a common discipline, because without such discipline no progress is made, no leadership becomes effective. We are, I know, ready and willing to submit our lives and property to such discipline, because it makes possible a leadership which aims at a larger good. This I propose to offer, pledging that the larger purposes will bind upon us all as a sacred obligation with a unity of duty hitherto evoked only in time of armed strife.

With this pledge taken, I assume unhesitatingly the leadership of this great army of our people dedicated to a disciplined attack upon our common problems.

Action in this image and to this end is feasible under the form of government which we have inherited from our ancestors. Our Constitution is so simple and practical that it is possible always to meet extraordinary needs by changes in emphasis and arrangement without loss of essential form. That is why our constitutional system has proved itself the most superbly enduring political mechanism the modern world has produced. It has met every stress of vast expansion of territory, of foreign wars, of bitter internal strife, of world relations.

It is to be hoped that the normal balance of executive and legislative authority may be wholly adequate to meet the unprecedented task before us. But it may be that an unprecedented demand and need for undelayed action may call for temporary departure from that normal balance of public procedure.

I am prepared under my constitutional duty to recommend the measures that a stricken nation in the midst of a stricken world may require. These measures, or such other measures as the Congress may build out of its experience and wisdom, I shall seek, within my constitutional authority, to bring to speedy adoption.

But in the event that the Congress shall fail to take one of these two courses, and in the event that the national emergency is still critical, I shall not evade the clear course of duty that will then confront me. I shall ask the Congress for the one remaining instrument to meet the crisis—broad Executive power to wage a war against the emergency, as great as the power that would be given to me if we were in fact invaded by a foreign foe.

For the trust reposed in me I will return the courage and the devotion that befit the time. I can do no less.

We face the arduous days that lie before us in the warm courage of the national unity; with the clear consciousness of seeking old and precious moral values; with the clean satisfaction that comes from the stern performance of duty by old and young alike. We aim at the assurance of a rounded and permanent national life.

We do not distrust the future of essential democracy. The people of the United States have not failed. In their need they have registered a mandate that they want direct, vigorous action. They have asked for discipline and direction under leadership. They have made me the present instrument of their wishes. In the spirit of the gift I take it.

In this dedication of a Nation we humbly ask the blessing of God. May He protect each and every one of us. May He guide me in the days to come.

Winston Churchill

1874–1965

*Churchill delivered the famous phrase of this speech,
"I have nothing to offer but blood, toil, tears, and sweat,"
to the House of Commons in his first statement as Prime
Minister, May 13, 1940. It was an historic day, event, and
speech. The new ministry had been formed to include
parties until then opposed; they had found their spokesman in Winston Churchill, in whom there was confidence
and for whom there was loyalty. He represented all that
was best and brave in the English people.*

*In this speech, given under grave circumstances, read-
ers are apt to forget the momentous times, the great danger, the low ebb of faith. New blood was needed; new
energies restored afresh, leadership with a certainty of purpose and all these the experienced, the eloquent Churchill
possessed. Yet it was through the dynamism of his activity
and the use of his eloquence that all the members of the
British Empire responded.*

Blood, Toil, Tears, and Sweat

On Friday evening last I received from His Majesty the
mission to form a new administration.

It was the evident will of Parliament and the nation
that this should be conceived on the broadest possible basis
and that it should include all parties.

I have already completed the most important part of
this task. A war cabinet has been formed of five members,
representing, with the Labor, Opposition and Liberals, the
unity of the nation.

It was necessary that this should be done in one single
day on account of the extreme urgency and rigor of events.
Other key positions were filled yesterday. I am submitting

a further list to the King tonight. I hope to complete the appointment of principal Ministers during tomorrow.

The appointment of other Ministers usually takes a little longer. I trust when Parliament meets again this part of my task will be completed and that the administration will be complete in all respects.

I considered it in the public interest to suggest to the Speaker that the House should be summoned today. At the end of today's proceedings, the adjournment of the House will be proposed until May 21 with provision for earlier meeting if need be. Business for that will be notified to M. P.'s at the earliest opportunity.

I now invite the House by a resolution to record its approval of the steps taken and declare its confidence in the new government. The resolution:

"That this House welcomes the formation of a government representing the united and inflexible resolve of the nation to prosecute the war with Germany to a victorious conclusion."

To form an administration of this scale and complexity is a serious undertaking in itself. But we are in the preliminary phase of one of the greatest battles in history. We are in action at many other points—in Norway and in Holland—and we have to be prepared in the Mediterranean. The air battle is continuing, and many preparations have to be made here at home.

In this crisis I think I may be pardoned if I do not address the House at any length today, and I hope that any of my friends and colleagues or former colleagues who are affected by the political reconstruction will make all allowances for any lack of ceremony with which it has been necessary to act.

I say to the House as I said to Ministers who have joined this government, I have nothing to offer but blood, toil, tears, and sweat. We have before us an ordeal of the most grievous kind. We have before us many, many months of struggle and suffering.

You ask, what is our policy? I say it is to wage war by land, sea and air. War with all our might and with all the strength God has given us, and to wage war against a monstrous tyranny never surpassed in the dark and lamentable catalogue of human crime. That is our policy.

You ask, what is our aim? I can answer in one word. It is victory. Victory at all costs—victory in spite of all terrors—victory, however long and hard the road may be, for without victory there is no survival.

Let that be realized. No survival for the British Empire, no survival for all that the British Empire has stood for, no survival for the urge, the impulse of the ages, that mankind shall move forward toward his goal.

I take up my task in buoyancy and hope. I feel sure that our cause will not be suffered to fail among men.

I feel entitled at this juncture, at this time, to claim the aid of all and to say, "Come then, let us go forward together with our united strength."

John Fitzgerald Kennedy

1917–1963

*John Fitzgerald Kennedy, thirty-fifth President of the
United States, won the Democratic nomination for President at Los Angeles, July 14, 1960. He was the first Roman Catholic ever to become President; he was the youngest President the United States ever had; he was already
the author of* Why England Slept *(1940) and had received a Pulitzer prize for* Profiles in Courage *(1956). He
was a vigorous speaker, and the debates on television with
his opponent for the presidency, Richard M. Nixon, found
him equally good in front of the cameras and on the quick,
energetic replies full of information and sharpness of
speech and wit.*

*In his "Inaugural Address" as one heard it and as one
now reads it there is a polish, a firm declaration, a full
eloquence which had not been heard during the preceding
administration. It, again, was a new and vital voice. Some
listeners did not like or approve of it, but they were willing to admit that it had vigor and strength. It had something else, indeed, which the listeners did not perceive.
Readers now can point to passages that are almost prophetic. Whatever one sensed about this speech, that sense
included a vision, like that of Jefferson, for the United
States of America.*

Inaugural Address

Vice President Johnson, Mr. Speaker, Mr. Chief Justice,
President Eisenhower, Vice President Nixon, President
Truman, Reverend Clergy, Fellow Citizens:—We observe
today not a victory of party but a celebration of freedom
—symbolizing an end as well as a beginning—signifying renewal as well as change. For I have sworn before you and

Almighty God the same solemn oath our forebears prescribed nearly a century and three-quarters ago.

The world is very different now. For man holds in his
mortal hands the power to abolish all forms of human
poverty and all forms of human life. And yet the same
revolutionary beliefs for which our forebears fought are
still at issue around the globe—the belief that the rights of
man come not from the generosity of the state but from
the hand of God.

We dare not forget today that we are the heirs of that
first revolution. Let the word go forth from this time and
place to friend and foe alike, that the torch has been
passed to a new generation of Americans—born in this century, tempered by war, disciplined by a hard and bitter
peace, proud of our ancient heritage—and unwilling to witness or permit the slow undoing of those human rights to
which this nation has always been committed, and to
which we are committed today at home and around the
world.

Let every nation know, whether it wishes us well or ill,
that we shall pay any price, bear any burden, meet any
hardship, support any friend, oppose any foe to assure the
survival and the success of liberty.

This much we pledge—and more.

To those old allies whose culture and spiritual origins
we share, we pledge loyalty of faithful friends. United,
there is little we cannot do in a host of new cooperative
ventures. Divided, there is little we can do—for we dare
not meet a powerful challenge at odds and split asunder.

To those new states whom we welcome to the ranks of
the free, we pledge our word that one form of colonial
control shall not have passed away merely to be replaced
by a far more iron tyranny. We shall not always expect
to find them supporting our view. But we shall always hope
to find them strongly supporting their own freedom—and
to remember that, in the past, those who foolishly sought
power by riding the back of the tiger ended up inside.

To those peoples in the huts and villages of half the
globe struggling to break the bonds of mass misery, we
pledge our best efforts to help them help themselves, for

whatever period is required—not because the Communists may be doing it, not because we seek their votes, but because it is right. If a society cannot help the many who are poor, it cannot save the few who are rich.

To our sister republics south of our border, we offer a special pledge—to convert our good words into good deeds —in a new alliance for progress—to assist free men and free governments in casting off the chains of poverty. But the peaceful revolution of hope cannot become the prey of hostile powers. Let all our neighbors know that we shall join with them to oppose aggression or subversion anywhere in the Americas. And let every other power know that this hemisphere intends to remain the master of its own house.

To that world assembly of sovereign states, the United Nations, our last best hope in an age where the instruments of war have far outpaced the instruments of peace, we renew our pledge of support—to prevent it from becoming merely a forum for invective—to strengthen its shield of the new and the weak—and to enlarge the area in which its writ may run.

Finally, to those nations who would make themselves our adversary, we offer not a pledge but a request: that both sides begin anew the quest for peace, before the dark powers of destruction unleashed by science engulf all humanity in planned or accidental self-destruction.

We dare not tempt them with weakness. For only when our arms are sufficient beyond doubt can we be certain beyond doubt that they will never be employed.

But neither can two great and powerful groups of nations take comfort from our present course—both sides overburdened by the cost of modern weapons, both rightly alarmed by the steady spread of the deadly atom, yet both racing to alter that uncertain balance of terror that stays the hand of mankind's final war.

So let us begin anew—remembering on both sides that civility is not a sign of weakness, and sincerity is always subject to proof. Let us never negotiate out of fear. But let us never fear to negotiate.

Let both sides explore what problems unite us instead of belaboring those problems which divide us.

Let both sides, for the first time, formulate serious and precise proposals for the inspection and control of arms—and bring the absolute power to destroy other nations under absolute control of all nations.

Let both sides seek to invoke the wonders of science instead of its terrors. Together let us explore the stars, conquer the deserts and encourage the arts and commerce.

Let both sides unite to heed in all corners of the earth the command of Isaiah—to "undo the heavy burdens . . . [and] let the oppressed go free."

And if a beachhead of cooperation may push back the angles of suspicion, let both sides join in creating a new endeavor not a new balance of power, but a new world of law, where the strong are just and the weak secure and the peace preserved.

All this will not be finished in the first 100 days. Nor will it be finished in the first 1,000 days, nor in the life of this Administration, nor even perhaps in our own life time on this planet. But let us begin.

In your hands, my fellow citizens, more than mine, will rest the final success or failure of our course. Since this country was founded, each generation of Americans has been summoned to give testimony to its national loyalty. The graves of young Americans who answered the call to service surround the globe.

Now the trumpet summons us again—not as a call to bear arms, though arms we need—not as a call to battle, though embattled we are—not a call to bear the burden of a long twilight struggle year in and year out, "rejoicing in hope, patient in tribulation"—a struggle against the common enemies of man: tyranny, poverty, disease and war itself.

Can we forge against these enemies a grand and global alliance, north and south, east and west, that can assure a more fruitful life for all mankind? Will you join in that historic effort?

In the long history of the world, only a few generations have been granted the role of defending freedom in its hour of maximum danger. I do not shrink from this responsibility—I welcome it. I do not believe that any of us would exchange places with any other people or any other generation. The energy, the faith, the devotion which we bring to this endeavor will light our country and all who serve it—and the glow from that fire can truly light the world.

And so, my fellow Americans: ask not what your country can do for you—ask what you can do for your country.

My fellow citizens of the world: ask not what America will do for you, but what together we can do for the freedom of man.

Finally, whether you are citizens of America or citizens of the world, ask of us here the same high standards of strength and sacrifice which we ask of you. With a good conscience our only sure reward, with history the final judge of our deeds, let us go forth to lead the land we love, asking His blessing and His help, but knowing that here on earth God's work must truly be our own.

PART EIGHT

MODERN PROBLEMS

Barry Morris Goldwater

1909–

Barry Goldwater, Senator from Arizona (1953–64), was nominated by the Republican Party to be its candidate for the presidency in 1964. In his acceptance speech delivered at the San Francisco party convention, Senator Goldwater set forth the principles on which his subsequent campaign was to be based.

This was a notable acceptance speech for two reasons. First, despite a sharp ideological split between the wings of his party, the senator surprised many in his audience by not delivering the "unity" speech customarily used to heal such breeches. Secondly, much controversy was stirred up in the campaign by the sentence in this speech: "I would remind you that extremism in the defense of liberty is no vice." The senator was called upon to explain, clarify, and develop this sentence until it became itself one of the most important issues of the campaign.

EXTREMISM IN DEFENSE OF LIBERTY

My good friend and great Republican Dick Nixon and your charming wife, Pat; my running mate—that wonderful Republican who has served us so well for so long—Bill Miller and his wife, Stephanie; to Thruston Morton, who's done such a commendable job in chairmaning this convention; to Mr. Herbert Hoover, who I hope is watching, and to that great American and his wife, General and Mrs. Eisenhower. To my own wife, my family, and to all of my fellow Republicans here assembled, and Americans across this great nation:—

From this moment, united and determined, we will go forward together dedicated to the ultimate and undeniable greatness of the whole man.

Together we will win.

I accept the nomination with a deep sense of humility. I accept, too, the responsibility that goes with it, and I seek your continued help and your continued guidance. My fellow Republicans, our cause is too great for any man to feel worthy of it. Our task would be too great for any man did he not have with him the heart and the hands of this great Republican party.

And I promise you tonight that every fibre of my being is consecrated to our cause, that nothing shall be lacking from the struggle that can be brought to it by enthusiasm, by devotion and plain hard work.

In this world no person, no party can guarantee anything, but what we can do and what we shall do is to deserve victory and victory will be ours. The Good Lord raised this mighty Republican—Republic to be a home for the brave and to flourish as the land of the free—not to stagnate in the swampland of collectivism, not to cringe before the bully of Communism.

Now my fellow Americans, the tide has been running against freedom. Our people have followed false prophets. We must, and we shall, return to proven ways—not because they are old, but because they are true.

We must, and we shall, set the tide running again in the cause of freedom. And this party, with its every action, every word, every breath and every heartbeat, has but a single resolve, and that is freedom.

Freedom made orderly for this nation by our constitutional government. Freedom under a government limited by laws of nature and of nature's God. Freedom balanced so that order lacking liberty will not become the slavery of the prison cell; balanced so that liberty lacking order will not become the license of the mob and of the jungle.

Now, we Americans understand freedom. We have earned it: we have lived for it, and we have died for it. This nation and its people are freedom's models in a searching world. We can be freedom's missionaries in a doubting world.

But, ladies and gentlemen, first we must renew freedom's mission in our own hearts and in our own homes.

During four futile years the Administration which we shall replace has distorted and lost that faith. It has talked and talked and talked and talked the words of freedom but it has failed and failed and failed in the works of freedom.

Now failure cements the wall of shame in Berlin; failures blot the sands of shame at the Bay of Pigs; failures marked the slow death of freedom in Laos; failures infest the jungle of Vietnam, and failures haunt the houses of our once great alliances and undermine the greatest bulwark ever erected by free nations, the NATO community.

Failures proclaim lost leadership, obscure purpose, weakening wills and the risk of inciting our sworn enemies to new aggressions and to new excesses.

And because of this Administration we are tonight a world divided. We are a nation becalmed. We have lost the brisk pace of diversity and the genius of individual creativity. We are plodding along at a pace set by centralized planning, red tape, rules without responsibility and regimentation without recourse.

Rather than useful jobs in our country, people have been offered bureaucratic make-work; rather than moral leadership, they have been given bread and spectacles, they have been given spectacles, and yes, they've even been given scandals.

Tonight there is violence in our streets, corruption in our highest offices, aimlessness among our youth, anxiety among our elderly, and there's a virtual despair among the many who look beyond material success toward the inner meaning of their lives. And where examples of morality should be set, the opposite is seen. Small men seeking great wealth or power have too often and too long turned even the highest levels of public service into mere personal opportunity.

Now, certainly simple honesty is not too much to demand of men in government. We find it in most. Republicans demand it from everyone.

They demand it from everyone no matter how exalted or protected his position might be.

The growing menace in our country tonight, to personal

safety, to life, to limb and property, in homes, in churches, on the playgrounds and places of business, particularly in our great cities is the mounting concern or should be of every thoughtful citizen of the United States. Security from domestic violence, no less than from foreign aggression, is the most elementary and fundamental purpose of any government, and a government that cannot fulfill this purpose is one that cannot long command the loyalty of its citizens.

History shows us, demonstrates that nothing, nothing prepares the way for tyranny more than the failure of public officials to keep the streets safe from bullies and marauders.

Now we Republicans see all this as more—much more— than the result of mere political differences, or mere political mistakes. We see this as the result of a fundamentally and absolutely wrong view of man, his nature and his destiny.

Those who seek to live your lives for you, to take your liberty in return for relieving you of yours; those who elevate the state and downgrade the citizen, must see ultimately a world in which earthly power can be substituted for Divine Will. And this nation was founded upon the rejection of that notion and upon the acceptance of God as the author of freedom.

Now those who seek absolute power, even though they seek it to do what they regard as good are simply demanding the right to enforce their own version of heaven on earth, and let me remind you they are the very ones who always create the most hellish tyranny.

Absolute power does corrupt, and those who seek it must be suspect and must be opposed. Their mistaken course stems from false notions, ladies and gentlemen, of equality. Equality, rightly understood as our founding fathers understood it, leads to liberty and to the emancipation of creative differences; wrongly understood, as it has been so tragically in our time, it leads first to conformity and then to despotism.

Fellow Republicans, it is the cause of Republicanism to

resist concentrations of power, private or public, which enforce such conformity and inflict such despotism.

It is the cause of Republicanism to insure that power remains in the hands of the people—and, so help us God, that is exactly what a Republican President will do with the help of a Republican Congress.

It is further the cause of Republicanism to restore a clear understanding of the tyranny of man over man in the world at large. It is our cause to dispel the foggy thinking which avoids hard decisions in the delusion that a world of conflict will somehow resolve itself into a world of harmony, if we just don't rock the boat or irritate the forces of aggression—and this is hogwash.

It is, further, the cause of Republicanism to remind ourselves, and the world, that only the strong can remain free: that only the strong can keep the peace.

Now I needn't remind you, or my fellow Americans regardless of party, that Republicans have shouldered this hard responsibility and marched in this cause before. It was Republican leadership under Dwight Eisenhower that kept the peace, and passed along to this Administration the mightiest arsenal for defense the world has ever known.

And I needn't remind you that it was the strength and the believable will of the Eisenhower years that kept the peace by using our strength, by using it in the Formosa Strait, and in Lebanon, and by showing it courageously at all times.

And I needn't remind you, but I will, that it's been during Democratic years that our strength to deter war has been stilled and even gone into a planned decline. It has been during the Democratic years that we have weakly stumbled into conflicts, timidly refusing to draw our own lives against aggression, deceitfully refusing to tell even our own people of our full participation and tragically letting our finest men die on battlefields unmarked by purpose, unmarked by pride or the prospect of victory.

Yesterday it was Korea; tonight it is Vietnam. Make no bones of this. Don't try to sweep this under the rug. We are at war in Vietnam. And yet the President, who is the

Commander in Chief of our forces, refuses to say, refuses to say mind you, whether or not the objective over there is victory, and his Secretary of Defense continues to mislead and misinform the American people, and enough of it has gone by . . .

Today—today in our beloved country we have an Administration which seems eager to deal with Communism in every coin known—from gold to wheat; from consulates to confidence, and even human freedom itself.

Now the Republican cause demands that we brand communism as the principal disturber of peace in the world. Indeed, we should brand it as the only significant disturber of the peace. . . .

And I want to make this abundantly clear—I don't intend to let peace or freedom be torn from our grasp, because of lack of strength, or lack of will—and that I promise you Americans.

I can see a day when all the Americas—North and South—will be linked in a mighty system—a system in which the errors and misunderstandings of the past will be submerged one by one in a rising tide of prosperity and interdependence. . . .

Balance, diversity, creative difference—these are the elements of Republican equation. Republicans agree, Republicans agree heartily, to disagree on many, many of their applications. But we have never disagreed on the basic fundamental issues of why you and I are Republicans.

This is a party—this Republican party is a party for free men. Not for blunt followers and not for conformists.

Back in 1858 Abraham Lincoln said this of the Republican party, and I quote him because he probably could have said it during the last week or so: It was so composed of strained, discordant, and even hostile elements. . . .

Yet all of these elements agreed on one paramount objective: to arrest the program of slavery, and place it in the course of its ultimate extinction.

Anyone who joins us in all sincerity we welcome. Those, those who do not care for our cause, we don't expect to enter our ranks in any case. And let our Republicanism so focused and so dedicated not be made fuzzy and futile by unthinking and stupid labels.

I would remind you that extremism in the defense of liberty is no vice!

And let me remind you also that moderation in the pursuit of justice is no virtue!

Our Republican cause is not to level out the world or make its people conform in computer-regimented sameness. Our Republican cause is to free our people and light the way for liberty throughout the world. Ours is a very human cause for human goals. This party, its good people, and its unquestionable devotion to freedom will not fulfill the purposes of this campaign which we launch here and now until our cause has won the day, inspired the world, and shown the way to a tomorrow worthy of all our yesteryears.

I repeat, I accept your nomination with humbleness, with pride, and you and I are going to fight for the goodness of our land. Thank you.

Winston Churchill

1874–1965

Sir Winston Leonard Spencer Churchill, at the time of this speech at Westminster College, Fulton, Missouri, March 5, 1946, had retired from office, had been knighted, and was, as he said, a visiting civilian to the United States. He had been in the country some time visiting Washington, where he saw President Truman for long conferences, and then he went to Florida for rest and painting.

This speech, containing the "iron curtain" phrase, brought to the consciousness of all men the fact that Russia and her satellites were more or less fused into a common front. At present this idea does not seem new, but one must realize that in 1946 World War II was just over and the wartime Allies were assumed still to be allies. Here was a phrase that startled all men into viewing two, if not three, worlds. It was a controversial speech and was criticized in many countries. Churchill felt it was necessary to fuse Anglo-American relations so that they would present as solid a front as did the Russian-satellite nations.

An Iron Curtain Has Descended

I am glad to come to Westminster College this afternoon and am complimented that you should give me a degree. The name Westminster is somehow familiar to me. I seem to have heard it before. Indeed it was at Westminster that I received a very large part of my education in politics, dialectic, rhetoric and one or two other things.

It is also an honor, perhaps almost unique, for a private visitor to be introduced to an academic audience by the President of the United States. Amid his heavy burdens, duties and responsibilities—unsought but not recoiled from

—the President has traveled a thousand miles to dignify and magnify our meeting here today and give me an opportunity of addressing this kindred nation, as well as my own countrymen across the ocean and perhaps some other countries, too. The President has told you that it is his wish, as I am sure it is yours, that I should have full liberty to give my true and faithful counsel in these anxious and baffling times. I shall certainly avail myself of this freedom and feel the more right to do so because any private ambitions I may have cherished in my younger days have been satisfied beyond my wildest dreams. Let me, however, make it clear that I have no official mission or status of any kind and that I speak only for myself. I can, therefore, allow my mind, with the experience of a lifetime, to play over the problem which beset us on the tomorrow of our absolute victory in arms, and try to make sure that what has been gained with so much sacrifice and suffering shall be preserved for the future glory and safety of mankind.

The United States stands at this time at the pinnacle of world power. It is a solemn moment for the American democracy. With primacy in power is also joined an awe inspiring accountability to the future. As you look around you, you must feel not only the sense of duty done but also feel anxiety lest you fall below the level of achievement. Opportunity is here now, clear and shining, for both our countries. To reject it or ignore it or fritter it away will bring upon us all the long reproaches of the aftertime. It is necessary that consistency of mind, persistence of purpose and the grand simplicity of decision shall guide and rule the conduct of the English-speaking peoples in peace as they did in war. We must and I believe we shall prove ourselves equal to this severe requirement.

When American military men approach some serious situation they are wont to write at the head of their directive the words, "over-all strategic concept." There is wisdom in this as it leads to clarity of thought. What, then, is the over-all strategic concept which we should inscribe today? It is nothing less than the safety and welfare, the freedom and progress of all the homes and families of all the men and women in all lands. And here I speak particularly of the myriad cottage and apartment homes, where the wage earner strives amid the accidents and difficulties of life, to guard his wife and children from privation and bring the family up in the fear of the Lord or upon ethical conceptions which often play their potent part.

To give security to these countless homes they must be shielded from the two gaunt marauders—war and tyranny. We all know the frightful disturbance in which the ordinary family is plunged when the curse of war swoops down upon the breadwinner and those for whom he works and contrives. The awful ruin of Europe, with all its vanished glories, and of large parts of Asia, glares in our eyes. When the design of wicked men or the aggressive urge of mighty states dissolve, over large areas, the frame of civilized society, humble folk are confronted with difficulties with which they cannot cope. For them all is distorted, broken or even ground to pulp.

When I stand here this quiet afternoon I shudder to visualize what is actually happening to millions now and what is going to happen in this period when famine stalks the earth. None can compute what has been called "the unestimated sum of human pain." Our supreme task and duty is to guard the homes of the common people from the horrors and miseries of another war. We are all agreed on that.

Our American military colleagues, after having proclaimed the "over-all strategic concept" and computed all available resources, always proceed to the next stop, namely the method. Here again there is widespread agreement. A world organization has already been erected for the prime purpose of preventing war. United Nations Organization, the successor of the League of Nations, with the decisive addition of the United States and all that means, is already at work. We must make sure that its work is fruitful, that it is a reality and not a sham, that it is a factor for action and not merely a frothing of words, that it is a true temple of peace in which the shields of many nations can some day be hung and not merely a cockpit in a tower of Babel. Before we cast away the solid assurances of national armaments for self-preservation, we must be certain that our temple is built not upon shifting sands or quagmires, but upon the rock. . . .

I have, however, a definite and practical purpose to make for action. Courts and magistrates cannot function without sheriffs and constables. The United Nations Organization must immediately begin to be equipped with an international armed force. In such a matter we can only go step by step; but we must begin now. I propose that each of the powers and states should be invited to dedicate a certain number of air squadrons to the service of the world organization. The squadrons would be trained and prepared in their own countries but would move around in rotation from one country to another. They would wear the uniform of their own country with different badges. They would not be required to act against their own nation but in other respects they would be directed by the world organization.

It would nevertheless be wrong and imprudent to intrust the secret knowledge or experience of the atomic bomb, which the United States, Great Britain and Canada now share, to the world organization.

I now come to the second danger which threatens the cottage home and ordinary people, namely tyranny. We cannot be blind to the fact that the liberties enjoyed by individual citizens throughout the British Empire are not valid in a considerable number of countries, some of which are very powerful. In these states, control is enforced upon the common people by various kinds of all-embracing police governments, to a degree which is overwhelming and contrary to every principle of democracy . . . It is not our duty at this time, when difficulties are so numerous, to interfere forcibly in the internal affairs of countries whom we have not conquered in war, but we must never cease to proclaim in fearless tones, the great principles of freedom and the rights of man, which are the joint inheritance of the English-speaking world and which, through Magna Carta, the Bill of Rights, the *habeas corpus,* trial by jury and the English common law, find their most famous expression in the Declaration of Independence.

All this means that the people of any country have the right and should have the power by constitutional action, by free, unfettered elections, with secret ballot, to choose or change the character or form of government under which they dwell, that freedom of speech and thought should reign, that courts of justice independent of the executive, unbiased by any party, should administer laws which have received the broad assent of large majorities or are consecrated by time and custom. Here are the title deeds of freedom which should lie in every cottage home. Here is the message of the British and American people to mankind. Let us preach what we practice and practice what we preach.

A shadow has fallen upon the scenes so lately lighted by the Allied Victory. Nobody knows what Soviet Russia and its Communist international organization intends to do in the immediate future, or what are the limits, if any, to their expansive and proselytizing tendencies. I have a strong admiration and regard for the valiant Russian people and for my war-time comrade Stalin. . . . We understand the Russians' need to be secure on her western frontiers from all renewal of German aggression. We welcome her rightful place among the leading nations of the world. Above all we welcome constant, frequent and growing contacts between the Russian people and our own people on both sides of the Atlantic. It is my duty, however, to place before you certain facts about the present position in Europe—I am sure I do not wish to, but it is my duty, I feel, to present them to you.

From Stettin in the Baltic to Triest in the Adriatic, an iron curtain has descended across the continent. Behind that line lie all the capitals of the ancient states of central and eastern Europe. Warsaw, Berlin, Prague, Vienna, Budapest, Belgrade, Bucharest and Sofia, all these famous cities and the populations around them lie in the Soviet sphere and all are subject in one form or another, not only to Soviet influence but to a very high and increasing measure of control from Moscow. Athens alone, with its immortal glories, is free to decide its future at an election under British, American and French observation. The Russian-dominated Polish government has been encouraged to make enormous and wrongful inroads upon Germany, and mass expulsions of millions of Germans on a scale grievous and undreamed of are now taking place. Police governments are prevailing in nearly every case, and so far, except in Czechoslovakia, there is no true democracy. An attempt is being made by the Russians in Berlin to build up a quasi-Communist party in their zone of occupied Germany by showing special favors to groups of Left-Wing German leaders. At the end of the fighting last June, the Americans and British armies withdrew westward, in accordance with an earlier agreement, to a depth at some points 150 miles on a front of nearly 400 miles to allow the Russians to occupy this vast expanse of territory which the western democracies had conquered. If now the Soviet government tries, by separate action, to build up a pro-Communist Germany in their areas this will cause new serious difficulties in the British and American zones, and will give the defeated Germans the power of putting themselves up to auction between the Soviets and western democracies.

The safety of the world, ladies and gentlemen, requires a new unity in Europe from which no nation should be permanently outcast.

In front of this iron curtain which lies across Europe are other causes for anxiety. In Italy the Communist party is seriously hampered by having to support the Communist trained Marshal Tito's claims to favor Italian territory at the head of the Adriatic. Again one cannot imagine a regenerated Europe without a strong France . . . However, in a great number of countries, far from the Russian frontier and throughout the world, Communist fifth columns are established and work in complete unity and absolute obedience to the directive they receive from the Communist center. These are somber facts for anyone to have to recite as the morrow of a victory gained by so much splendid comradeship in arms and in the cause of freedom and democracy, and we should be most unwise not to face them squarely while time remains.

I repulse the idea that a new war is inevitable; still more that it is imminent.

If the population of the British English-speaking Commonwealth be added to that of the United States, with all that such cooperation implies in the air, on the sea and in science and industry, there will be no quivering, precarious balance of power to offer its temptation to ambition or adventure. On the contrary, there will be an overwhelming assurance of security. If we adhere faithfully to the charter of the United Nations and walk forward in sedate and sober strength, seeking no one's land or treasure, or seeking to lay no arbitrary control on the thoughts of men, if all British moral and material forces and convictions are joined with your own in fraternal association, the high roads of the future will be clear, not only for us but for all, not only for our time but for a century to come.

John Fitzgerald Kennedy, PRESIDENT OF THE UNITED
STATES

Dr. Edward Roland Annis, MIAMI, FLORIDA

*These two speeches are not in any sense a formal or
informal debate; they present two sides of the question of
medical care through Social Security: why it should be
supported and why it should not be supported. President
Kennedy had sponsored the plan and gave his address
not as a legislator but as a man speaking for the citizens
of his country. Note that the Kennedy address was delivered to a Madison Square Garden rally of the National
Council of Senior Citizens, in New York City, May 19,
1962. Dr. Annis' "rebuttal," taking another view of the
same problem and citing his objections, was delivered the
following day over the television network of the National
Broadcasting Company. Dr. Annis broadcast from the
same podium the President had used but before an empty
auditorium rather than the cheering throng of the day
before.*

MEDICAL CARE THROUGH SOCIAL SECURITY:
WHY IT SHOULD BE SUPPORTED

I am very proud to be here today at one of our thirty-
three meetings which are being held across the United
States.

I have come to New York because I believe the effort
in which we are engaged is worth the time and effort of
all of us. I come from Boston, Mass., near Faneuil Hall,
where for a whole period of years meetings were held by
interested citizens in order to lay the groundwork for
American Independence.

And while there may be some who say that the business
of government is so important that it should be confined to

those who govern, in this free society of ours the consent and, may I say, the support of the citizens of this country is essential, if this, or any other piece of progressive legislation, is going to be passed. Make no mistake about it. Make no mistake about it.

Now why are we here? What is the issue which divides and arouses so much concern? I will take a case which may be typical, a family which may be found in any part of the United States. The husband has worked hard for his life, and he is retired. He might have been a clerk or a salesman or on the road or worked in a factory, stores or whatever. He's always wanted to pay his own way. He does not ask anyone to care for him; he wants to care for himself. He has raised his own family; he has educated it; his children are now on their own. He and his wife are drawing Social Security. It may run $75, $100, $125 in the higher brackets; let's say it's $100. And he has a pension from where he worked, the results of years of effort.

Now therefore his basic needs are taken care of. He owns his house. He has $2,500 or $3,000 in the bank. And then his wife gets sick.

And we're all going to be in a hospital—nine out of ten of us—before we finally pass away. And particularly when we're over 65.

Now she is sick—not just for a week but for a long time. First goes the $2,500. That's gone. Next he mortgages his house, even though he may have some difficulty making the payments out of his Social Security.

Then he goes to his children, who themselves are heavily burdened because they're paying for their house; and they're paying for their sickness, and they want to educate their children. Then their savings begin to go. This is not a rare case.

I talked to a member of the Congress from my own state a week ago who told me he was going to send his daughter away to school, but because his father had been sick for two years, he could not do it. And Congressmen are paid $22,500 a year. And that's more than most people get.

So, therefore, now what is he [the typical case] going to do? His savings are gone, his children's savings—they're contributing, though they have responsibilities of their own—and he finally goes in and signs a petition saying he's broke and needs assistance.

Now what do we say? We say that during his working years he will contribute to Social Security, as he has in the case of his retirement, twelve or thirteen a month. [This was apparently a slip of the tongue—under the measure this would be the annual payment.]

When he becomes ill, or she becomes ill, over a long period of time—he first pays $90 [of the hospital costs], so that people will not abuse it [the Social Security program]. But then, let us say, he has a bill of $1,500.

This [legislative] bill does not—that we're talking about, Mr. Anderson's bill and Mr. King's—solve everything. But let's say it's $1,500, of which a thousand dollars are hospital bills.

The [legislative] bill will pay that $1,000 in hospital bills, and then, I believe that he and the effort he makes in his family can meet his other responsibilities. Now that does not seem such an extraordinary piece of legislation twenty-five years after Franklin Roosevelt passed the Social Security Act.

Well, let's hear what some people say. First we read that the A.M.A. [American Medical Association] is against it, and they're entitled to be against it, though I do question how many of those who speak so violently about it have read it. But they are against it, and they are entitled to be against it, if they wish.

In the first place, there isn't one person here who isn't indebted to the doctors of this country. Children are not born in an eight-hour day. All of us have been the beneficiaries of their help. This is not a campaign against doctors, because doctors have joined with us. This is a campaign to help people meet their responsibilities.

There are doctors in New Jersey who say they will not treat any patient who receives it. Of course they will! They are engaged in an effort to stop the bill. It is as if I took out somebody's appendix.

The point of the matter is that the A.M.A. is doing very well in its effort to stop this bill and the doctors of New Jersey and every other state may be opposed to it, but I know that not a single doctor, if this bill is passed, is going to refuse to treat a patient.

No one would become a doctor just as a business enterprise. It's a long, laborious discipline. We need more of them. We want their help—and generally we're getting it. The problem, however, is more complicated because they do not comprehend what we're trying to do.

We do not cover doctors' bills here. We do not affect the freedom of choice—you can go to any doctor you want. The doctor and you work out your arrangements with him. We talk about his hospital bill. And that's an entirely different matter!

And I hope that one by one the doctors of the United States will take the extraordinary step of not merely reading the journals and the publications of the A.M.A., because I do not recognize the bill when I read those descriptions.

But, instead, to write to Secretary Ribicoff in Washington, or to me—and you know where I live—or to Senator Anderson or to Congressman King, if you are a doctor or opposed to this bill, and get a concise explanation and the bill itself and read it.

All these arguments were made against Social Security at the time of Franklin Roosevelt. They're made today. The mail pours in, and at least half of the mail which I receive in the White House and—on this issue and others —is thoroughly misinformed.

Last week I got 1,500 letters on a revenue measure, 1,494 opposed and six for. And at least half of these letters were completely misinformed about details of what they wrote—and why is that so?

Because there are so many busy men in Washington who write. Some organizations have 600, 700 and 800 people spreading mail across the country asking doctors and others to write in and tell your Congressman you're opposed to it.

The mail pours into the White House, into the Congress

and Senator's office. Congressmen and Senators feel people are opposed to it. Then they read a Gallup Poll which says 75 per cent of the people are in favor of it, and they say, "What has happened to my mail?"

The point of the matter is that this meeting and the others indicate that the people of the United States recognize—one by one, thousand by thousand, million by million—that this is a problem whose solution is long overdue. And this year, I believe, or certainly as inevitably as the tide comes in, next year, this bill is going to pass.

This bill serves the public interest. It involves the Government because it involves the public welfare. The Constitution of the United States did not make the President or the Congress powerless. It gave them definite responsibilities to advance the general welfare, and that is what we are attempting to do.

And then I read that this bill will sap the individual self-reliance of Americans. I can't imagine anything worse —or anything better—to sap someone's self-reliance than to be sick, alone, broke or to have saved for a lifetime and put it out in a week, two weeks, a month, two months.

I visited twice today—yesterday—and once today a hospital where doctors labor for a long time, to visit my father. It isn't easy. It isn't easy. He can pay his bills. But otherwise, I would pay it. And I'm not as well off as he is.

But what happens to him and to others when they put their life savings out in a short time?

[The] argument that the Government should stay out, that it saps our pioneer stock—I used to hear that argument when we were talking about raising the minimum wage to $1.25.

I remember one day being asked to step out into the hall, and up the corridor came four distinguished-looking men with straw hats on and canes. They told me they had just flown in from a state in a private plane, and they wanted me to know that if we passed the bill providing for time and a half for service-station attendants who were then working about fifty-five to sixty hours at straight time, it would sap their self-reliance.

The fact of the matter is what saps anyone's self-reliance

is working sixty hours at straight time or working at 85 or 95 or \$1 an hour, depending upon filling out a pauper's oath and going up and then getting it free. Nobody in this hall is asking for it for nothing. They are willing to contribute during their working years. That is the important principle which has been lost sight of.

I understand that . . . this week . . . an English physician is going to talk about how bad their plans are. It may be. But he ought to talk about it in England, because this plan—this plan, and what they do in England, is entirely different.

In England the entire cost of medicine for the people of all ages, all of it—doctors, the choice of doctors, hospitals, from the time you are born to the time you die—are included in a government program.

The fact of the matter is that what we are now talking about doing, most other countries of Europe did years ago. The British did it thirty years ago.

We are behind every country pretty nearly in Europe in this matter of medical care for our citizens. And then [there are] those who say that this should be left to private efforts!

In those hospitals in New Jersey, where the doctors said they wouldn't treat anyone who paid their hospital bills through Social Security, those hospitals and every other new hospital, the American people, all of them, contribute one-half, one- or two-thirds to every new hospital—the National Government.

We pay 55 per cent of all the research done. We help young men become doctors. We are concerned with the progress of this country, and those who say that what we are now talking about spoils our great pioneer heritage should remember that the West was settled with two great actions of the National Government.

One, in President Lincoln's Administration where he gave a homestead to everyone who went West. And in 1862 he set aside Government property to build our land-grant colleges. This cooperation between an alert and progressive citizenry and a progressive government is what has made this country great, and we shall continue as long as we have the opportunity to do so.

This matter should not be left to a mail campaign. Where Senators are inundated, or Congressmen, 25- and 30,000 letters, the instructions go out: "Write it in your own hand. Don't use the same words." The letters pour in in two or three weeks—half of them misinformed.

What we are concerned about is not the person who has not got a cent, but those who saved and worked and then get hit. Then there are those who say, "Well, what happens if you die before you're 65?" Well, there isn't— you really don't care—you have no guarantee.

But what we are talking about is: our people are living a long time; their housing is inadequate; in many cases their rehabilitation is inadequate.

We've got great unfinished business in this country.

We don't, aren't able overnight to solve all the problems that this country faces, but is that any good reason why we should say, "Let's not even try?" That's what we're going to do today. We are trying. We are trying.

But I refuse to see us live on the accomplishments of another generation. I refuse to see this country and all of us shrink from these struggles which are our responsibility in our time, because what we are now talking about in our children's day would seem to be the ordinary business of government.

So I come here today as a citizen asking you to exert the most basic power which is contained in the Constitution of the United States and the Declaration of Independence: the right of a citizen to petition his Government. And I ask your support in this effort.

This effort will be successful, and it will be successful because it is soundly based to meet a great national crisis. And it is based on the efforts of responsible citizens.

In closing, might we say that on this issue and many others, we depend upon your help. This is the only way we can secure action to keep this country moving ahead; to have places to educate our children; to have decent housing; to do something about the millions of young children who leave our schools before they graduate.

Every day I am reminded of how many things were left undone.

Thirty years ago they provided that no drugs be put on the market which were unsafe for hogs and for cattle. We want to take the same radical step of doing the same for human beings. Anyone who says that Woodrow Wilson, as great a President as he was, and Franklin Roosevelt and Harry Truman, that they did it all and we have nothing left to do now, are wrong.

We ask you, the citizens of this country, the responsible and thoughtful doctors, the hospital administrators—all those who face this challenge of educating our children, finding work for our older people, finding security for those who have retired, all who are committed to this great effort and are moving this country forward—come and give us your help.

MEDICAL CARE THROUGH SOCIAL SECURITY: WHY IT SHOULD NOT BE SUPPORTED

My colleagues asked me: Would I feel nervous or foolish addressing 18,000 empty seats in this hall? My answer: No. I understand the reason for it. They said: But those empty seats won't applaud. Won't the television audience compare that silence with the cheers President Kennedy got yesterday?

I said: I'm not a cheer leader. I'm a physician.

Yesterday's mass rally in this very arena—how did it all come to happen? Spontaneously? You and I know better. Let's start in Washington. Whatever a President of the United States says—Whatever he opposes or proposes, argues about, worries about or jokes about—goes out to millions by newspapers, magazines, television, and radio.

That kind of publicity goes with the office. And so does the administrative direction over thousands of people in the huge Executive Branch of the Federal Government.

Men and women of America, I appeal to your sense of fairness! Nobody—certainly not your doctors—nobody can compete in this unfamiliar art of public persuasion against such massive publicity, such enormous professional machinery, such unexplained money, and such skillful manipulations! Of course, it's unfair when the proponents of King-Anderson—by having the President address their rally —get their story and their show televised over all three networks, free of charge, as a news event!

Of course it's unfair when your doctors, asking for equal time to make reply, got turned down and have to pay for a half-hour on one network to tell you the other side of the story.

Unfair, yes—not to us so much, but to you.

We doctors fear that the American public is in danger of being blitzed, brainwashed and bandwagoned into swallowing the idea that the King-Anderson Bill is the only proposal—the only program that offers medical care for the aged—that there is nothing else. Well, let's put that outrageously false idea on the bandwagon and send it back where it came from!

Just two years ago your Congress in Washington enacted into law the Kerr-Mills medical aid to the aged program. The Kerr-Mills Law has already been accepted by thirty-eight states and is being considered by others. It's on the books. It's a brand new national law. Why aren't you hearing more about it? It works!

Out in Lansing, Mich., at their comfortable little home at 528 Avon Street, Dr. John Packer has asked one of his elderly patients, Mrs. Helen Cole, to tell you what the Kerr-Mills Law has meant to her.

[At this point a film clip showed Mrs. Cole saying that under the Kerr-Mills Program her entire $4,000 bill had been paid, without "Never any embarrassment at all" in the question asked her.]

Four thousand dollars in medical assistance to a woman who was really in need! Under the Kerr-Mills Law! It works wherever responsible public leaders want it to work. This new law could be doing its job in a lot more states by now, I assure you, if somebody hadn't changed the signals in Washington because they had something else in mind.

The American Medical Association and most doctors in this country supported and do support the Kerr-Mills Law, because we see it as a desirable supplement to one of the greatest social advances of our generation—I mean the spectacular growth of private, voluntary health insurance systems, to which millions of Americans already belong.

Of our 17,000,000 people past 65, over half—53 percent, or 9,000,000—three times as many as ten years ago —already are covered by some form of voluntary health insurance or prepayment plan. This is a spectacular forward movement. Insurance actuaries estimate that by 1970, 80 to 90 percent of the aged will be covered by private programs.

Of course there will always be a number of people who are truly indigent or who just cannot pay for their medical needs. That is where the Kerr-Mills Medical Aid for the Aged Law comes in.

The worst thing the King-Anderson crowd find to say about the Kerr-Mills Law is that it requires a "means test." The charge is made that the means test is degrading and undignified. Well, let's look at that.

Where you apply for the low-rent benefit of public housing don't you have to prove that your income is below a certain level? This is a "means" test. A test of your means.

And when you apply for Social Security, aren't you asked to prove that your wage earnings are below a certain amount? Is this degrading or undignified? Well, that's a means test, isn't it? A means test for Social Security itself.

A means test is a desirable protection for those who are really needy, or against those who are merely greedy.

Please, do not be blinded by the scarewords of propagandists.

Now let's make an x-ray examination of what they are attempting to sell you—the King-Anderson Bill—H.R. 4222. Yesterday you heard the President say—well, no, let's listen to his own words.

[Tape insert: "Well, let's hear what some people say. First we read that the A.M.A. is against it, and they're entitled to be against it. But I do question how many of those who speak so violently about it have read it."]

First I read the title—the "Health Insurance Benefits Act." Is it genuine insurance? No, it is not. The Supreme

Court has held more than once that the Social Security system is not an insurance system. It is the way we have chosen to cushion the general economic needs of old people in this country.

The Social Security tax collected from those under 65 pays the benefits to those over 65. Why not be honest about it? I say any health program that calls itself insurance and isn't has to be bad to begin with.

Do people under 65 get ill? Does nobody get a serious illness at 60, or 61, or 62? This great humanitarian measure shuts its eyes, turns its back, cares not—says, "Come back when you're 65." And yet the King-Anderson Bill would destroy many of those genuine insurance systems which do have provisions taking care of people under 65: Say, that's real progress, isn't it?

And what about those who would be covered—meaning everyone over 65 eligible for Social Security? That means everyone—the rich, the well-to-do and the comfortable as well as those of low income; whether they need it or not, whether they want it or not—they'd be in. The American taxpayer, whose payroll tax would be hiked by as much as 17 percent to start with in order to pay for this program, certainly has a right to question the free ride those who do not need these benefits would be taking at the expense of his children.

Now there is some more interesting reading in here for those on Social Security who genuinely need medical aid. Just what would you get under King-Anderson? You can read it as we did.

For a hospital room containing one, two, or three other people, it would still cost you $10 a day for the first nine days of your hospitalization. That's $90.

After you left the hospital or nursing home, you would not be eligible for further hospital benefits for at least three months. Don't have a relapse or get sick again!

To get into the hospital you'd apply in writing and get a certification from a doctor. You'd have to pay for your doctor and you'd have to pay for a private-duty nurse if needed.

And you can also read if your illness required hospitalization for more than thirty days, it'd have to be passed on by a special committee who'd have to consider a lot of other people, too, don't you know? After all, the Government has to treat everyone fair and equal, don't you know?

Do you know, my friends, that you'd have to pay the first $20 of each diagnostic study you'd get at the hospital as an outpatient?

Do you know that in order to get into a nursing home for your maximum or 150 "units of service" you'd have to go to the hospital first?

This bill would put the Government smack into your hospitals! Defining services, setting standards, establishing committees, calling for reports, deciding who gets in and who gets out, what they get and what they don't—even getting into the teaching of medicine—and all the time imposing a Federally administered financial budget on our house of mercy and healing.

The American system of medicine is a system of quality medicine, not mass-production medicine. It is a system of private medicine, practiced by private doctors treating private patients, free to make decisions based on the patient's specific medical needs—and nothing else.

Under King-Anderson let's say your doctor believes you should be in a hospital immediately, but the facilities utilization committee force you to wait, to go by number instead of by need. What can your doctor do? You are his patient. He is responsible for bringing you back to health. Not the committee.

Why are most doctors so opposed to King-Anderson? Our fees are not involved! Our practice of quality medicine is! Our health is!

If our Government wants to move now toward welfare state medicine, then let them tell us so honestly.

The King-Anderson crowd intends to take us all the way down the road to a new system of medicine for everybody—and don't mistake it England's nationalized medical program is the kind of thing they have in mind for us eventually.

Today, after fourteen years of national medicine, more and more people in England are buying health insurance —on top of paying the heavy compulsory tax for government medicine they don't use. These people want private medical care. That's what we have here.

Laurance S. Rockefeller

1910–

*Laurance S. Rockefeller has shown his interest in con-
servation of wildlife, in particular, but also of scenic pleasures which people of the whole nation enjoy. He has tried
to preserve the Palisades in New Jersey and the west side
of the Hudson River as natural parks unspoiled by apart-
ments and other buildings. He has worked as Interstate
Park Commissioner and given special attention to the Jackson Hole Wildlife Park. Wherever wildlife and objects of
natural beauty are endangered, Mr. Rockefeller is present
to battle for protection and preservation.*

*Parallel with the preservation of wildlife and nature is
the use of the parks for recreation, and the recreation
within the parks means also how people spend their time.
Since more time seems to be on people's hands in automation, the problem of the proper use of time and leisure
needs careful consideration.*

*Mr. Rockefeller, as Chairman of the Outdoor Recreation
Resources Review Commission, delivered this speech at
the "Newsmakers Luncheon" of the Radio and Television
Society, in New York City, October 26, 1960.*

LEISURE: THE NEW CHALLENGE

I am most grateful for the invitation to speak to you on
the constructive use of leisure time and the relationship to
it of radio and television. I know the subject of leisure
holds more than casual attraction for you as leaders in
broadcasting. And it is of course an integral part of the
field of outdoor recreation in which I am especially interested.

The American people spend more of their free time
watching television than in any other leisure activity. You

are the men and women who constantly make the judgments that determine what they see. This is an awesome power, and it involves tremendous responsibility, of course.

I believe wise use of leisure time is of extreme importance to the American people as individuals and as a nation. For leisure is more than a by-product of work. It is an asset produced by work. At our time in history we cannot afford to waste it as too many of us are doing.

Leisure and constructive use: these are the key words, and definition of them is in order.

There is no difficulty with the word leisure. An acceptable if unpoetic definition is: time which is not spent working or sleeping.

While constructive use is a matter of individual taste and interest, there can be agreement on the elements involved. Leisure should be a time for healthful relaxation, self-improvement, enjoyment of the best in the arts and literature, and of community service.

This means that leisure involves basic human values.

The outdoors, for example, is more than a place to acquire a suntan. Along with physical activity, which is an important element, the outdoor experience should be a re-creative experience. It should recharge our emotional and spiritual batteries. Otherwise it is providing nothing more than an escape.

The machine has liberated Western man from the kind of toil which precludes leisure.

But there are no machines that automatically insure the consumption will benefit the consumer, that guarantee the leisure use will be constructive.

In this area we are on our own, so to speak. And we have not kept pace in educating and persuading ourselves to make creative and wise use of expanded free time.

A deplorable number of Americans actually search for ways to kill time. And there are such things as "Sunday Frustration"—a phrase which sums up the fact that too many of us spend Sundays and other days off in pointless activities.

The need to end this waste of leisure time opportunities represents what I regard as a new challenge. I believe it is tied up vitally to the question of where we are as a nation and where we are going.

Viewed from this angle, and looking ahead, the challenge of what we do with leisure takes on added dimensions. All of us are familiar with predictions that automation is going to change our lives as much as the Industrial Revolution did.

One result, so we are told, will be a steady decline in the work week to perhaps half of today's standard. It is my belief that further reduction of the work week will be modest.

Work gives dignity and meaning to our individual lives. We need to ponder the possibly damaging effects to character and initiative if work is relegated to a minor position in daily life.

The immediate challenge is to make wise use of the leisure time available to us. This time may, if abused, be not only wasteful but also destructive. The plainest proof of this is the problem of juvenile delinquency.

The experiment of a manufacturing plant in California helps to bring the challenge into focus. The company tried a four-day week, once a month. The experiment was so unrewarding and unsatisfactory that—at the end of a year —the company abandoned the project after taking a referendum in the plant.

What the experiment brought home was that increased leisure is not automatically desirable. And it is valueless when people have not learned to use it constructively.

The whole problem is made more urgent by the growing size of our elderly population. These are people with large amounts of time—and generally with very little preparation for its wise use.

All of this—killing time and Sunday Frustration, the four-day week experiment, the experience of the elderly—point to the importance of an early start in what might be called education for leisure.

One most encouraging development is the growing interest in outdoor recreation. This includes many activities: sports such as boating and skiing, hunting and fishing, and what is sometimes called the back-to-nature movement, camping.

But the growing popularity of outdoor activities is a mixed blessing. It has brought heavy pressures on available facilities. In fact, crowd pressures are becoming so great on our parks, ski slopes, campgrounds and other outdoor areas that leisure use benefits are seriously impaired.

Recognition that our outdoor facilities, public and private, were overloaded prompted the Federal government to action. Thus, in 1958, the Outdoor Recreation Resources Review Commission was created by Congress.

I have the good fortune to be chairman of this Commission. Our job is to project, to the years 1976 and 2000, the rapidly growing needs of our people.

One fact already stands out: the central area of planning in this field involves the preservation today of open space for tomorrow. The swift growth of our population and the speedup in urbanization of America have given an urgency to this problem as never before. To stake out and preserve open space before the contractor's bulldozer takes over, that's the problem. The race for open space is one name for it.

The Federal government, the states, local communities and private interests all have a part of the race to run.

The extent of commercial television's influence on contemporary American life is obviously tremendous. There is TV in nearly every home and viewing time is calculated at an average of six hours a day per family. And this is leisure time.

Another vital consideration is TV's huge audience of children and young people and its impact on this particular audience.

What these facts reveal is the enormous importance of television as a most significant vehicle for the constructive use of leisure time.

Television has literally brought the world into the home. The printed word is powerful. But how can it match the knowledge conveyed by the sight and sound of [a] Khrushchev at the United Nations?

If upgrading means anything, it means presentation of

more and more programs of a recognized high standard of excellence—whether it be in comedy, drama, music, news, or public affairs.

Upgrading also should include the showing of more programs of out-and-out constructive nature—more documentaries and more educational programs.

I would like to make a few further suggestions:

One is that conscious effort be made to include a constructive message in programs of various kinds. It can be done without preaching. The power of suggestion can involve a recognition of values.

The Father Who Knows Best could take his family to the art museum, or hiking through the woods, or on a visit to the zoo or aquarium.

The next suggestion deals with public service programs.

The thought is that educational material of high quality be put on films for showing on TV at other than prime times. But that one showing would not be the end. The networks could make these films available for showing in schools and at meetings of P.T.A.'s, religious organizations and clubs.

Some commercial TV stations around the country are assisting non-profit education TV stations in their communities. This seems both a laudable and far-seeing practice.

I am certain there would be concern about our use of leisure even if our time in history were serene. Given present circumstances—the tensions of the nuclear and missile era, the very real challenge to our way of life—there obviously is reason for the most urgent concern.

Our nation is rich and powerful. To match our material standard of living is the goal of all other people around the world. We have evolved an economy which provides our people more hours of leisure than is required for them for work. However, without some fundamental changes in our use of leisure, the effects on the American character could be severe. Misuse, waste of leisure, if allowed to persist, might easily prove the Achilles heel of our free society.

The physical, cultural and spiritual benefits of leisure wisely used, can give new meaning and purpose to our lives—and help us to become a spiritual, as well as material, example to the people of all nations.

James B. Conant

1893–

James Bryant Conant, first a chemist, then educator, President of Harvard University, Ambassador to Germany, and at present viewing American education in all of its varied forms as well as the myriad problems besetting the youth of America, is a faithful servant of his country and mankind.

To name but a few of his works on education is an education in itself: General Education in a Free Society *(1945),* Education in a Divided World *(1948),* Modern Science and Modern Man *(1952),* Education and Liberty *(1952),* The American High School *(1959),* Slums and Suburbs *(1961). His stamp will be upon high school, college, and graduate education for the next century. When he speaks and writes, he writes with greater authority than any former professor or teacher of teachers.*

This speech was delivered before the Conference on Unemployed, Out-of-School Youth in Urban Areas, sponsored by the National Committee for Children and Youth in Washington, D.C., May 24, 1961.

SOCIAL DYNAMITE IN OUR LARGE CITIES: UNEMPLOYED, OUT-OF-SCHOOL YOUTH

I appreciate the opportunity of serving as Keynote speaker and chairman of this workshop Conference on Unemployed, Out-of-School Youth in Urban Areas sponsored by the National Committee for Children and Youth. It is a sobering responsibility. I make this statement principally because I am convinced that the problem you ladies and gentlemen are here to discuss poses a serious threat to our free society. I submit that the existence in the slums of our large cities of thousands of youths ages 16–21 who are both out-of-school and out-of-work is an explosive situation. It is social dynamite.

In preparation for this Conference, a few special studies were conducted in slum areas of large cities to find out what the facts really were. In a slum section composed almost entirely of Negroes in one of our largest cities the following situation was found. A total of 59 percent of the male youth between the ages of 16 and 21 were out of school and unemployed. They were roaming the streets. Of the boys who graduated from high school 48 percent were unemployed in contrast to 63 percent of the boys who had dropped out of school. In short, two-thirds of the male dropouts did not have jobs and about half of the high school graduates did not have jobs. In such a situation, a pupil may well ask why bother to stay in school when graduation for half the boys opens onto a dead-end street?

An even worse state of affairs was found in another special study in a different city. In a slum area of 125,000 people, mostly Negro, a sampling of youth population shows that roughly 70 percent of the boys and girls ages 16–21 are out of school and unemployed. When one stops to consider that the total population in this district is equal to that of a good-sized independent city, the magnitude of the problem is appalling and the challenge to our society is clear.

In the slum area where over half the male youth are unemployed and out of school we are allowing a grave danger to the stability of our society to develop. A youth who has dropped out of school and never has had a full-time job is not likely to become a constructive citizen of his community. Quite the contrary. As a frustrated individual he is likely to be anti-social and rebellious. Some of this group of youths will end as juvenile delinquents. I suggest that full employment would have a highly salutary effect. Moreover, I offer the following hypothesis for professional social workers and sociologists to demolish; namely, that the correlation between desirable social attitudes (including attitudes of youth) and job opportunities are far higher than between the former and housing conditions, as measured by plumbing facilities, heating, and space per family.

Leaving juvenile delinquency aside, the existence of gangs of unemployed out-of-school youth in some neighborhoods of our large cities creates social problems acute enough by themselves. The adverse influence of the "street" is largely a consequence of the existence of these gangs. I doubt if anyone familiar with a slum district would deny that, if all the male youth by some miracle were to find employment, the social climate would change dramatically for the better. Some juvenile delinquents would remain, gangs might not wholly disappear, but the whole attitude of the neighborhood would alter in such a way as to make more effective the teachers in every classroom.

Consider for a moment the long-run consequence of persistent failure of underprivileged youth to find work. Out of work and out of school since they turned 16, these youths behave in ways that may have serious political consequences, similar behavior of youth in smaller cities would be far less serious. It is a matter of geography in the last analysis. Three factors are significant: first, the total size of the group of youth to whom I am referring—the larger the group, the more dangerous; second, the density of the population—the number of frustrated youth per block; third, the isolation of the inhabitants from other kinds of people and other sorts of streets and houses.

I know there are those who maintain that, on the average, Negro children are inferior to white children in academic ability. I have seen no evidence to support any such contention. In considering the relative abilities of whites and Negroes, let us examine the situation in an all-white slum in a city of considerable size. A careful study of a group of children in grade 4 of one such school showed that their average achievement level was a full year below their grade placement—a typical situation in any slum area.

The principal [of this school] writes, . . . "The parents of at least one-third of the children are either in penal institutions, are on probation, or have prison records. At least 100 children are on probation to the Juvenile Court . . .

"Less than 10 percent of the children have private

doctors or dentists. A dental examination of 900 children in the fall of 1959 reveals only forty-five free of cavities. The eyes of every child in the school were examined and about 300 showed some vision defects, and thirty had such serious vision loss that they were referred for partially-seeing teaching. At least one-third of the children are on welfare rolls or are recipients of very small social security and/or veteran benefits checks."

I am quoting from an official report which, in acknowledging the generally low achievement of the white children in this school, makes the interesting statement that "there is no reason to believe that these students as a group are inherently or genetically less capable than average students, but apparently because of some types of experiences in their lives they have been unable to develop their intellectual skills." *I should argue strongly that to date we have no evidence to indicate that the assumption* [made above] *should not be broadened to include both white and Negro students.* [italics his.] I start with the belief that, given a satisfactory socio-economic background and educational opportunity, Negro children can be just as successful in academic work as any other group.

Visits to a wealthy suburb and impoverished slums only a few minutes away jolt one's notions of the meaning of equality of opportunity. On the one hand, there is likely to be a spacious, modern school staffed by as many as 70 professionals for 1,000 pupils; on the other hand, one finds a crowded often dilapidated and unattractive school staffed by 40 professionals for 1,000 pupils. Expenditure per pupil in the wealthy suburban school is likely to be over $1,000; often it is less than half that in the slum school. To my mind, in view of the problems one finds, conditions in the slum school necessitate more staff and more money than in the suburban school.

The growth of Negro slums in big cities is alarming. I wish that I could do more than direct attention. For without being an alarmist, I must say that when one considers the total situation that has been developing in the Negro slums since World War II, one has reason to worry about the future. The building up of a mass of unemployed and frustrated Negro youth in congested areas of a city is a social phenomenon that may be compared to the piling up of inflammable material in an empty building in a city block. Potentialities for trouble—indeed, possibilities of disaster—are surely there.

I have so far referred only to white and Negro slums. In addition, a few words are necessary to point out that in some cities, New York in particular, there are slum areas inhabited by recent arrivals from Puerto Rico. In these sections, the problems are similar to those I have described but complicated by the difference in language. Unlike the American Negro from the South, these recent arrivals bring with them a set of social mores closely associated with their own methods of communication. At the same time, they often, if not always, come with children where schooling has been bad. These problems [of language] are so special I shall not attempt to discuss them here. Add to these tasks the possibilities of interracial hostility and gang warfare between Negroes and Puerto Ricans and the resentment of both toward the whites and one has a veritable witches' brew which comes to boil with unsavory vehemence in certain schools in certain areas—particularly in the junior high school years. The amazing feature of the whole situation is that pupils make any progress in schools in certain areas of the city.

In closing, I should like to express my own views on a very few of the subjects just mentioned about which I feel strongly. In the first place, there are those who would say that what goes on in the schools should not have any direct connection with the community or the employment situation. I completely reject this idea. The school, the community, and the employment picture are and should be closely tied together. *I submit that in a heavily urbanized and industrialized free society the educational experience of youths should fit their subsequent employment.* This should be so whether a boy drops out of school in grade 10, after graduation from high school, or after graduation from college or university. In any case, there should be a smooth transition from full-time schooling to a full-time job.

When we examine the situation at the high school level, we find that in many high schools a half or more of the graduates seek employment immediately on graduation, only in a few cities does one find an effective placement service. The obligation of the school should not end when the student either drops out of school or graduates. At that point the cumulative record folder concerning a student's educational career is usually brought to an end. It should not be. To my mind, *guidance officers, especially in the large cities, ought to be given the responsibility for following the post-high school careers of youth from the time they leave school until they are 21 years of age.* It is with the unemployed out-of-school youths that I am especially concerned—especially the boys, for whom the unemployment problem is more severe than for girls. This expansion of the school's function will cost money and will mean additional staff; but the expense is necessary, for vocational and educational guidance must be a continuing process to help assure a smooth transition from school to work. What I have in mind suggests, of course, a much closer relationship than now exists between school, employers, and labor unions, as well as social agencies and employment officers.

In short, there is much that schools are doing but much more that they should do. Money in many instances is the key—remedial reading teachers, smaller classes, guidance counselors cost money.

But even if the schools were to improve their services drastically, there should remain what seems to me the crux of the situation—the presence or absence of employment opportunity. Whereas I have indicated my conviction that the problems of Negro education are no different from those of all underprivileged socio-economic groups, the problems of Negro employment are distinctly different. The enforcement of anti-discrimination laws has proved a most difficult undertaking. I have heard it said that only those projects which are supported by public funds can really be operated on a truly non-discriminatory basis. Therefore, it seems to me that unless local management and labor take up the challenge, it may be necessary for

Congress to appropriate funds for public work programs to alleviate the problem of unemployment among youth 16 to 21 in the large cities. In view of the past discriminatory employment practices by both management and labor, action at the federal level may become a necessity. Even if there were no discrimination, it might become a necessity if the private sector of the economy is unable to provide sufficient jobs.

In conclusion, let me repeat my sense of shock as I contemplate conditions in our big cities with respect to youth in slum neighborhoods. The problems are the result of a social situation the roots of which run back to the days of slavery and the result of an economic problem which is in part a reflection of the total unemployment situation and is part a result of racial discrimination among labor unions and employers. To improve the work of the schools requires an improvement in the lives of the families who inhabit these slums, but without a drastic change in the employment prospects for urban Negro youth, relatively little can be accomplished. I close by urging that our large-city problems be analyzed in far more detail than in the past and with far greater degree of frankness. Neighborhood by neighborhood we need to know the facts, and when these facts indicate a dangerous social situation the American people should be prepared to take drastic measures before it is too late.

Thomas J. Watson, Jr.

1914–

*Thomas J. Watson, Jr., corporation executive and phi-
lanthropist, has followed the footsteps of his father,
Thomas J. Watson, the founder, executive, and inspirer of
the International Business Machines complex. He graduated from Brown University in Providence, Rhode Island,
in 1937 and immediately went to IBM, where he thoroughly learned the business from 1937 to 1940. After the
war interval he returned to IBM in 1946.*

*With all of his business interests and philanthropic pur-
suits, he has continued to have a lively interest in education and in speaking to young people in education and
business.*

Self-Protection: Individualism

Twenty-seven years ago I sat where you now sit in the
graduating class of 1937 at Brown University. I'm sure I
seem several generations away from you in age, but these
twenty-seven years have gone so quickly that it's not at
all hard for me to remember that vivid day of my own
graduation. Strangely enough, the one thing about that
day that I cannot remember is what the commencement
speaker had to say. My thoughts, like yours, were tar-
geted upon my family and my friends and my plans for
the summer. But of one thing I'm sure: If the speaker
made a short speech, I know I blessed him.

Therefore, I surmise, there is only one sure way to earn
a place in your memory and that is to be brief. I will.

My subject today is in the general area of self-protec-
tion. I want to spend a few moments contrasting the drive
for physical protection in and out of college with the great

difficulty all of us have through life in protecting the non-physical parts of our being.

In college sports, one is constantly protecting one's body with all kinds of devices, from shoulder pads to shin guards. Even in later life, we continue this drive for physical safety with such things as padded dashboards and shatter-proof windshields. All these things help to keep one's body safe and unmarked, and they are good things.

However, all of you graduating today possess something much more important to you than your body. I am speaking to you of your mind, your spirit, your ability to think and speak independently, and your ability at this point as college seniors to stand up and be counted with a clear and firm position on nearly any of the issues which affect your life or the life of the nation.

The fundamental convictions and principles which help you to form your firm, clear position are your most precious possession. Paradoxically, all the wonderful equipment available for shielding the body is worthless for protecting the spirit and the mind.

What then can you do to protect these priceless personal assets? You can't hide them; you can't smother them; you can't rely on some kind of padding. On the contrary, you can protect them only by exposing them to danger, only by defending your personal beliefs regardless of opposition and, like tempered steel, toughening your convictions by the hot shock of conflict.

If you succeed in preserving your principles in the years ahead, without becoming so radical that nobody will listen or follow your example, you will become a part of that elite group in the world which Crawford Greenwalt, Chairman of the DuPont Company, calls the "uncommon man."

The world's destiny will, to a great extent, depend on how many of these uncommon men and women we have. If there are enough of them and they assume their rightful role of leadership, our future will be secure. If we fail to produce them in sufficient numbers, we will fail as a nation.

It may seem fantastic to you that you could lose this

outspoken ability you have been developing throughout your scholastic career. Yet it's a fact that the mass world in which we live tends to etch away the tough hard bumps of conviction and belief. I venture to predict that not one of you will be at work very many years before you will have to look into your heart and answer some very difficult questions. Your answers will, in a very real sense, begin to determine whether your parents, this institution, and the world in which you have lived have produced a common or uncommon human being.

You will have to choose between the safe, conservative silent position and the choice of speaking your mind, of stating your true position and thereby earning yourself some enemies.

Will you develop the reputation of being outspoken, sometimes uncooperative but always honest in supporting what your beliefs indicate is right?

Or will you be a steadfast, reliable fellow who can always be counted on to cooperate?

If you take the safe choice, you may well get a promotion or two, and get it faster than less diplomatic people, but in the end you will never fulfill the best that's in you.

If you take the bold choice, you may find yourself temporarily stymied, but a quote which was a favorite of President Kennedy's suggests the importance of the bold choice. It is from Dante and goes

> "The hottest places in Hell are reserved for those who, in times of moral crisis, preserved their neutrality."

If you make the bold choice you will be taking the only road men have ever found toward true success and greatness. And I might even say—true happiness.

All the great men of history have had to answer the same critical questions. Each had to choose between the safe protection of the crowd and the risk of standing up and being counted. And you can find no truly great men who took the easy way.

For their courage some suffered abuse, imprisonment,

and even death. Others lived to win the acclaim of their fellow men. But all achieved greatness.

Through history, examples are abundant:

—Columbus

—Charles Darwin

—Galileo, who confirmed the theory that the earth traveled about the sun, and who for his affirmation became a prisoner of the Inquisition.

—Socrates, who told his judges at his trial: "Men of Athens, I honor and love you; but I shall obey God rather than you, and while I have life and strength, I shall never cease from the practice and teaching of philosophy."

If we turn to our own times, we can all of us recall other men of other lands who refused to take the easy way out, who stood up against the current for what they believed right and just. Nehru in India, de Gaulle in France, Churchill in England.

And in our own country, it wasn't easy in 1956 when the British, French and Israeli forces invaded Egypt—in the midst of an American presidential election—for the President of the United States, Dwight D. Eisenhower, to condemn the use of force and to call upon the aggressors to get out. But he did it—and the electorate overwhelmingly upheld his courage.

And it wasn't easy for another American President of a different political party—John F. Kennedy—to take an unequivocal stand on civil rights, when that stand might have cost him votes of the South, which in the 1960 election gave him his tiny margin of victory. But he did it and thereby added a post publication chapter to *Profiles in Courage*.

All these men, despite their great variety, had something in common. Every single one of them put principle first, safety second; individuality first, adjustment second; courage first, cost second.

We need more such men, more than ever before, living at this hour. The issues are the biggest in history—the need for courageous dialogue greater than ever.

I'm not arguing for nonconformity in everything. I'm not urging you, for example, to refuse to be polite, to pay your bills, to stand in the line at a supermarket. I'm not even suggesting that you should debate every issue, for if you take a minority position on everything, you won't be a leader—you'll be a crank. But I am calling on you to be shrewd enough to recognize these things upon which agreement and compromise are sensible, and bold enough to take a stand on those issues on which you feel disagreement and differences are not only possible but necessary.

Now suppose you try, in your own manner, to follow this course. What will happen to you?

Well, Nicholas Murray Butler, the great President of Columbia University at the beginning of this century, said that the world is made up of three groups of people.

A small elite group who make things happen.

A somewhat larger group who watch things happen.

And the great multitude who don't know what happens. This means that the leaders, the makers of opinion in the world, are a very limited group of people.

So as you stand and are counted you will first run into the group who equate newness with wrongness. If it's a new idea, it's uncomfortable and they won't like it. These are the conventionalists.

Second, you're sure to meet cynics, people who believe anyone who sticks his neck out is a fool. I am sure all of you have heard of measures which passed the Congress in a breeze on a voice vote, and later go down to crashing defeat where some Congressman insists that every vote be recorded in the *Congressional Record*.

Third, you'll run into the group of people who believe that there are certain taboo questions that should not be debated. These suppressors of dissent think that once a stand has been taken it is forever settled. Disarmament, the admission of Red China to the U.N., a change in policy toward Castro or Vietnam—all such touchy subjects, these people warn, should be left alone.

A few months ago, the Chairman of the Senate Foreign Relations Committee, Senator William Fullbright, raised some of these questions and gave his own answers in a forthright speech on the Senate floor. He called upon Americans to think some "unthinkable thoughts." Some Senators and some writers attacked his opinions, as is their right and indeed their duty. But others refused to discuss the questions and instead merely condemned the Senator for mentioning them in public.

Now, what's wrong with shutting off all such discussion? John Stuart Mill in his *Essay on Liberty* gave an argument for freedom of speech which described three possible effects of speaking out—and I would apply these to Senator Fullbright's action:

In the first place, the Senator may be a hundred percent right. If so, the popular current opinion is nearly a hundred percent wrong, and in the national interest it deserves rejection.

Second, the Senator may be partially right. If so, the current opinion is partly wrong and in the national interest requires revision.

Third, the Senator may be a hundred percent wrong. If so, he still serves the national interest. How? By driving the defenders of the current opinion to go back and look at the facts, to rethink their reasons, to express their conclusion so that people can accept it with greater conviction.

Now, if you back the conventionalists, the cynics and the suppressors of dissent, here's what may well happen: Sometimes you may look foolish; sometimes you may lose some money or even your job; sometimes you may give offense to others. There's no getting around it.

Strangely, the expounders of many of the great new ideas of history frequently were considered on the lunatic fringe for some or all of their lives.

If you stand up and are counted, from time to time you may get yourself knocked down. But remember this: A man flattened by an opponent can get up again. A man flattened by conformity stays down for good.

Therefore, I'd like to reverse a traditional piece of commencement time advice. You know it well, it goes: "Make no little plans." Instead, I'd like to say this: Make no little enemies—people with whom you differ for some petty, insignificant, personal reason. Instead I would urge you to cultivate "mighty opposites"—people with whom you disagree on big issues, with whom you will fight to the end over fundamental convictions. And that fight, I can assure you, will be good for you and your opponent.

Follow the path of the unsafe, independent thinker. Expose your ideas to the dangers of controversy. Speak your mind and fear less the label of "crackpot" than the stigma of conformity. And on issues that seem important to you, stand up and be counted at any cost.

Clare Boothe Luce

1903–

*Clare Boothe Luce has had a multifaceted career as a
magazine editor, playwright, Congresswoman from Con-
necticut (1943–47) and U. S. Ambassador to Italy
(1953–57). She continues to be an active figure in the
national political arena.*

*This address, which reflects her views on the means of
achieving lasting peace, was delivered as the Given Foundation Lecture, at Wilson College, Chambersburg, Pennsylvania, in October 1961.*

AMERICAN MORALITY AND NUCLEAR DIPLOMACY

Today the two strongest nations in the world are drawn
up in full array, facing one another across half the world.
Their bombs testing in air, their rockets' red glare, seem
proof to the world that war may be near.

Wrote Churchill in *The Gathering Storm,* "statesmen
are not called upon to settle easy questions . . . it is when
balance quivers, and the proportions are veiled in mist
that the opportunity for world-saving decisions presents
itself."

The same opportunity presents itself to the American
people.

In a democracy, the vital decisions of statesmen are
seldom taken in defiance of the Public Will. Whoever
changes his own opinion in a national crisis, by just so
much changes the Public Will and, by just so much, in-
fluences the decisions of statesmen.

The purpose of this paper is to raise the question of the
morality of America's attitude in this century toward the
uses of force, in international affairs, to submit that our
morality has been a fuzzy if not false one, and to suggest

that unless that attitude does not soon change, we dare not hope that American diplomacy can win the cold war.

What *is* the historic American attitude toward force, toward the purpose of force, the possession of force, and the use of force? In speaking of force, I am speaking not only of America's armies-in-being at any given moment since the turn of the century, but of America's war-making *capacity*, its total realizable military potential.

Until most recent times America's attitude was that the sole purpose of American force was the military self-defense—of America; that the possession of force was solely for deterrent to military aggression—against America; and that the only use to which American force could ever *morally* be put was retaliation against military aggression —*on* America.

Morality in respect of force, consisted in *not striking the first military blow*. Conversely, any nation who struck the first military blow against America, *ipso facto* established its own morality.

Consequently, the only moral *casus belli*, or cause of war which the Public Will has fully supported is the initiation of war on the United States. For almost a century, statesmanship has been constrained, diplomacy has been confined, and patriotism itself has been defined, by the moral necessity of waiting for Pearl Harbors.

There are, of course, many explanations of this attitude. Even if there were time I could not do justice to this whole complex problem. A review of it would begin with General George Washington's unique role in insuring that the military forces should be absolutely subject to the civil government; that the two hats the President wears, his Commander-in-Chief hat should be kept in the closet of Congress. The scholar could then go on to show that one of the strongest of American feelings was always its antipathy toward the militaristic tradition of Europe. Indeed, throughout most of history, the flaunting of military power was closely tied to old world dynastic, monarchial and feudal institutions and rivalries. From the beginning, the United States sought to set a new example to the world, an example not only of democracy but also of repudiation of war as the normal, more or less continuous, instrument of government policy. To all such considerations of these, most historians would add the fact of America's geographical isolation . . .

Consequently America in this century has twice failed, with a third time threatening, to prevent the outbreak of world war as our moral duty and our prime task as the world's strongest nation. America failed because the Public Will would seldom support a foreign policy or a diplomacy which would permit our statesmen to introduce the subject of the war-making capacity of the United States into the normal conduct of international negotiations. We would not allow—we positively forbade—our diplomats to convert our tremendous physical power into diplomatic or political victories for peace.

Have we always been blind to this necessity? No, we have not.

Let me give you an elegant historical example of wise American statesmanship: the proclamation of the Monroe Doctrine, on December 2nd, 1823. This was a clearly stated political and diplomatic warning to all the nations of the world that the United States would rapidly raise armies to fight any nation which, for any reason good or bad, sought any conquest in this hemisphere . . . "There is such a thing as a man being too proud to fight," said Woodrow Wilson in the Spring of 1915. This was certainly a statement which the embattled French and British heard with dismay and contempt and bitterness. How can a man be proud *not* to fight while his friends are being killed and even conquered in a war *they* did not start? America was not too proud to sell guns, make loans, ship supplies to the Allied side, and to heap abuse on Kaiser Bill—a procedure which American morality permitted us nevertheless to call "neutrality," since neutrality also consisted entirely in *not* joining the fighting until "war came."

Even after World War I, America clung to the idea that the unilateral renunciation—America's renunciation of the First Use of Force—would preserve peace in the world.

But by 1937, World War II was plainly in the making. Once again American statesmanship and diplomacy were confronted with the stern necessity of taking a firm stand against the outbreak of hostilities in Europe. What stand did we take? I do not know how clearly you remember Franklin Roosevelt's famous "quarantine" speech in that year. But let me read a sentence to you. (Said President Roosevelt) . . . "the mere fact that we *rightly* decline to intervene with arms to prevent acts of aggression does not mean that we must act as if there were no aggression at all . . . There are many methods short of war, but *stronger and more effective* than mere words, of bringing home to aggressor governments the aggregate sentiments of our own people."

The quietly spoken words of American diplomats in Rome and Berlin and Tokyo and Moscow—that if Hitler plunged Europe into war, Germany would have to reckon with American military power because America *would rightly decide to intervene on the side of the Allies.* This warning never came.

Despite the warnings of history, we have held to our morality, and we have done so until this present hour. The Kaiser and Hitler began our education in the political uses of military power. They were not tough enough to finish it. It is now being finished by Mr. Khrushchev and Mao Tse-tung.

The United States emerged from that war as the first atomic power in history. One American A-bomb was a thousand times more destructive than any blockbuster dropped in World War II. Never before in the story of mankind had one nation possessed such a monopoly of decisive military power, and the means of delivering it to anywhere on the globe.

How did we view the *purpose* of this power? As self-defense, quite proper. How did we view the *possession* of this power? As a deterrent to the use of force against ourselves and our allies, by others. So far, excellent. But what political or diplomatic use did we make of this power? Very little.

The war had no sooner ended in 1945 than it became plain . . . that Soviet Russia had *not* abandoned her dream of ideological conquest of the world.

American foreign policy promptly geared itself to fight the war Russia chose to fight—the cold war.

Nor was the United States laggard in responding to Soviet world propaganda. Tooling up the most formidable propaganda machinery that the United States Congress would buy, the United States struggled valiantly to save the ears of the world from Red contamination USIS, the Voice of America, Radio Free Europe, the Voice of Liberty, delivered a tittle for every Russian tattle.

In 1949 Russia detonated her first atomic bomb and ended our atomic monopoly. There was no question in any American's mind what target her bombs, when they came in sufficient numbers, were designed to find. The fallout of 30- and 50-megaton bombs exploded by Russia *inside* Russia, is headed our way now. Our frontiers have been militarily crossed, have they not, by death-dealing Russian fallout?

As proof of the sincerity of our position and the purity of our intentions, we pursued a long series of disarmament negotiations which began with the Baruch plan, but which have today ended in utter nothingness.

The idea that a nation, although the mightiest power on earth, has no moral obligation to warn, no less to punish the international hoodlum who is raping the independence of nations whose interests are closely tied to its own, until it is first attacked, the idea that by waiting until its own shores are bombarded, it then gains a moral advantage which gives it the right to plunge everyone into all-out war, *guerre à l'outrance*—all this is so far from being moral, that it has long been viewed in the Chanceries of the world as a moral aberration, of a peculiar stupid—and dangerous—sort. And indeed, some *hubris*, or pride, ignorance and selfishness do lie close to the root of it.

A correct *moral* attitude toward force must begin by the clear and never-to-be-forgotten truth that force is itself neutral. The fact that men can now make use of nuclear energy does not alter this truth by one jot. Nuclear energy is *force*. Force is neutral. It is not something that uses man. Man uses it. In international questions force can be used to exert *diplomatic* pressures which can, and often have prevented wars.

Our moral attitude toward nuclear war must be that there *are* moral values worth dying for. Our moral attitude toward the cold war must be that there are moral values worth great economic sacrifices. For if this be not true, then morality itself will die at our own hands.

Said Abraham Lincoln, 100 years ago. America is "the last best hope of earth . . ." It still is.

The one great and decisive force which we must now translate into political and diplomatic action is the force of our free spirits.

John Fitzgerald Kennedy

1917–1963

President Kennedy delivered this speech on the future of the United Nations organization on September 25, 1961, before the UN General Assembly in New York City. The entire speech is not given here, only those parts which offer a view of the best ways to accomplish peace. As will be seen, the ideas set forth in this speech are quite in contrast to those offered by Mrs. Luce.

Just prior to this speech the UN's Secretary General, Dag Hammarskjold, had been killed in a plane crash in the Congo.

PEACE THROUGH THE UNITED NATIONS

We meet in an hour of grief and challenge. Dag Hammarskjold is dead. But the United Nations lives. His tragedy is deep in our hearts, but the tasks for which he died are at the top of our agenda. A noble servant of peace is gone. But the quest for peace lies before us.

So let us here resolve that Dag Hammarskjold did not live—or die—in vain. Let us call a truce to terror. Let us invoke the blessings of peace. And, as we build an international capacity to keep peace, let us join in dismantling the national capacity to wage war.

This will require new strength and new roles for the United Nations. For disarmament without checks is but a shadow—and a community without law is but a shell.

But the great question which confronted this body in 1945 is still before us—whether man's cherished hopes for progress and peace are to be destroyed by terror and disruption—whether the "foul winds of war" can be tamed in time to free the cooling winds of reason—and whether the pledges of our Charter are to be fulfilled or defied:

pledges to secure peace, progress, human rights and world law.

In this hall there are not three forces, but two. One is composed of those who are trying to build the kind of world described in Articles 1 and 2 of the Charter. The other, seeking a different world, would undermine this Organization in the process.

Today, every inhabitant of this planet must contemplate the day when this planet may be no longer habitable. Every man, woman and child lives under a nuclear sword of Damocles, hanging by the slenderest of threads, capable of being cut at any moment by accident or miscalculation or by madness. The weapons of war must be abolished before they abolish us.

Men no longer debate whether armaments are a symptom or a cause of tension. The mere existence of modern weapons—ten million times more powerful than any that the world has ever seen, and only minutes away from any target on earth—is a source of horror and discord and distrust. Men no longer maintain that disarmament must await the settlement of all disputes—for disarmament must be part of any permanent settlement. And men may no longer pretend that the quest for disarmament is a sign of weakness—for in a spiralling arms race, a nation's security may be shrinking even as its arms increase.

For fifteen years this Organization has sought the reduction and destruction of arms. Now that goal is no longer a dream—it is a practical matter of life or death. The risks inherent in disarmament pale in comparison to the risks inherent in an unlimited arms race.

It is in this spirit that the recent Belgrade Conference —recognizing that this is no longer a Soviet problem or an American problem, but a human problem—endorsed a program of "general, complete and strictly internationally controlled disarmament." It is in this same spirit that we in the United States have labored this year, with a new urgency and with a new, now statutory agency fully endorsed by Congress, to find an approach to disarmament which would be so far-reaching yet realistic, so mutually balanced and beneficial, that it could be accepted by every nation. And it is in this spirit that we have presented, with the agreement of the Soviet Union—under the label which both nations now accept of "general and complete disarmament" a statement of newly agreed principles for negotiation. . . .

Such a plan [as devised] would not bring a world free from conflict and greed—but it would bring a world free from the terrors of mass destruction. It would not usher in the era of the super State—but it would usher in an era in which no State could annihilate or be annihilated by another.

The logical place to begin is a treaty assuring the end of nuclear tests of all kinds, in every environment, under workable controls. The United States and the United Kingdom have proposed such a treaty that is both reasonable and effective and ready for signature. We are still prepared to sign that treaty today.

But to halt the spread of these terrible weapons, to halt the contamination of the air, to halt the spiralling nuclear arms race, we remain ready to seek new avenues of agreement. Our new disarmament program includes the following proposals:

First, signing the test-ban treaty by all nations. This can be done now. Test ban negotiations need not and should not await general disarmament.

Second, stopping the production of fissionable materials for use in weapons, and preventing their transfer to any nations now lacking in nuclear weapons.

Third, prohibiting the transfer or control over nuclear weapons to states that do not own them.

Fourth, keeping nuclear weapons from seeding new battlegrounds in outer space.

Fifth, gradually destroying existing nuclear weapons and converting their material to peaceful uses; and

Finally, halting the unlimited testing and production of strategic nuclear delivery vehicles, and gradually destroying them as well.

To destroy arms, however, is not enough. We must create even as we destroy—creating world-wide law and law enforcement as we would outlaw world-wide war and weapons. In the world we seek United Nations emergency forces which have hastily assembled, uncertainly supplied and inadequately financed will never be enough.

Therefore, the United States recommends that all member nations earmark special peace-keeping units in their armed forces—to be on call to the United Nations, to be specially trained and quickly available, and with advance provision for financial and logistic support.

In addition, the United States Delegation will suggest a series of steps to improve the United Nations machinery for the peaceful settlement of disputes—for on-the-spot fact-finding, mediation and adjudication—for extending the rule of international law. For peace is not solely a matter of military or technical problems—it is primarily a problem of politics and people. And unless man can match his strides in weapons and technology with equal strides in social and political development, our great strength, like that of the dinosaur, will become incapable of proper control—and, like the dinosaur will vanish from the earth.

But I come here today to look across this world of threats to a world of peace. In that search we cannot expect any final triumph—for new problems will always arise. We cannot expect that all nations will adopt like systems—for conformity is the jailer of freedom and the enemy of growth. Nor can we expect it to reach our goal by contrivance, by fiat or even by the wishes of all.

But however close we sometimes seem to that dark and final abyss, let no man of peace and freedom despair. For he does not stand alone. If we can in every land and office look beyond our own shores and ambitions, then surely the age will dawn in which the strong are just and the weak secure, and the peace is preserved.

Index